BEING FOR THE OTHER

EMMANUEL LEVINAS, ETHICAL LIVING AND

PSYCHOANALYSIS

For Helen and Harvey,
For two very good
friends. Affectionately,
Paul

PAUL MARCUS

BEING FOR THE OTHER
EMMANUEL LEVINAS, ETHICAL LIVING AND
PSYCHOANALYSIS

MARQUETTE
UNIVERSITY
PRESS

MARQUETTE STUDIES IN PHILOSOPHY
NO. 65
ANDREW TALLON, SERIES EDITOR

LIBRARY OF CONGRESS CATALOGING-IN-PUBLICATION DATA

Marcus, Paul, 1953-
  Being for the other : Emmanuel Levinas, ethical living and psychoanalysis / Paul Marcus.
    p. cm.—(Marquette studies in philosophy ; no. 65)
  Includes bibliographical references and index.
  ISBN-13: 978-0-87462-763-3 (pbk. : alk. paper)
  ISBN-10: 0-87462-763-X (pbk. : alk. paper)
  1. Levinas, Emmanuel. 2. Psychoanalysis. 3. Ethics. 4. Other (Philosophy) I. Title.
  B2430.L484M365 2008
  170.92—dc22

                                                              2008041411

© 2008 Marquette University Press
Milwaukee, Wisconsin 53201-3141
All rights reserved.
www.marquette.edu/mupress/

FOUNDED 1916

♾The paper used in this publication meets the minimum requirements of the
American National Standard for Information Sciences—
Permanence of Paper for Printed Library Materials, ANSI Z39.48-1992.

MARQUETTE UNIVERSITY PRESS
MILWAUKEE

The Association of Jesuit University Presses

TABLE OF CONTENTS

TO MY LATE MOTHER

"Freud was consulted by a young poet and university student, Bruno Goetz, who suffered from persistent headaches. After an hour's discussion, in which it emerged that Goetz spent what little money he had on books, Freud gave him a sealed envelope, containing a prescription, and also warned him that psychoanalysis might not be good for poetry. When Goetz opened the envelope, he found both diagnosis and cure: the headaches were caused by hunger, and money was enclosed to spend on food."

D.J. Enright,
Interplay

"The only morality is therefore one of kindness."

Emmanuel Levinas
Difficult Freedom

ACKNOWLEDGEMENTS

I would like to thank a number of friends and colleagues who have been very generous in their willingness to be helpful to me during the writing of this book. My good friend, William B. Helmreich, Professor of Sociology and Judaic Studies, graciously read every word of the manuscript, made constructive criticisms and always made time in his busy life to discuss his comments. Levinas scholar, Professor B.C. Hutchens and Levinasian-inspired psychologist, Professor George Kunz also read the entire manuscript and provided me with valuable comments for which I am most grateful. Thanks also go to Levinas scholars, Professors Richard A. Cohen, David Ross Fryer and Edith Wyschogrod who have read specific chapters and offered very useful comments as did psychoanalyst, Charlotte Schwartz from the National Psychological Association for Psychoanalysis (NPAP). Professor Richard N. Williams also made thoughtful comments during and after a presentation I made at George Kunz's yearly conference, "Psychology For the Other: Emmanuel Levinas and Psychology" at Seattle University. Michael Eigen, the editor of the NPAP's Psychoanalytic Review also deserves appreciation for encouraging me to do a special issue of the journal on Levinas and Psychoanalysis.

Finally, my beloved wife Irene, a child and adult psychoanalyst, and the mother of our two wonderful children. For her kindness, support, and overwhelming reasonableness, I am grateful beyond words.

Paul Marcus

ABOUT THE AUTHOR

Paul Marcus, Ph.D., is a supervising and training analyst for the National Psychological Association for psychoanalysis. He is the author of *Ancient Religious Wisdom, Spirituality and Psychoanalysis*, and *Autonomy in the Extreme Situation: Bruno Bettelheim, the Nazi Concentration Camps and the Mass Society*, among other books.

I

LEVINAS'S CHALLENGE TO PSYCHOANALYSIS

"The thought of Emmanuel Levinas makes us tremble."
Jacques Derrida[1]

W hile the work of the great French philosopher and Jewish scholar Emmanuel Levinas (1906-95) is beginning
to become better known in this country,[2] he is regarded
in France "as the most important ethical thinker of the twentieth
century,"[3] recognized alongside such giants as Martin Heidegger,
Maurice Merleau-Ponty and Jean-Paul Sartre. Philosopher Philippe
Nemo further describes Levinas as "the philosopher of ethics, without
doubt the sole moralist of contemporary thought," while Derrida has
indicated that "the reverberations of his thought will have changed the
course of philosophical reflection in our time, and of our reflection

---

1 Jacques Derrida, *Writing and Difference*, trans. Alan Bass (Chicago: University of Chicago Press, 1978), 82.

2 The most accessible introductions to Levinas's difficult philosophy are two
conversations with him: *Ethics and Infinity. Conversations with Philippe Nemo*,
trans. Richard A. Cohen (Pittsburgh: Duquesne University Press, 1985) and *Is
It Righteous to Be? Interviews with Emmanuel Levinas*, ed. Jill Robbins (Stanford:
Stanford University Press, 2001). The best introductory secondary sources are
Colin Davis, *Levinas: An Introduction* (Cambridge: Polity Press, 1996); Benja-
min C. Hutchens (London: Continuum International Publishing Group, 2004),
Levinas, A Guide for the Perplexed; Adriaan Peperzak, *To the Other. An Introduc-
tion to the Philosophy of Emmanuel Levinas* (West Lafayette: Purdue University
Press, 1993); Peter Atterton and Matthew Calarco, *On Levinas* (Pittsburgh,
PA: Duquesne University Press, 2004); Michael B. Smith, *Toward the Outside:
Concepts and Themes in Emmanuel Levinas* (Pittsburgh: Duquesne University
Press, 2005); John Llewelyn, *Emmanuel Levinas: The Genealogy of Ethics* (New
York: Routledge, 1995); Edith Wyschogrod, *Emmanuel Levinas. The Problem of
Ethical Metaphysics*, 2^d ed. (New York: Fordham University Press, 2000).

3 Davis, *Levinas*, 120.

on philosophy…"[4] Levinas has also influenced important philosophers who have a strong appreciation for psychoanalysis, such as Jacques Derrida, Paul Ricoeur, Jean Francois Lyotard, and Luce Irigaray (who also practices as an analyst). Thus, his work has "attained classic status…for his attempt to explore the meaning of ethics from a phenomenological starting point."[5]

Despite Levinas's major significance on the European continent, he is hardly known, let alone read or cited, in the mainstream psychoanalytic community in America, except perhaps, by a few in the Lacanian camp and some other scattered references.[6] This despite the fact that Levinas's oeuvre cogently deals with issues that are central to psychoanalysis, namely, the "deep" structure of subjectivity, intersubjectivity and human flourishing. Most importantly, Levinas's account of "ethical subjectivity,"[7] contained in his hugely disruptive critique of the Western philosophical tradition, the tradition in which psychoanalysis is lodged, not only challenges many of the taken-for-granted assumptions that guide much of psychoanalytic theorizing and practice, but also shows how this Western tradition, and by extension psychoanalysis, inadvertently does violence to the human self. As Fryer wisely points out, there are many important "unappreciated connections…to be made between Levinas and Freudian thought…"[8] This book strives

4 Levinas, *Ethics and Infinity*, viii; Derrida, *Adieu to Emmanuel Levinas*, 4.

5 Robert Bernasconi, "Levinas, Emmanuel," in *Routledge Encyclopedia of Philosophy*. Edward Craig, ed., volume 5 (London: Routledge, 1998), 579.

6 *Levinas and Lacan. The Missed Encounter*, ed. Sarah Harasym (Albany: SUNY Press, 1998); David Ross Fryer, *The Intervention of the Other: Ethical Subjectivity in Levinas and Lacan* (New York: Other Press, 2004). See also Michael Eigen, "On the Significance of the Face," *Psychoanalytic Review*. 67 (1980): 427-442, and *Emotional Storm* (Middletown, CT: Wesleyan University Press, 2005).

7 Fryer very aptly defines ethical subjectivity: "It means that in studying both ethics and subjectivity, our focus is on the ways in which those things that structure us (social law, language, the Unconscious, ideology) make us, fail to make us ethical—ethical in the sense of responsible for others and responsible to ourselves, ethical in the sense of being originally bound to each other in ways that cannot, or least should not, be denied or ignored, ethical in the sense that, at our very core, we, as subjects, have commitments that we need to be aware of, that we need to nurture and cultivate, and that it is these commitments that make us who and what we are." (Ibid., 18).

8 Fryer, *The Intervention of the Other*, 76.

to discern some of the worthwhile unappreciated connections between Levinas and psychoanalysis. However, it goes much further. My claim is that Levinas's "ethical transcendentalism," his "ethics of responsibility," as it has been called, imposes a challenge to psychoanalysis that I believe needs to be taken up in order to make a "better" psychoanalysis. That is, Levinas provides the intellectual resources and insights for creating a psychoanalysis that is "truer" to Freud's humanistic vision at its best, namely, one that makes ethics and living a moral life central to its theorizing and practice. By doing so, I believe, psychoanalysis can become a more robust and compelling life- and identity-defining narrative of the human condition and form of psychotherapy. In psychoanalytic parlance, this means, in part, a psychotherapy that centrally involves helping analysands live their lives not simply with greater ethical maturity, an accepted goal in nearly every major "school" of psychoanalysis. Perhaps even more fundamentally, extrapolating Levinas's radical thesis, helping analysands live according to an ethic in which the self's responsibility for the other is more fundamental than its liberty and decision[9], and perhaps most importantly, the other's needs, in a metaphysical and real-life sense, takes precedence over one's own.

DEFINING PSYCHOANALYSIS AND THE PROBLEM OF "TRANSLATING" LEVINAS INTO PSYCHOANALYTIC LANGUAGE

Before laying out the rudiments of my argument, that a Levinasian-animated psychoanalysis is a potentially productive and useful alternative way of thinking about our discipline's theory and practice, one that can be greatly beneficial to our analysands, I want to clarify what I mean by the term psychoanalysis. I also want to comment on the problem of "translating" Levinas's philosophical and phenomenological insights into a usable psychoanalytic language, so that, perhaps, Levinas's insights will be more accessible and meaningful to the typical psychoanalyst not familiar with the extremely dense, if not tortuous language that he uses.

DEFINING PSYCHOANALYSIS

I conceive of psychoanalysis as more than a body of thought and type of psychotherapy. By psychoanalysis I mean a widely accepted theoretico-practical matrix, an intellectual technology for rendering

9 Hutchens, *Levinas*, 8.

existence "thinkable and predictable."[10] Psychoanalysis is not merely a
body of thought, but a certain form of life, one that gives its followers a language to articulate themselves and their own action, "to judge
and evaluate their existence," to give their experience a meaning, and
"to act upon themselves."[11] Many individuals appropriate the life and
identity-defining narrative of psychoanalysis when they seek to understand, endure and possibly conquer the problems that assail the
human condition such as despair, loss, tragedy, anxiety and conflict. In
effect, they try to synthesize the affectively discrepant experiences of
life through a psychoanalytic calculus and ethic. In this sense, psychoanalysis is similar to what Michel Foucault called a "technology of the
self" or a "practice of the self": "an exercise of the self, by which one attempts to develop and transform oneself, and to attain a certain mode
of being."[12] According to Pierre Hadot (writing in another context),
psychoanalysis can be viewed as a "spiritual exercise," a tool for living
life correctly. The aim of a spiritual exercise is to foster a deep modi-
fication of the individual's way "of seeing and being," a decisive change
in how he or she lives his or her practical, everyday life.[13] My hope is
that psychoanalysis can be enhanced and made more vigorous, livelier
and more poetic, as a self-sustaining narrative of self-identity through
better understanding of the form of life that Levinas insinuated in his
account of ethical subjectivity and in his general ethical reflections.

"TRANSLATING" LEVINAS INTO
PSYCHOANALYTIC LANGUAGE

To the reader steeped in the mainstream psychoanalytic "language
game," Levinas's poetic, stark and dramatic phenomenological descriptions of the human condition and self-experience, at least at first encounter, are hardly intelligible, let alone appealing and useful. Indeed,
the widespread "problem of reading" Levinas, says Davis, referring to
his seemingly deliberate "elusiveness," his "lapidary, aphoristic prose,"

---

10   Nikolas Rose, *Inventing Our Selves* (Cambridge: Cambridge University
press, 1996), 83.

11   Ibid., 62, 65.

12   Michele Foucault, "The Ethics of the Concern for the Self as a Practice
of Freedom," in *Foucault Live: Collected Interviews, 1961-1984*, ed. Sylvère
Lotringer (New York: Semiotexte, 1989), 433.

13   Pierre Hadot, *Philosophy as a Way of Life* (Oxford: Blackwell Publishers,
1997), 83.

which "makes few gestures towards patient exposition, and even gram-
matical links between sentences," seems "essential to the texture and
writing of his thought."[14] As Davis further notes, such an approach is
extremely hard going and discouraging for Levinas readers, including
I would add, the psychoanalytically-informed reader.

There is of course, no right or definitive way of explicating Levinas,
especially an explication that does not over-simplify in an attempt to
make narratively smooth his extremely elusive, elliptical and paradoxical prose. Mindful of this point, that Levinas is fiercely resistant to the
uninitiated, I will nevertheless attempt a "metaphoric redescription,"
to quote Mary Hess, of those Levinasian notions that have what I take
to have, a specifically psychoanalytic and psychological significance, especially to the practicing analyst and analysand. Indeed, contemporary psychoanalysis, a discipline that has been described by Marshall
Edelson as a "theory in crisis" characterized by a "profound malaise,"
by Nathan G. Hale as a "crisis of clashing theories, competing modes
of therapy, and uncertainties of professional identity," and by Edith
Kurzweil as marked by considerable theoretical "fragmentation,"[15] suffers from a scarcity of resonating and useful metaphors[16] that are more
relevant to our socio-moral zeitgeist. That is, metaphors are lacking
for more aptly talking about the human condition, ethical subjectivity,
and problems in living, that are more relevant to our current psychological, social and moral contexts. Levinas's evocative phenomenological language and penetrating understanding can contribute to improving this limitation in the current psychoanalytic intellectual landscape.
Moreover, as I will show, a Levinasian gloss on psychoanalysis offers new insights into some of the key thematics that are relevant to
analysands' troubled lives, such as embracing greater responsibility for
ourselves and especially for others, the nature of guilt and anxiety, giv-

---

14 Davis, *Levinas*, 129-136.

15 Marshall Edelson, *Psychoanalysis: a Theory in Crisis* (Chicago: University
of Chicago Press, 1988), xiv; Nathan G. Hale, *The Rise of and Crisis of Psychoanalysis in the United States* (New York: Oxford University Press, 1955),
360; Edith Kurzweil, *The Freudians: A Comparative Perspective* (New Haven: Yale University Press, 1989) 283.

16 Edwin E. Gantt and Richard N. Williams, "Pursuing Psychology as Science of the Ethical," in Edwin E. Gantt and Richard N. Williams, *Psychology-for-the-Other: Levinas, Ethics, and the Practice of Psychology* (Pittsburgh:
Duquesne University Press, 2002), 31.

ing and receiving love, enduring suffering, and the quest for spiritual transcendence.

In other words, only after Levinas's descriptions, observations and formulations are cautiously translated into another language, a more psychoanalytic and psychological one in our case, will they be more accessible, more illuminating and, I hope, more useful to the psychoanalyst and others interested in analysands' struggle for self-transfiguration, self-mastery and greater ethicality. In a certain sense, this book may be viewed as a collection of "retellings," to use Roy Schaefer's term,[17] of Levinas's descriptions that can help us fashion the important insights emanating from his elusive work. As Richard Rorty has pointed out, a "new vocabulary makes possible, for the first time, a formulation of its own purpose. It is a tool for doing something which could not have been engaged prior to the development of a particular set of descriptions, those which it itself helps to provide."[18] The problem for the explicator of Levinas is how to "retell" his narrative in a way that clearly conveys his insights but does not undermine his philosophical project by overly schematizing and systematizing it. Moreover, to make matters more difficult, Levinas tends to focus on what is conscious, phenomenological and holistic, whereas psychoanalysis is mainly concerned with unconscious processes and dynamics, the vicissitudes of the sexual and aggressive drives, and the internal object world. However, as Freud noted, while consciousness is a notoriously untrustworthy criterion to guide behavior, in the end, at least in a certain sense, it is all we have, especially as we engage the other: "Actions and consciously expressed opinions are as a rule enough for practical purposes in judging men's characters."[19] I will leave it to the reader to decide if my efforts at "retelling" Levinas into a more psychoanalytic and psychological language have been more or less "true" to the spirit of Levinas and reasonably illuminating and useful.

17   Roy Schaefer, *The Analytic Attitude* (New York: Basic Books, 1983), 255.

18   Richard Rorty, *Contingency, Irony and Solidarity* (New York: Cambridge University Press, 1989), 13

19   Freud, S.E., Vol. 5, *The Interpretation of Dreams*, 621. While consciousness is, in a way, all we have, the question for the psychoanalyst is what kind of consciousness? For Levinas, as for many of the great ancient religious wisdom traditions and spiritualities, and some philosophies, it is moral consciousness that matters the most.

ETHICS AND PSYCHOANALYSIS

Freud always wanted ethics and the goal of living a more moral life to be at the center of psychoanalysis. Such was implied in his letters to James Jackson Putnam: "That psychoanalysis has not made the analysts themselves better, nobler, or of stronger character remains a disappointment for me. Perhaps I was wrong to expect it." Freud answered his own question, "…Why should analyzed men and women in fact be better than others?" by saying that "[a]nalysis makes for integration, but does not of itself make for goodness." He also notes that "[o]ur art consists in making it possible for people to be moral and to deal with their wishes philosophically." It is well known that Freud tried to live an exemplary ethical life and, without arrogance, believed that he did: "…I consider myself a very moral human being, who can subscribe to the excellent maxim of Th. Visher: What is moral is always self-evident. I believe that in a sense of justice and consideration for one's fellow men, in discomfort at making others suffer or taking advantage of them, I can compete with the best men I have known. I have never done anything shameful or malicious, nor do I find in myself the temptation to do so." In light of Freud's strong ethical commitments and self-appraisal it is not surprising that he wrote in his paper "On Psychotherapy," that an important qualification for the treating analyst is that "his own character be irreproachable."[20]

My point is that though for Freud the development of an ethical outlook, or more aptly, living an ethical life, was always a central concern of his vision of psychoanalysis, in general, this aspect of his work has not been adequately appreciated or integrated into mainstream Freudian psychoanalysis. There is of course, a long and productive history of the psychoanalytic study of ethics and morality and the like, but as far as I know, no theorist has made ethical subjectivity, at least as Levinas conceives it—the ethical demand of the other, especially before oneself—as the grounding, animating, definitive hermeneutic horizon.

I have no intention of reviewing the very interesting and useful work done by psychoanalysts and psychoanalytic scholars on ethics, morality, the ethics of and in psychoanalysis, and other subjects on the inter-

---

20 Nathan G. Hale, editor, *James Jackson Putnam and Psychoanalysis*, trans. J.B. Heller (Cambridge: Cambridge University Press, 1971); Letters from Freud to Putnam, 11/13/13, pages 163-164; 6/7/15, page 188; 5/14/11, page121; 8/7/15, page 189; S.E., Volume 7, 267.

face of psychoanalysis and ethics. The works of Freud, Flügel, Fromm, Hartmann, Rieff, Winnicott, Erikson and Lacan are aptly summarized by Meissner, and both he and Wallwork, for example, offer good introductions to some of the ethical aspects of psychoanalysis.[21] What I want to do is provide the reader with a description of what Levinas means by ethics, for it very much departs from the usual use of the term in psychoanalytic circles. I then want to present some of the main themes of Levinas's writings, themes that I will detail in the later chapters. To begin with I want to convey to the reader a "sense" of, a "feel" for, the compelling nature of the Levinasian narrative without worrying about its technical aspects and complex conceptualizations. It is this "Levinasian effect,"[22] an openness to the ethical realm as Levinas conceives it, that I want to evoke.

A LEVINASIAN DEFINITION OF ETHICS

Before offering a definition of ethics as Levinas uses the term, it is necessary to contextualize such a definition in Levinas's wider project. One of the main reasons that Levinas is such a significant thinker is that his philosophy is possibly the most important attempt to go beyond the phenomenology of Edmund Husserl and Martin Heidegger, leading to his audacious assertion that ethics and alterity (otherness), "the Other...is what I am not,"[23] rather than ontology (knowledge of being and reality), is "first philosophy."[24] That is, whereas Heidegger asserted that in the way we comport ourselves toward the world, man's primary relation is with Being, and that "anguish" is the basic existential mood of existence, Levinas believed, in part, via the study of the Hebrew Bible and its Talmudic and other classical commentaries, that only the ethical relation permits us to transcend the isolation and aloneness of Being. Ethics, says Wirzba is "first philosophy" "because every pursuit of wisdom, if it is attentive to the integrity, even sanctity,

---

21   W.W. Meissner, *The Ethical Dimensions of Psychoanalysis* (Albany: State University of New York Press, 2003); Ernest Wallwork, *Psychoanalysis and Ethics* (New Haven: Yale University Press, 1991); Ernest Wallwork, "Ethics in Psychoanalysis," in *Textbook of Psychoanalysis*, eds. Ethel S. Person, Arnold M. Cooper and Glen O. Gabbard (Washington, DC: American Psychiatric Publishing, Inc., 2005), 281-300.

22   Davis, *Levinas*, 122.

23   *Levinas, Existence and Existents*, 98.

24   "Ethics as First Philosophy," in *The Levinas Reader*, 75-87.

of the other arises out of a moral claim placed upon the knower."[25] Thus, Levinas is mainly concerned with describing a relation with the other person that cannot be reduced to thematization and conceptualization, that is, to comprehension. As we shall see, he locates this in what he calls the "face-to-face" relation.[26] By claiming that ethics and morality are not divisions of philosophy but first philosophy, Levinas began a far-reaching critique of the Western philosophical tradition, proposing that philosophy, in a sense similar to psychoanalysis, is not simply the "love of wisdom," as the Greeks would have it, but rather, the "wisdom of love at the service of love."[27] Freud says in one of his letters to Carl Jung, psychoanalysis is actually "a cure by love."[28]

Wallwork, a professor of ethics, and a practicing analyst gives a reasonable and straightforward definition of ethics as conventionally understood in his review article on ethics in psychoanalysis: ethics is a "critical reflection about right and 'wrong' actions and 'good' and 'bad' character traits and other states of affairs."[29] Meissner, a Jesuit priest and analyst, defines ethics as "directives for a general pattern of life, a set of rules or codes governing right and wrong behavior, or an inquiry into the basis of rules of conduct (metaethics)."[30] While Levinas would probably agree that in a certain sense, both of these definitions are good ones, he would, however, most likely claim that they are not nearly complete, and certainly do not include what Levinas disruptively means by ethics.[31] Levinas's notion of ethics cuts much deeper than Wallwork's and Meissner's standard definitions of ethics.

25 Norman Wirzba, "Emmanuel Levinas," in *World Philosophers and Their Works*, ed. John K. Roth (Pasadena: Salem Press, 2000), volume 2, 1092.

26 Critchley, "Introduction," in *The Cambridge Companion to Levinas*, 8.

27 Levinas, *Otherwise Than Being*, 162.

28 William McQuire, editor, *The Freud/Jung Letters* (Princeton: Princeton University Press, 1974), 12-13.

29 Wallwork, "Ethics in Psychoanalysis," 281. While ethics offers disputations on behalf of our most fundamental "normative standards," morality is a more descriptive notion referring to how people actually think and behave within specific cultural settings (ibid).

30 Meissner, *The Ethical Dimensions of Psychoanalysis*, 2.

31 Wallwork and Meissner do not even list Levinas in their references.

In *Totality and Infinity*, Levinas defines ethics as follows: "We name this calling into question of my spontaneity by the presence of the Other ethics."[32] In an interview he elaborates that ethics is

> a comportment in which the other, who is strange and indifferent to you, who belongs neither to the order of your interest nor to your affections, at the same time matters to you. His alterity [otherness] concerns you. A relation of another order than that of knowledge, in which the object is given value by knowing it, which passes for the only relation with beings. Can one be for an I without being reduced to an object of pure knowledge? Placed in an ethical relation, the other man remain other.[33]

And in another interview, taken from the same book, Levinas further sharpens his definition of ethics:

> …ethics is no longer a simple moralism of rules which decree what is virtuous. It is the original awakening of an I responsible for the other; the accession of my person to the uniqueness of the I called and elected to responsibility for the other.[34]

Thus, says Simon Critchley, "ethics, for Levinas, is critique. It is the putting into question of the liberty, spontaneity and cognitive emprise of the ego that seeks to reduce all otherness to itself. Ethics is the location of a point of otherness, or what Levinas calls 'exteriority,' that cannot be reduced to the same."[35] Most importantly, "it is this putting into question of the same [the "I"] by the Other, this strangeness of the Other [that] puts everything that we are into question,"[36] that awakens us, compels us to responsibility for the Other.[37] Levinas says further that "ethics is an 'optics,'"[38] "an unmediated relation with the Other," the very "spiritual condition" and state "of ethical life."[39] Put simply, "ethics is the practical relation of one to an other, a relation which is prior to

---

32   Levinas, *Totality and Infinity*, 43.

33   Levinas, *Is It Righteous to Be?* 48.

34   Ibid., 182

35   Critchley, "Introduction," in *The Cambridge Companion to Levinas*, 15.

36   Wyschogrod, *Emmanuel Levinas*, 103.

37   Levinas rarely so clearly defines "ethics": "consciousness of a responsibility toward others," Levinas, *Proper Names*, 76).

38   Levinas, *Totality and Infinity*, 29.

39   Wyschogrod, *Emmanuel Levinas*, 245.

ontology."[40] As Derrida paradoxically sums it up, "It is true that Ethics, in Levinas's sense, is an Ethics without law and without concept.... Levinas does not seek to propose laws or moral rules, does not seek to determine *a* morality, but rather the essence of the ethical relation in general. But as this determination does not offer itself as a *theory* of Ethics, in question then, is an Ethics of Ethics...Is this Ethics of Ethics beyond all laws? Is it not the Law of laws?"[41]

SOME MAJOR THEMES IN LEVINAS'S PHILOSOPHY

There are two major texts, both extremely dense, that embody the core of Levinas's philosophical position: *Totality and Infinity: An Essay on Exteriority*,[42] which puts forth Levinas's views on ethics and alterity, and *Otherwise Than Being or Beyond Essence*, which focuses on the modalities that orient a subject that is sensitive and responsible to otherness. In other words, there is a conceptual transition from *Totality and Infinity* to *Otherwise Than Being*, from concentrating on the radical and overwhelming alterity of the other to concentrating on the impact of that alterity on the subjectivity of the person.[43] I will now summarize a few of the main ideas that are contained in these books so as to better contextualize my effort at suggesting the significance of Levinas's philosophy for psychoanalysis, and to familiarize the reader with Levinas's strange, evocative language. This summary does not aim to be comprehensive or heavily technical, and my hope is that it does not do violence to Levinas's summoning texts.

TOTALITY AND INFINITY

As Wirzba points out,[44] *Totality and Infinity* can perhaps be viewed as Levinas's response to both a cultural and philosophical crisis. The book was written in 1961, after Europe had come through two barbaric wars, which showed to an unimaginable degree, the violence and inhumanity that men and women are capable of. In particular, what

---

40 John Lechte, *Fifty Key Contemporary Thinkers* (London; Routledge, 1994), 117.

41 Derrida, "Violence and Metaphysics," 111.

42 Exteriority is Being, otherness, that which cannot be reduced to the same.

43 Cohen, translator's introduction, in Levinas, *Time and the Other*, 10-11.

44 Wirzba, "Emmanuel Levinas," 1093.

was especially troubling was the fact that some of the nations that perpetrated the violence and Holocaust were supposed to epitomize the highest development of Western tradition and culture. In response to this cultural crisis, Levinas wondered if there was an "eschatological hope," a relation with being beyond totality and history, towards the infinite that transcends totality, available to people. Could there be a hope maintained and nurtured by living a life of responsibility, not only for oneself, but firstly, for the other, that could possibly transform the pessimism and despondency of those who lived through these wars?[45]

That he had such a goal is not surprising given the fact that Levinas was personally devastated by the Holocaust. During World War II he was incarcerated for five years, mainly in Fallingpostel (north Germany), in a Nazi-administered prisoner of war camp for French soldiers. He did forced labor as an officer member of a Jewish labor force, the Jewish prisoners being separated from the non-Jewish ones, their uniforms marked with the word "JUD." Levinas's wife and daughter survived in France, as they were hidden in Paris and in a Vincentian convent outside Orleans, respectively, with the help of Levinas's non-Jewish friend and writer, Maurice Blanchot, and others. Levinas's parents, his two brothers and his mother and father-in law, however, were not so lucky, but were murdered by French and Lithuanian collaborators of the Nazis. Moreover, most of Levinas's community was also wiped out. These experiences, especially the premature and grotesque deaths of his loved ones, most likely influenced Levinas's return to the Lithuanian Orthodox Judaism of his upbringing, his career in Jewish education as the director of The École Normale Israelite Orientale (an organization created to train teachers for Jewish day schools in the Mediterranean Basin), his highly regarded Jewish scholarship with an emphasis on translating Hebraic or biblical wisdom into the language of Greece (Western philosophical discourse), and the "Jewish texturing" of many of his philosophical works. In fact, Levinas indicated that his life had been "dominated by the presentiment and the memory of

---

45 Wyschogrod, *Emmanuel Levinas*, 213. The term "totality" refers to those modes of thought and philosophies that erect some all-encompassing concept in relation to which all else must be understood. For Levinas, "ontology is conceptual" and metaphysics is a "passion for the infinite." See John Macquarrie, *Twentieth-Century Religious Thought* (Harrisburg: Trinity Press, 2001), 463.

the Nazi horror."[46] Moreover, on the memorial page in *Otherwise Than Being*, Levinas wrote "To the memory of those who were closest among the six million assassinated by the national Socialists, and of the millions of all confessions and all nations, victims of the same hatred of the other man, the same anti-Semitism." At the bottom of the page, written in traditionally-phrased Hebrew, is a personal memorial to those loved ones who were murdered. Levinas said he would never set foot in Germany again and he kept his promise. In other words, Levinas's philosophical and Jewish writings, can both, in part, be regarded as a post-Holocaust response from two overlapping perspectives: one written by a survivor[47] who aims both to bear witness to the horror he and others experienced, while affirming Jewish life, continuity and survival, the other to try to get at the "roots of hatred within Western thought" and society so "as to reverse its deadly logic."[48]

With regards to the philosophical crisis, Levinas was reacting to the important contributions of Husserl and Heidegger, which attempted to move philosophy in a novel, more demanding and exacting direction. Husserl, in his universal and transcendental approach to experience, conceived phenomenological philosophy as the science that would guide people beyond "relativism and naturalism" that dominated philosophical thinking at the time.[49] According to Heidegger's "fundamental ontology," phenomenology evoked and renewed an adequate sense of recognition and engagement with ourselves, that is, with the sense of Being. By doing so, phenomenology would lead us to "take hold of ourselves" in an authentic "resolution" of our own existence. It would help humanity to move away from inauthenticity—oneself as

---

46   Levinas, *Difficult Freedom*, 291.

47   In Holocaust scholarship and among "survivors," the question of who is a survivor has been debated. In my view, though Levinas was not in a concentration camp or a death camp, his experiences in as prisoner of war camp, including being separated out as a Jewish prisoner, the extreme disruption of his life while in Nazi Europe, and the enormous personal losses he suffered at the hands of the Nazis and their collaborators, make him a "survivor." Moreover, as I will quote in a later chapter, he viewed himself as a "survivor" of the Holocaust.

48   Susan Shapiro, "Emmanuel Levinas," in *Holocaust Literature*, ed. S. Lillian Kremer, (New York: Routledge, 2003), volume 2, 759-760.

49   Wirzba, "Emmanuel Levinas," 1093.

a merely generalized, undistinguished, and anonymous "anyone," towards authenticity –"resoluteness of being in the face of death."[50]

Levinas claimed that neither Husserl nor Heidegger actually focused
on what he thought was the key philosophical, and I would add, social
and psychological problem, after the world wars: how to intellectually and morally engage and transform the violent, brutal and inhu-
mane tendencies that underlie the Western philosophical outlook? As
Levinas viewed it,[51] the Western philosophical outlook and method,
including psychoanalysis to some extent, is intrinsically totalitarian;
it tends to refuse, deny and conceal "the otherness of reality, reducing
it to sameness in thought," that is, to all-inclusive totalities. By not
recognizing, acknowledging and affirming the otherness, integrity
and transcendence of the one disrespected and violated, totalization
is operative. Nothing "'outside' or 'beyond' the totality" is allowed to
interrogate, challenge or dispute it. Humane rational thought, critical reason and moral process is thus not possible.[52] In terms of the
intersubjective encounter this means engaging the other with an eye
to "knowing what makes him or her tick," rather than attempting to
reduce his or her existence to a personality or character type, social
stereotype or diagnostic category. It is to be receptive and responsive,
with the fullness of one's being, to the fundamentally evocative, mysterious, autonomous otherness of the Other. Levinas tries to develop
a modality of reflection that is both receptive and responsible to the
Infinite (something-outside-everything, e.g., the Other, ethics, transcendence, God). Such "a responsiveness to the otherness [and dif-
ference] of things" is not characterized by mindless domination by
means unreflectively judged as "good," appropriate, or "proper"; nor is
it characterized by the imposition of, or conformity with, normative
standards and identities.[53] Levinas calls this the "face to face" encounter. The face is his term for "moral consciousness" or "the personality."[54]

---

50   David Carr, "Husserl and Phenomenology," in *The Columbia History of
     Western Philosophy*, ed. Richard H. Popkin (New York: Columbia Univer-
     sity Press, 1999), 679.

51   Wirzba, "Emmanuel Levinas," 1093.

52   Ibid.

53   Scott, "Continental Philosophy at the Turn of the Twenty-First Century,"
     752.

54   Levinas, *Entre Nous. Thinking-Of-The-Other* (London: the Athlone Press,

Levinas's yearning was that such a new way of thinking and being in the world would lead to greater tolerance for difference and peaceful co-existence and away from hatred, atrocity, genocide and war.

Levinas's situating of the foundation of ethics in the face-to-face relation where the other challenges and questions me means that my obligations to the other are neither negotiated nor consented to by me. My obligations not only are prior to the debts and liabilities I amass, but also go beyond anything I could possibly fulfill. In *Otherwise Than Being* Levinas further explores the "I" that is challenged and put into question in the engagement with the other. Ultimately, what Levinas discerns is alterity, otherness within the self: "In the form of responsibility, the psyche in the soul is the other in me, a malady of identity, both accused and *self*, the same for the other, the same by the other."[55] As Kunz points out, "the soul is the other in me" means that the nature of the self is to seek the good revealed in others, and, by doing so, the self finds itself, genuinely working for the sake of others, for their best interests. "The self finds the Other-in-the-self, or, the self finds itself-in-the-Other"; both formulations mean that fundamentally, ontologically, we are moved to find ourselves in the Other while the Other maintains his or her absolute uniqueness and otherness.[56] Most importantly, says Levinas, we are originally, indeclinably responsible for the Other. In other words, Levinas has developed a metaphysics based on ethical considerations by demonstrating that "man's being in the world" is a "moral being."[57]

As Bernasconi points out,[58] perhaps most importantly, Levinas is claiming that in the face-to-face encounter one's self-confidence and self-efficacy diminish, if not vanish, and one finds oneself living in bad faith experiencing guilt. Levinas does not appeal to conventional ethics to reestablish good faith and conscience, nor does he believe that one has the comfort of knowing that one did the right thing in any given context. One can always do more for the other, and this awareness is, in part the basis for man's guilt and bad conscience. He also maintains

---

1998), 11; *Proper Names*, 95.

55   Levinas, *Otherwise than Being*, 69.

56   Kunz, *The Paradox of Power and Weakness*, 31-32.

57   Wyschogrod, *Emmanuel Levinas*, 228.

58   Robert Bernasconi, "Levinas, Emmanuel," in *Encyclopedia of Philosophy*, ed. Edward Craig (London: Routledge, 1998), volume 5, 580.

that it is not simply a matter of cognitive understanding and conscious knowledge. Rather, what Levinas is getting at is the notion that one's obligations to the Other are infinite, asymmetrical, non-reciprocal and non-dialogic, at least in the sense that one does not have the right to request, let alone demand, from the other what the other requests of me. As I suggest in Chapter 4, "Love without Lust," in many ways such a view of the face-to-face encounter is opposed to a broadly conceived psychoanalytic outlook, perhaps most evidently in relational psycho-analysis, which tends to assume that adult relationships should be symmetrical and reciprocal,[59] that relationships are characterized by mutual utility: "I love fully only if the other loves."[60]

Rather, Levinas is getting at something more originary, "an-archic,"[61] and summoning, the responsibility for the other that is antecedent to one's freedom. Levinas succinctly makes this point by often quoting Aloysha Karamazov in Dostoyevski's *The Brothers Karamazov*: "We are guilty for all and for all men before all, and I more than the others." And again in another version, "We are all responsible for everyone else—but I am more responsible than all the others."[62]

The face of the Other, then, represents what Levinas refers to as exteriority (otherness, infinity, what cannot be made intelligible by consciousness)—"The absolutely other is the Other," says Levinas,[63] with the face signifying the opportunity for channeling one's freedom and autonomy to responsibility for the Other. The face, not to be tak-en literally as physicality, is Levinas's term for that which disrupts, de-stabilizes and defamilarizes thought and its tendency towards totality and sameness; it is the "disincarnate presence of the Other,"[64] "a relation whose terms do not form a totality can hence be produced within the

---

59   Paul Marcus and Alan Rosenberg, eds, *Psychoanalytic Versions of the Hu-man Condition. Philosophies of Life and Their Impact on Practice* (New York: New York University Press, 1998), chapters 6, 7, 9, 10.

60   Levinas, *Totality and Infinity*, 266.

61   "Arche," says Smith, means beginning, rule or principle, "a past that never was present" (Smith, *Toward the Outside*, 12). "An-archic" thus means "out-side of synchronous time and re-presentational being," and outside and prior to language (Fryer, *The Intervention of the Other*, 225).

62   Levinas, *Ethics and Infinity*, 101; Levinas, *Face to Face with Levinas*, 31.

63   Levinas, *Totality and Infinity*, 85.

64   Wychogrod, *Emmanuel Levinas*, 244.

economy of being only as proceeding from the I to the other, as a *face to face*…"[65] Most obviously, this tendency to totalization is seen in political totalitarianism, dogmatic religious and philosophical ideologies, formal logic, and psychological and sociological categories that aim to capture the so-called essence or nature of the human condition, personality and social interaction. "Sociology, psychology and physiology are deaf to exteriority."[66] The face is thus the perfect term for Levinas in that perhaps better than anything else, the face of the Other refuses to be constrained, pinned down, or trapped by any totalizing effort that tries to make it utterly intelligible, transparent, predictable and controllable. It is "the source of revelation of the other who cannot be encompassed in cognition," and "it calls separated being, egoity, the self into question."[67] There is thus a traumatic, affectively-infused immediacy in the encounter with the Other, the ethical relation conceived as "the original traumatism," says Levinas.[68]

I should remind the reader that the actual face of skin and bones is not what mainly interests Levinas philosophically, though it is not irrelevant either, as Levinas is concerned with the ethical and moral outlook and behavior of real people in the real world, especially in terms of the "third party," all others, that is, the concrete operations of justice. Levinas's texts are replete with references to our obligations to the vulnerable, disenfranchised and powerless clusters of people whom we are obliged, if not commanded, to honor, protect and take care of. Thus, for Levinas, the modality of the Other's presence is de-

---

65   Levinas, *Totality and Infinity*, 39.

66   Ibid., 291.

67   Wyschogrod, *Emmanuel Levinas*, 244.

68   Levinas, *Basic Philosophical Writings* (Bloomington, IN: Indiana University Press, 1996), 90. By conceiving of the relation with the Other as traumatic Levinas means that the Other decisively erodes, if not removes ones self-assurance and stability. The encounter with the Other divests one of the time necessary to assess what has taken place and to choose how to respond to it. The Other "devastates and awakens", "compels me to Goodness." Precisely how the Other does this is not known to Levinas (*Otherwise Than Being*, 148-149). Perhaps it is to psychoanalysis that we must turn to understand how the compelling and commanding Other dwells, forms, and changes the heart and mind of the hearer.

scribed most directly, concretely and poignantly by a biblical criterion and sensibility; the Other is the stranger, the widow and orphan.[69]

OTHERWISE THAN BEING

In *Otherwise Than Being,* published in 1974, Levinas picks up where he left off in *Totality and Infinity*: in what ways the other challenges the very sense of what it means to be an "I." But where *Totality and Infinity* mainly dealt with the other, *Otherwise Than Being* is more focused on the existential orientation and "meaning of the subject,"[70] what psychoanalysts usually refer to as self-identity or selfhood. To Levinas, being-for-the-Other, having an unending responsibility for the Other, implies a loss, if not eradication, of one's taken-for-granted, normative, felt sense of self-identity and selfhood.[71] In other words, Levinas rejects the Western tradition initiated by Réne Descartes, including its psychoanalytic expression, which largely characterizes human existence, the human subject, as an ego or an I.[72] To the contrary, Levinas attempts to demonstrate that the human self has a structure other than the one that was established by Descartes. Moreover, he does this without eliminating "human subjectivity and autonomy," as many French philosophers and others have done, suggesting instead that the conventional way of problematizing subjectivity and autonomy needs to be radically changed.[73] Levinas's notion of substitution, what he calls the "centerpiece" of *Otherwise than Being*, is a key element in this effort.[74]

As Bernasconi points out, Levinas claims that at the center of subjectivity is not a "for itself," but what Levinas describes as "the one-for-the-Other." Alterity is at the center of subjectivity and, according to Levinas, it is characterized by ethicality. It should be pointed out that while Levinas moves beyond egoism, he does so without folding his argument into advocating altruism, at least as altruism is usually understood: "beyond egoism and altruism it is the religiosity of the

---

69   Ibid., 105.

70   Davis, *Levinas*, 70.

71   Bernasconi, "Levinas, Emmanuel," 580.

72   Peperzak, *To the Other*, 25.

73   Ibid.

74   Levinas, *Otherwise than Being*, xivii.

self," that is, the self as infinitely responsible.[75] Levinas is not claiming that one should be altruistic, though I have no doubt that he had the highest regard for such behavior and his philosophy certainly points in that direction.[76] Rather, or in addition, his philosophical effort is aimed at accounting for the possibility of sacrificing oneself,[77] of being roused to the fundamental imperative, the "ought" of ethics, prior to choice, of living for-the-Other before oneself. Drawing on Platonic doctrine, in particular, the "form of the Good," and Descartes' notion of the "idea of the infinite," the other's "highness" or "infinity" ruptures my existence by a fundamental command, "Do not kill me" (literally and figuratively), help me to live, to flourish.[78]

According to Levinas,

> to substitute oneself does not amount to putting oneself in the place of the other man in order to feel what he feels [as psychoanalysis tends to conceptualize empathy]; it does not involve becoming the other or, if he be destitute and desperate, the courage of such a trial. Rather, substitution entails bringing comfort by associating ourselves with the essential weakness and finitude of the other; it is to bear his weight while sacrificing one's interestedness and complacency-in-being, which then turns into responsibility for the other.[79]

As Hand succinctly points out,[80] what is important to note about substitution is that for Levinas responsibility for the other is viewed as "a pre-original or an-archic fact." It antecedes "any act through which one might assume responsibility for" an action or social role and goes

---

75   Ibid, 117.

76   Levinas, *Proper Names*, 73. "The election [the putting in question of the I by the Other] signifies the most radical commitment there is, total altruism."

77   Bernasconi, "What is the question to which 'substitution' is the answer?" *The Cambridge Companion to Levinas*, 235.

78   Adriaan Peperzak, "Emmanuel Levinas," in *The Cambridge Dictionary of Philosophy*, ed. Robert Audis (New York: Cambridge University Press, 2005), 488. "Do not kill me," includes all the ways that we dishonor, disrespect and hurt others in our everyday lives. Rudeness, gossiping, backbiting and mean-spiritedness are good examples.

79   Levinas, *Is It Righteous to Be*, 228.

80   Hand, *The Levinas Reader*, 88.

"beyond my death in its" significance and ramifications. Levinas, continues Hand, is thus moving beyond the ontology of *Totality and Infinity* into what he calls "Otherwise than being," a relation established not
on death as Heidegger claimed, but rather, on alterity. As Hand puts
it, "The *original* form of openness is therefore my exposure to alterity
in the face of the other. I literally put my self in the place of another,"
more than, and different than, the psychological experience of caring
and compassion. Moreover, such substitution is not a renunciation "of
responsibility, but a passivity" that endures the weight "of everything
for which the other is responsible." In other words, according to Hand,
"I become a subject in the physical sense of being hostage to the other.
The unconditionality of this responsibility means that we are always
already beyond essence." Thus, for Levinas, a subject or self that has
given up the need for comprehensive thematization and systematic ob-
jectification, for understanding and control, will be so responsible for
the other as to be substituted for the other, including to the point of
the other's suffering and even death.[81]

For Levinas, though ontology is the realm of being, relationships to
others do not fit within being so conceived. The rupture of being, the
face of the other that summons me to responsibility, is beyond ontology, it points to alterity and transcendence, to "otherwise than being."

"To be oneself, otherwise than being, to be dis-interested,[82] is to
bear the wretchedness and bankruptcy of the other, and even the responsibility that the other can have for me. To be oneself, the state
of being a hostage, is always to have one degree of responsibility, the
responsibility for the responsibility of the other." Elsewhere, he says,
"I exist through the other and for the other, but without this being
alienation: I am inspired."[83]

In light of this description of substitution, Levinas does not shy
away from asking perhaps the most fundamental question, the one
that skeptical analysts with their interest in human motivation would
surely wonder about: "Why does the other concern me in the first
place? Am I "really" my brother's keeper?" He says that

---

81 Wirzba, "Emmanuel Levinas," 1092.

82 "Dis-interested," says Levinas, means "disengaged from all participation"
    (*Totality and Infinity*, 109). In other words, "taking on oneself the being of
    the other," i.e., responsibility (*Is It Righteous to Be?* 108).

83 Levinas, "Substitution," in *The Levinas Reader*, 107, 104.

these questions have meaning only if one has already supposed that the ego is concerned only with itself, is only a concern for itself. In this hypothesis it indeed remains incomprehensible that the absolute outside-of-me, the other, would concern me. But in the 'prehistory' of the ego posited for itself speaks a responsibility. The self is through and though a hostage, older than the ego, prior to principles. What is at stake for the self, in its being, is not to be. Beyond egoism and altruism is the religiosity of the self,[84] [i.e., assuming responsibility for the Other is a testimonial to the ethical, to the glory of the Infinite.][85]

What Levinas is getting at is that such questions as "why does the other concern me?" in the ethical sense, assume a concept of the ego that is derivative from my proximity to the Other. Proximity, a frequently used Levinasian term, refers to the approach to the Other, though it is a much more complex notion.[86] In this view, human subjectivity is not the separate and isolated ego of modern philosophy, and to some extent, certain versions of psychoanalysis maintain aspects of this underlying presupposition about the human condition. Rather, subjectivity conceived as being hostage, is the unsettledness, the experience of being provoked, deeply troubled, summoned by the Other to help him. This means acting without concern for symmetricality and reciprocity, two of the key aspects of most psychoanalytic concepts of love. "Proximity is quite distinct from every other relationship, and has to be conceived as a responsibility for the other, it might be called humanity, or subjectivity, or self."[87]

LEVINAS AND PSYCHOANALYSIS

"I am definitely not a Freudian," declared Levinas in an interview.[88] Levinas rarely, if ever, makes any mention, let alone sustained and/ or positive discussion, of Freud or psychoanalysis. Likewise, he does

---

84 Levinas, *Otherwise than Being*, 117.

85 Levinas, *Ethics and Infinity*, 113.

86 Lingis says in his translator's introduction to *Otherwise than Being*, "But the subject is exposed to alterity before it can gather itself up and take a stand. This closeness without distance, this immediacy of an approach which remains approach without what approaches being circumscribable, locatable there, Levinas calls proximity" (xxv).

87 Levinas, *Otherwise than Being*, 46.

88 Levinas, *Is It Righteous to Be?* 174.

not cite the work of Lacan, who wrote and lectured at about the same time in Paris, often to the same audiences and colleagues, about similar themes.[89] Levinas points out that his early exposure to Freud was by a professor who had developed a "Bergsonian psychology quite hostile to Freud—a hostility that made a deep and lasting impression on me."[90] Despite Levinas's ambivalence toward Freud and disinterest in psychoanalysis, he did indicate that psychoanalysis helped critique and deconstruct consciousness as we know it.[91] It is also worth noting that, unfortunately, not only did Levinas not draw from Freud and divergent mainstream post-Freudian psychoanalysis in developing his philosophy, but he also never considered those psychoanalytic thinkers who were steeped in the same intellectual tradition as he was, that of phenomenology, including Heidegger. The names of European psychiatrists Ludwig Binswanger, Medard Boss, Jan Linschoten and Jan Van den Berg come to mind as does the work of psychologists Adrian Van Kaam and Rollo May in the United States. One wonders what Levinas would have made of these important phenomenologically-based thinkers and what his philosophy would have looked and felt like if he had integrated their work and other insights from psychoanalysis into his philosophy. That this book aims to show Levinas's transformational significance for psychoanalysis is an irony that is worth noting.

My claim in this book is that psychoanalysis can be enhanced on a theoretical and clinical level by intellectually engaging Levinas's path-breaking ethical writings. More specifically, my argument is that like Freud, Levinas was focused on personal existence, on those issues of ultimate value and meaning that are central to what it means to be a human being at its best. According to Levinas, it was the strength and "certainty" of the "inner self" that was the primary source of strength for Jews and non-Jews resisting Nazi barbarism.[92] Both Levinas and Freud can be read as thinkers who were interested in helping to create the conditions of possibility for human beings to be kinder, gentler, stronger, and more reasonable in the face of the harshness, chaos, and moral challenges that we all face in our personal lives and on the world scene.

---

89   As far as I know, in his writings Lacan never cited let alone discussed Levinas's work, nor did they correspond with each other.

90   Levinas, *Face to Face with Levinas*, 13.

91   Levinas, *Entre Nous*, 33-34.

92   Levinas, *Proper Names*, 121-122.

This book aims to contribute to the development of an alternative paradigm, or at least, a complementary paradigm to mainstream psychoanalysis, one that is based on the Levinasian assumption that the call, or better yet the command for responsibility to others delineates the fundamental cast of the human mind. In contrast, with the partial exception of Lacan's famous critique of ego psychology,[93] mainstream psychoanalysis tends to describe human experience and behavior as events of an ego-centered, self-centric being solely and/or firstly concerned with itself. That is, either an ego or self propelled, as Freud says, by biological and instinctual causes, similar to animals, or a willing ego empowering itself to enhance personal self-esteem and self-efficacy. A Levinasian-animated psychoanalysis offers an alternative view of human experience, one that has been described as a "radical altruism" by one Levinasian-inspired psychologist.[94] While Levinas's notion of "otherwise than being"—a person's withdrawal of its interestedness in being toward the Other—includes altruism as conventionally understood as a part of an orienting modality, Levinas is getting at something more primordial, what he calls responsibility for the Other. Psychoanalysis, viewed as a value-laden technology of the self, advocates a way of being in the world that seems to encourage us to orient and justify our actions and efforts to be responsible for ourselves, and only secondarily and instrumentally to others largely for reasons of mutual utility. In contrast, Levinas points us away from self-interest, egoism and infantile narcissism as first principle, towards selfless-like service[95]

93   In contrast to the so-called ego or "I," which is a distorting, deforming, estranging screen, Lacan offers us a "decentered" subject. See Marion M. Oliner, "Jacques Lacan: The Language of Alienation," in Paul Marcus and Alan Rosenberg, *Psychoanalytic Versions of the Human* Condition: *Philosophies of Life and Their Impact on Practice* (New York: New York University Press, 1998), 362-391.

94   Kunz, *The Paradox of Power and Weakness*, 3-29.

95   I say selfless-like service because psychoanalytically speaking, even the most seemingly selfless act has some narcissistic gratification on some level. Moreover, there is a certain truth to the paradox that the search for selflessness is inevitably self-referential and often selfish. Similarly, as Ambrose Bierce noted, an abstainer is a weak individual who gives in to the temptation of denying himself a pleasure. While in a certain sense all of this is semantically true, it is one's intention, whether one's action is largely motivated by the needs of the Other or of the self, that is the crucial element in making such a determination about how selfless an action is, especially pragmatically speaking.

and unconditional giving and serving as a basis for reasonable, decent and satisfying living. In other words, where the psyche of modern psychoanalysis is the ego or self establishing itself in the center of the individual personality, configuring its own identity, manipulating its environment to satisfy its needs, and enjoying the pleasure of gratifying those strivings (in a certain sense, legitimate strivings), I argue, following Levinas, that modern psychoanalysis needs to advance to the study of the human psyche's ability to transcend its self-centric needs to find a deeper and stronger desire than those of self-interest, self-sufficiency, individualism. This new view, the one I will be describing and detailing in the rest of this book, emanates from a different presupposition, of the self "having its identity inspired by others, animated by others, and empowered and sustained by others,"[95a] to establishing its fundamental identity of responsibility towards, and for others. It is the idea that the center of the self is the Other, not the ego or "I" as psychoanalysis usually assumes, that is one of the most important guiding metaphors of this book.

Psychoanalysis has put forth at least three broadly conceived versions of the subject/self or what I have called elsewhere, "versions of the human condition"[96] that tend to guide and delimit clinical practice: man as fundamentally pleasure-seeking (Freud), object-seeking (e.g., Melanie Klein and Donald Winnicott), and meaning-seeking (e.g., Roy Schaefer and Donald Spence).[97] Moreover, we have further variations on these versions of the subject as depicted by Heinz Kohut's famous contrast between Freud's "Guilty Man" and "Tragic Man." Freud's Guilty Man continuously struggles toward satisfaction of his drives. He lives under the sovereignty of the pleasure principle, endeavoring to resolve inner conflict, and he is often frustrated in his objective of tension reduction by those who have brought him up. By dramatic contrast, Tragic Man struggles to satisfy the aspirations of his bi-polar nuclear self. Tragic Man strives to articulate the pattern of his very being, the ideals, ambitions and self-expressive goals that

---

95a Kunz, *The Paradox of Power and Weakness*, 148.

96 Marcus and Rosenberg, *Psychoanalytic Versions of the Human Condition: Philosophies of Life and Their Impact on Practice*, 3.

97 Fred Weinstein, *History and Theory After the Fall: An Essay on Interpretation* (Chicago: University of Chicago Press, 1990), 27.

go beyond the pleasure principle.[98] For Guilty Man the central anxiety is castration anxiety, while for Tragic Man it is the dread of complete disintegration.

Thus, we have a number of so-called "master narratives" about subjectivity, about the human condition, that tend to guide and animate clinical practice. To make matters even more complicated, not only do each of these perspectives have their advocates, but there are important differences within each perspective. As Roth points out, Freud offers us a narrative of the "taming of the beast within," while Kohut narrates according to "the discovery of the self within." Klein postulates the "mad person within raging about," and Schaefer's hermeneutic narrative focuses on the increasing of responsibility, from "self-as-victim of unknown psychic forces" to "master in one's own house."[99] While these master narratives have their appeal and usefulness, I am suggesting that the analytic community consider an alternative paradigm in its theorizing, one that is rooted in the evocative Levinasian angle of vision on existence: the sacrificing mother "who takes bread from her mouth and the milk from her body to give to...[her]child."[100] The powerful story of a mother and child in Turkey who were trapped under the earthquake ruble for days comes to mind. When her child became weak from loss of nourishing fluids, the woman cut the tip of her finger with a piece of broken glass for the child to suck her blood. Remarkably, they both survived.[101]

Such a Levinasian-inspired narrative of the human condition points psychoanalysis in a very different direction than is conventionally conceived. It emphasizes that the "responsibility for, and obligation to, the Other are absolute": they are greater than the individual's responsibility to satisfy them, there is always more demanded and required, and they are never accomplished by the fulfillment of any one deed.[102] In

---

98   Heinz Kohut, *The Restoration of the Self.* (New York: International Universities Press, 1977), 133.

99   Paul A. Roth, "The Cure of Stores, Self-Deception, Danger Situations, and the Clinical Role of Narratives in Roy Schaefer's Psychoanalytic Theory," in Marcus and Rosenberg, *Psychoanalytic Versions of the Human Condition*, 327.

100 Kunz, *The Paradox of Power and Weakness*, 148.

101 Ibid.

102 Davis, *Levinas*, 54.

other words, "as a moral subject," the individual is always found lacking, because ethics is not just a component of one's existence as psychoanalysis usually assumes, but delimits the entire realm in which
he resides.[103] Such a notion of the subject, formed, shaped and ultimately constituted by the encounter with the other, "the basis of ethical relations founded on" the encounter,[104] suggest a reorientation for
psychoanalysis in at least one fundamental way: a psychoanalysis that
moves away from viewing the Other as primarily a source of gratification of one's relational needs, whether for companionship, friendship, love and intimacy. Rather, following Levinas, I am imagining a
psychoanalytic subject that lives with a different sensibility, a different
way of being in the world, one in which he declares with the fullness
of his or her being, like Abraham—"Heneni"—"Here I am!" Such a
person, says Levinas, knows and feels with radical clarity and moral
passion that "the node of the subjective is knotted in ethics understood
as responsibility."[105] In my imaginings, this is a psychoanalytic subject
who is less driven by pleasure, meaning or even object seeking and attachment needs as analysts usually use these terms. Rather, in this new
psychoanalytic version of subjectivity it is the image of the panic and
horror-filled Turkish mother and her vulnerable, weak, near-death
child who lies helplessly under the rubble from the earthquake that
the Levinasian-inspired psychoanalytic subject is haunted by. Levinas's
notion of subjectivity is thus conceptualized in strictly ethical terms,
as responsibility for the Other, a "demand" or "commandment to giving and serving."[106] Moreover, it is important to note, Levinas's ethical
subject does not augment a preceding existential base as psychoanalysts usually assume in its various versions of subjectivity. Rather, the
subject is from the onset the responsible self-hostage to the other.

LAYOUT OF THE BOOK

The main purpose of this book is to help psychoanalysts and psychoanalytically informed mental health practitioners and interested others, to intellectually engage Levinas's ethical philosophy and to discern
its great significance for psychoanalytic theory, especially clinical prac-

103 Ibid.
104 Ibid., 79.
105 Levinas, *Ethics and Infinity*, 95.
106 Ibid., 119.

tice. As Todd has noted, "There is little in the way of extensive discussion of Levinas's work from a clinical psychoanalytic perspective."[107] Thus, rather than structure this book around strictly theoretical and technical lines, I have chosen to organize it along the "big themes" that frequently emerge within the treatment context, those "experience near" themes that constitute the heart of analysands' lives as they actually live them and describe them in the consultation room.

In Chapter Two, "Responsibility for the Other," I flesh out Levinas's key concept of responsibility for the Other, especially as it relates to two real-life human contexts, the concentration camp inmate's ordeal of surviving as a "person," and the treatment setting, in an attempt to understand the nature of genuine and neurotic guilt. It is in this chapter that I introduce the case of "John," an analysand whom I analyzed for many years and who is clinically discussed in all of the other chapters except the conclusion. These accompanying vignettes, located at the end of each chapter, suggest, at least in a rudimentary sense, how a Levinasian-inspired psychoanalysis might successfully animate the treatment context. Chapter Three, "The Horror of Existence," takes up Levinas's intriguing concept of the "there is," impersonal being, perhaps reasonably viewed as a sub-species of anxiety in psychoanalytic parlance. This chapter reviews various psychoanalytic accounts of anxiety and then offers Levinas's angle of vision on the "there is," anonymous being, and its significance for understanding the source, expression and meanings of certain forms of what analysts call anxiety. Chapter 4, "Love Without Lust," takes up Levinas's ethically-infused notion of love, conceived as mainly asymmetrical, non-reciprocal responsibility for the Other before oneself. This view is contrasted to a number of mainstream psychoanalytic notions of love, which largely locate it in the self, not in the other, as Levinas does. Chapter 5, "Eroticism and Family Love," considers love in terms of sexual passion, such as is manifested in eroticism, gender and family relations. Chapter 7, "Religion Without Promises," takes up Levinas's insights into the so-called spiritual realm, what he broadly calls biblical wisdom, and its associated notions of God, transcendence and holiness. Chapter 6, "Making Suffering Sufferable," again mainly by drawing on the concentration camp inmate's ordeal, concerns itself with the problem of how individuals can endure pain and suffering while maintain-

107 Sharon Todd, *Levinas, Psychoanalysis, and Ethical Possibilities in Education* (Albany: SUNY Press, 2005), 149.

ing their autonomy, integration and humanity. Chapter 8, "Towards a Levinasian-inspired, 'Ethically-infused' Psychoanalysis," I summarize and elaborate what Levinas offers psychoanalysis as it tries to transform itself into a radically ethical theory and technique. I do this, in part, by suggesting what a Levinasian conception of the human condition "looks and feels like," and most importantly, how such a conception impacts on understanding psychopathology and construing treatment. In all of the above chapters, the focus is always on Levinas's "ethics of ethics," "the ethical relation in general," as Derrida called it, and how such a way of seeing and understanding human experience can enhance psychoanalysis. Levinas is interested in how such biblical wisdom can be helpful to the analysand as he tries to transform his "ethically disabled" character and ethically disordered life, into one in which his "commitments," personal "concerns," "judgments" and actions are ethically significant[108]—the responsible self that is for the Other.

Finally, while for Levinas, "subjectivity-hostage"[109] is the unchosen groundless ground of being, the very structure of being, for it to be the ultimate source of significance in one's actual lived, authentic life, quite clearly, as in psychoanalysis, requires great personal effort at self-understanding and self-transformation. That is, as Gadamer points out, our self-understanding always involves self-transformation, since our engagement with the Other is the vehicle whereby we ourselves become something other, something more, and hopefully, something better than we were prior to the engagement. When we engage the disruptive texts of Levinas, and the demanding form of moral life that they point to, whose newness is a radical challenge to our conventional way of seeing and experiencing, what they say, what the Other says to us, in Gadamer's words, is "You must change yourself."[110]

---

108 Jonathan Jacobs, *Choosing Character. Responsibility For Virtue and Vice* (Ithaca: Cornell University Press, 2001), 1, 119.

109 Levinas, *Otherwise Than Being*, 197.

110 G.B. Madison, "Hermeneutics: Gadamer and Ricoeur," in Richard H. Popkin, ed, *The Columbia University History of Western Philosophy* (New York: Columbia University Press, 1999), 709.

2

RESPONSIBILITY FOR THE OTHER

I understand responsibility as responsibility for the Other,
thus as responsibility for what is not my deed, or for what does not even
matter to me; or which precisely does matter to me,
is met by me as face.[1]

Levinas

For nearly all psychoanalysts and insight-oriented psychotherapists, the notion of responsibility, in some form, is the bedrock to their clinical work. The analysand is invited to honestly confront himself, critically explore his internal world and take responsibility for what he encounters there. It is mainly through this taking responsibility for who one is, for who one was, and for who one aspires to be, that the potential for internal change and growth comes about. Consequential thinking is vital to this process. However, also permeating the analytic process, is the analysand's tendency to avoid taking responsibility for his inner life, a kind of flight from himself, which forms the basis for resistance. Resistance is here conceived as that elaborate system of hideouts that the analysand creates to protect himself from honest self-scrutiny; it is the many conscious and unconscious ways in which the analysand attempts to subvert the goal of change.

Analysts are of course, also concerned with the analysand's real life behavior outside the consultation room, in the external world. It is not only what one says in the analytic encounter that is important, but what one does in his everyday real life. An analysis is viewed as a success by many analysts by the extent to which the analysand can translate his psychological insights and self-understandings into changed behavior (thoughts, feelings and actions). This almost always involves assuming greater responsibility for one's behavior, including its consequences for others, or, as Levinas and the existentialists might say, for one's mode of being-in-the-world.

---

1 Levinas, *Ethics and Infinity,* 95.

The above formulation of responsibility for oneself is reasonable and useful. What does Levinas add to the conversation about responsibility that has bearing on psychoanalysis? I believe that Levinas would probably find the above-described clinical process, one that is mainly based on an autonomous selfhood notion, as good, though not complete, that psychoanalysis has only provided a partial answer in its understanding of responsibility for oneself, and more generally, of ethical existence. From a Levinasian point of view, psychoanalysis is not wrong to describe ethical experience in terms of an autonomous self-sufficient selfhood. Ideally, at least after a successful analysis, the analysand is better able to rationally and critically reflect and, thus, to discern the most morally commendable course of behavior available in a particular situation. Certainly, this notion of responsibility for oneself, at least in many contexts, is relevant and compelling to the person engaged in psychoanalytic psychotherapy who also attempts to live his or her life by a psychoanalytic calculus.

What Levinas contributes to psychoanalysis is an enriching portrait of a very different kind of selfhood, one not simply lodged within familiar notions of responsibility for oneself. In a sense, Levinas goes further than mainstream psychoanalysis in that he posits and describes a selfhood mainly based on its responsibilities for, and obligations to, others. Says Kunz: "The self finds its meaning, not centered in itself as an ego establishing its individual freedom and power, but as a self facing the other person who calls the self out of its center to be ethically responsible."[2] As I indicated earlier, psychoanalysis can enlarge and deepen itself by embracing the idea that responsibility for, and to, others, defines a basic, primary characteristic of the psyche, and more generally, human existence.

In this chapter I want to first flesh out the previous discussion of Levinas's key concept of responsibility for the Other, including his bold claim that freedom is secondary to responsibility, and not the other way around as psychoanalysts usually conceive it. The heart of this chapter is an exploration of how the concept of responsibility for the Other relates to two real-life human contexts. First, I describe its importance in a concentration camp inmate's struggle to survive his ordeal as a "person." Second, I want to suggest, at least in an elemental manner, a few ways that Levinas's formulation of responsibility for the

---

2 Kunz, *The Paradox of Power and Weakness*, 34.

Other can enhance the psychoanalytic understanding(s) of guilt, especially neurotic guilt, and clinical practice. While I present a clinical vignette, a more in-depth discussion of some of the ways a Levinasian outlook can, in general, further enrich psychoanalytic theory and practice will wait until the final chapter.

THE SELF, RESPONSIBILITY FOR THE OTHER, AND FREEDOM

It should be relatively clear by now that Levinas is challenging, if not subverting, the totalizing, Western rationalist modality of being and thinking of which psychoanalysis is to some extent, a part. In the psychoanalytic context, such a modality is manifested for example, in the tendency to look at affects and thoughts, sexual desire and pleasure, religious convictions and spiritual yearnings, and anything private and personal about the self as part of the "technical economy of rationalism." As Hutchens further notes, anything that cannot be "known, understood, synthesized, analyzed, utilized," in short, comprehended and made intelligible by the rationalistic method and outlook is viewed as largely irrelevant or threatening. As a result, the individual is to a large extent denuded of his uniqueness, individuality, mystery, and transcendence. For Levinas, it is ethics which resists and disrupts this totalizing tendency of rationalism, best understood and expressed in terms of its ultimate animating principle, responsibility.[3]

Levinas rather unclearly defines the psyche as "the other in the same, without alienating the same."[4] This notion of the psyche (roughly equivalent to self, ego, subjectivity, I and soul in Levinas's writings) has been reconceptualized in a way that puts into sharp focus his main thesis, his "ethics of responsibility," as well as one important difference between Levinas and Freud and most psychoanalysts. As Cohen points out,[5] for Levinas, "the self is a moral event, an event of sensibility deeper than rationality," the kind of rationality Freud put so much faith in. According to Cohen, it is not as Freud and others tended to believe, the node of interactions or transactions within a social network, social values, nor I would add, the instinctual, from which the self originally

---

3 Hutchens, *Levinas*, 14, 16, 17.

4 Levinas, *Otherwise Than Being*, 112.

5 Richard A. Cohen, "Maternal Psyche," in Gantt and Williams, *Psychology-for-the-Other*, 41, 42, 43.

emanates and is manifested. Rather, Cohen says, the self emerges as the bearer of absolute, undeclineable obligations and responsibilities for the other. Selfhood is thus "constituted by, constituted in, and constituted as—the inescapable exigencies of moral obligations and responsibilities."[6] The self, continues Cohen, "is pressed into service, service to others. It does not volunteer, it is enlisted,"[7] it is a privilege or an election, says Levinas. In sum, the self is originally "for-the-Other" prior to being "for-itself," chosen or commanded before choosing.

It is in *Otherwise Than Being* that Levinas takes up the human possibility of a subjectivity characterized firstly, and mainly, by responsibility, rather than by the experience of freedom, as mainstream psychoanalysis tends to conceive of subjectivity. According to Meissner, for a psychoanalyst, "Ultimately personal agency and autonomy is the root of ethical responsibility.... The reigning assumption among analysts is that responsibility only comes into question as decisional processes approach the border of awareness and conscious control."[8] In contrast to this received psychoanalytic wisdom, Levinas boldly claims that responsibility for the other is prior to freedom. Just as the "freedom of the subject" was demonstrated to be a specific mode of being-in-the-world, "so too the responsibility of the subject" shows a modality coming "from beyond being." In light of the significance for Levinas of the "critique of ontology" and its modality of freedom, his journey "towards the responsible subject" shows a modality "that is otherwise than ontology and freedom."[9]

For Levinas, "A free being alone is responsible, that is, already not free. A being capable of beginning in the present is alone encumbered with itself."[10] Hutchens wonderfully explicates this quotation:

> Modern rationality emphasizes the privilege of freedom over responsibility because the irreducible aspects of he human condition are either presumed intelligible or ignored. It establishes the ideal of the rational, autonomous (self-ruling) and free agent capable of deciding whether to be responsible and choosing which respon-

---

6 Ibid., 41.

7 Ibid.

8 Meissner, *The Ethical Dimension of Psychoanalysis: A Dialogue*, 196, 203.

9 Howard Caygill, *Levinas and the Political* (London: Routledge Books, 2002), 131.

10 Levinas, *Existence and Existents*, 78-79.

sibility to recognize. But, and this is a vital Levinasian objection, there is an infinite number of alternative courses of action upon which we decide or among which we choose. In a richly significant sense, although freedom may be determined by rationalistic criteria, rationality itself finds its opportunities in the network of social relationships in which the self is embedded. The self could not be self-ruling if it did not have some obligations to be so, and that obligation too is elicited by social arrangements. Furthermore, even the self's freedom is facilitated solely by dialogical opportunity. The opposition between freedom and responsibility, then, does not pose a question of exclusive alternatives, an 'either/or,' but rather a question of privilege and subordination.[11]

Thus, for Levinas, the Other challenges my selfhood by revealing to me that my freedom and powers for intervention and making a difference are limited and inadequate. However, while the face calls the self into question, it does not destroy the self, but rather, it is the basis of its separateness and individuation.

Where, for example, Sartre claims that the individual is condemned to freedom, and Freud dramatically depicts the unfreedom of neurosis, Levinas asserts that freedom is conferred, as an investiture, through the encounter with and entrance of the Other. Without the Other, freedom is without meaning or foundation. In the face-to-face encounter, the Other provides my freedom with purpose because I am confronted with the often tough choices between, on the one hand, responsibility and obligation towards the Other, and, on the other, contempt and violent rejection or indifference. In other words, the Other invests me with authentic freedom, and the Other will either be enhanced or subverted, depending on how I decide to use my freedom.[12] "For me, the freedom of the subject is not the highest or primary value" [as it is often viewed in psychoanalysis, e.g., freedom from neurosis]. The heteronomy of our response to the human other, or to God as the absolutely other, precedes the autonomy of our subjective freedom."[13]

Kunz succinctly elaborates Levinas's point when he says that belief in the importance of individual freedom over the importance of responsibility is an "idealistic myth" used to validate the practices of

---

11 Hutchens, *Levinas*, 18.

12 Ibid.

13 Levinas, *Face to Face with Levinas*, 27.

a self-centric, ego-valuing culture sustained by an "ideological infra-
structure." Against this cultural myth, says Kunz, we are called to be
culturally oppositional. Every one of us is summoned, "but I can only
speak for myself. I am appointed. I am ordained. I am named."[14]

What the above has to add to mainstream psychoanalysis is a shift,
or at least a broadening in the discipline's angle of vision of its understanding of the human condition, and its important implications for
psychoanalytic theory and practice. Where most versions of psychoanalysis tend to claim that the origin of a person's freedom emanates
from him, Levinas claims that a person's freedom is conferred on him
by the needs, worthiness and dignity of others. In this view, in a sense,
"the ultimate act of freedom is to give oneself," with the fullness of
one's being, to and for the other.[15] Levinas makes this point by quoting
the Jewish proverb credited to the Lithuanian rabbi, Israel Salanter
(1810-1883) who said that "The other's material needs are my spiritual needs."[16] In other words, we can say that, for Levinas, the psyche,
at least in part, is only "healthy"(to use a psychoanalytic term), to the
extent that its responsibility-driven search for the Good takes precedence over its freedom-driven search for the True.

RESPONSIBILITY FOR THE OTHER IN THE NAZI CONCENTRATION CAMPS

Thus far, Levinas's notion of responsibility for the Other has been
discussed in a somewhat detached, theoretical manner, with few references to real-life situations and/or clinical work. In this section, I
want to draw from the literature on survival in the concentration and
death camps in order to delineate more clearly what Levinas's notion
of responsibility for the Other looks and feels like in real life. I do this
being mindful of what Peperzak wrote in his important study of Levinas: "As long as philosophy [and I would add, psychoanalysis] ignores
and postpones [or underexplores] taking into account the ethical aspects of human existence, it condemns itself to an ontological and egological perspective for which the root of existence remains hidden."[17]

---

14 Kunz, *The Paradox of Power and Weakness*, 21-22.

15 Gantt and Williams, "Pursuing Psychology's Science of the Ethical," in
    Gantt and Williams, *Psychology-for-the-Other*, 8.

16 Levinas, *Nine Talmudic Lectures*, 99.

17 Peperzak, *To the Other*, 91.

For Levinas, this root is expressed in his foundational metaphor of the face and the absolute responsibility for the Other that it necessarily evokes.[18] Before proceeding, it should be noted that it is probably not by chance that we are face to face with the Holocaust in this discussion of responsibility for the Other. As I pointed out earlier, Levinas was incarcerated for many years in a Nazi-administered, POW labor camp, and was personally devastated by the loss of loved ones and nearly his entire religious community during the Holocaust. Most important, as Levinas has indicated, and other scholars have noted,

---

18 In a certain sense, Levinas does not really tell us how he "knows for sure," as it were, how he can effectively substantiate his claim that "responsibility is the essential, primary and fundamental structure of subjectivity" (*Ethics and Infinity*, 95). This lack of adequate substantiation, or at least clarification, is noteworthy, especially when we appreciate a crucial feature of language—that meaning is not fixed, it is emergent, tied to specific situations and constantly changing. That is, the concept of responsibility, like any concept or term, cannot itself convey to us how it is to be properly used. There is no set of rules or instructions that intrinsically comes with the concept, it is open-ended and revisable. Therefore, if the proper usage of a term or concept like responsibility is simply the usage communally judged to be proper, and is no more predetermined than idiosyncratic individual usage, than the "essential, primary and fundamental" nature of responsibility is questionable, ethically troubling. Put more starkly, if the meaning of language is really no more stable than the particular situations it may be used to describe, then one could conceivably claim that the Nazis were acting in a manner that reflected "responsible for the other" in killing the Jews, who were destroying the Aryan nation. That the concept of responsibility for the Other is radically philosophical, without a fixed ethical meaning, and therefore open to abuse, is not considered by Levinas so far as I know.
     A second psychoanalytically-oriented criticism of Levinas's claim that "responsibility for the Other is an essential, primary and fundamental structure of subjectivity" is that the notion of the other is not something that we come into the world with. As far as we know, the infant only apprehends or "knows" that there is an "other" well after birth. Therefore, to speak of "responsibility for the Other" as, in a sense, hardwired, does not take into consideration that the infant's sense of the "other" is a later developmental acquisition. Even more troubling is the fact that an infant's notion of "responsibility" as conventionally understood, and certainly in a Levinasian ethical sense, is an even much later developmental acquisition. All of this raises the question of whether it is reasonable to claim that "responsibility for the Other" can be described as an essential, primary and fundamental structure of subjectivity.

"every aspect of Levinas's thought is a valiant effort to find meaning in the Holocaust despite the deficiencies of philosophy."[19]

There is considerable anecdotal evidence that indicates that a being-for-the-Other orientation in the camps was the most effective way of staying psychologically intact. In psychoanalytic language, this has been described in part, as being autonomous (decision making) and integrated (the sense that the different parts of oneself are combined, organized and working together as a complex whole). Most importantly, however, the central problem in the camps expressed in most survivor and scholarly accounts, is that of "remaining human." As Leo Eitinger, an Auschwitz survivor/psychiatrist has pointed out, "it was those people who were capable of showing interest in others who, mentally, had the best chance of retaining their individuality—and perhaps also of surviving as integrated persons."[20]

Falk Pingel also notes, paraphrasing Auschwitz survivor Herman Langbein, that in the camps, "The struggle for the life of one's fellow prisoners had to be kept alive, because otherwise the strength to resist would atrophy and disappear completely."[21] Todorov makes a similar point and quotes a number of camp inmates to support his claim "that individuals find much more strength within themselves when looking after someone else than when they are taking care of themselves alone." He quotes Margarete Buber-Neumann, a Ravensbruck survivor, who explains her survival this way: "I was always able to find people who needed me. Again and again, I made friends. It is only under such conditions that the true meaning of friendship can be learnt." Another camp inmate cited by Todorov, from Robert Antelme's *Human Race* said, "In order to hang on, each one of us has got to get out of himself, he's got to feel responsible for everybody."[22] As Auschwitz survivor

19   Hutchens, *Levinas*, 84.

20   Leo Eitinger, *Concentration Camp Survivors in Norway and Israel* (London: Allen and Unwin, 1964), 80. The quotations and discussion in this chapter about camp behavior are taken in part, from my previous publication, *Autonomy in the Extreme Situation. Bruno Bettelhiem, the Nazi Concentration Camps and the Mass Society* (Westport: Praeger, 1999).

21   Falk Pingel, "The Destruction of Human Identity in Concentration Camps: The Contribution of the Social Sciences to the Analysis of Behavior under Extreme Conditions," *Holocaust and Genocide Studies*, 6, 2 (1991),178.

22   Tzevetan Todorov, *Facing the Extreme: Moral Life in the Concentration*

Anna Pawelcynska wrote, the inmate who passed through Auschwitz practicing the rule "Do not harm your neighbor and if at all possible, save him" salvaged the highest values.[23]

What all of these quotes indicate is how closely connected the self-less-like caring for others, a form of responsibility, and maintaining one's humanity were. This would include, as analysts would conceive it, maintaining one's autonomy and integration. Whether it was the difficult but life-sustaining act of sharing one's food, or other acts of generosity, protectiveness and selflessness, these actions not only helped the recipient but, as Todorov points out, were probably the best way to retain one's humanity and autonomy in the camp. As is well known, caring for others, psychoanalytically speaking, has its narcissistic gratifications though this fact should not diminish our assessment of the caring for others. In the camps caring about others raised one's own self-esteem, dignity and self-respect because one was doing something morally praiseworthy, and that feeling of increased self-esteem and dignity, in itself, reinforced one's ability to survive.[24] Also, caring about others provided a meaningful structure that transcended Nazi dehumanization and the objective of mere survival. Todorov quotes Olga Lengyel, who found a reason to live when she was asked to set up an infirmary. "I knew that I was doing something useful, something that was enough to give me strength [to go on]."[25] Jack Werber, incarcerated alone in Buchenwald for many years, when he found out about the death of his wife and children felt that there was no reason to go on, but the arrival of 700 children transformed his outlook and mobilized him out of his near-death depression. "Nothing helped, that is, until the children came to Buchenwald." He resolved to do everything in his power to protect them and prevent their murder.[26] Frequently, the well-known psychological paradox holds true: the more you give of

---

Camps (New York: Henry Holt and Company, 1966), 88.

23   Anna Pawelczynska, Values and Violence in Auschwitz: A Sociological Analysis, Trans. Catherine S. Leach (Berkeley, CA: University of California Press, 1979), 141.

24   Todorov, Facing the Extreme, 88.

25   Ibid.

26   Jack Werber and William B. Helmreich, Saving the Children: Diary of a Buchenwald Survivor and Rescuer (New Brunswick, N.J.: Transaction Publishers, 1996), 95.

yourself the more you find you have to give. And as I have suggested, in a certain sense, in the camps the more you gave to others, the more you received in terms of the psychic income necessary to remain human, autonomous and integrated. Responsibility for the Other did not limit the freedom of the inmate, a view that Levinas would most likely agree with. On the contrary, it set him free. By imposing on the inmate the burden of responsibility, the Other released him from the extreme emotional isolation and anonymous existence[27] (and possible anonymous death) in the camps. Through the act of caring for another, psychoanalytically speaking, one cares for oneself, emphasizing the interdependency between narcissistic gratification and egoism on the one hand and caring for others and altruism on the other. Ultimately, remaining human in the camps seems to have required the inmate struggling to flexibly calibrate his narcissism (being-for-oneself) and altruism (being-for-the-Other), depending on the context.[28]

The above discussion of camp inmate behavior emphasizes what I think Levinas tries repeatedly to convey to his reader from different viewpoints, that responsibility for the Other is unrefuseable and non-substitutable; it is more summoning, more demanding than the individual's capacity to honor and fulfill it, as there is always more love to give and justice to pursue. In a certain sense, as an ethical subject the person is always, to some extent, deficient and inadequate, because ethics is not simply an endeavor, something one self-consciously does in certain contexts. Rather, for Levinas, ethics is the very horizon of meaning that constitutes and permeates a person's existence. Such a

---

27 Levinas's notion of the "there is," described as anonymous, impersonal existence is discussed in the next chapter.

28 Levinas, the Orthodox Jew, was well aware that man's purpose on earth was meant not only "to repair the world" (*tikun olam* in Hebrew), through love and justice, for example, unselfishly serving the material and psychological needs of others (e.g., "showing concern for the widow, the orphan, the stranger and the beggar" (*Difficult Freedom*, 26), but also to enjoy worldly pleasures, though always in an ethically informed manner as described in sacred writings and tradition. In other words, Levinas never posited a simple polarity between narcissism and altruism (Peperzak, *To the Other*, 137), the first inherently bad and the latter inherently good. Living a worthwhile life inevitably requires both capacities, depending on the situation one is in. It does, however, seem that Levinas viewed enjoyment through selfless-like serving of others as the highest joy, more than any material or sensual pleasure.

view of the ethical subject points to a conceptual and valuative shift for psychoanalysis, from viewing the self firstly, and mainly, as for-itself, by reason or willfulness, to viewing the self as in its very sensibility as for-the-Other of responsibility.[29]

The significance of these observations for the analysand, and more generally, for the average western person living in "normal" times, is that one of the best ways to shield one's personal and moral integrity, to resist and fight back against the dangerous aspects of our contemporary "mass" society, especially its often mindless technological appropriation and exploitation, is to embrace the above-described responsibility-driven, for-the-Other orientation in the world. Levinas, as well as other scholars during and after his era, was concerned about the subtle, and not so subtle, aspects of modern social and technological control and violence that assault and erode the individual's humanity and autonomy. As I have argued elsewhere, following Bruno Bettelheim and others, these destructive social processes are to some extent analogous to the breaking down of the prisoner's humanity, autonomy and integration in the concentration camps.[30] These all-too-common malignant societal forces include, for example, the pressures of homogeneity and conformity, normative correctness, mechanical subservience, and perhaps most importantly for Levinas, lack of decency and morality. Thus, from a Levinasian point of view, part of the antidote to these dangerous societal tendencies is for the individual to create as Foucault would say, "new forms of subjectivity"[31] and values that refuse the kind of conformist, normalizing and dehumanizing pressures mentioned above. For Levinas, this, in part, means assuming a way of being in the world that is always mindful of the fact that the Other is the core of the self, emanating from a pre-originary ethical responsibility of what has been called "radical altruism."[32] A life saturated by such

29   Cohen, "Maternal Psyche," in Gantt and Williams, *Psychology-for-the-Other*, 42.

30   Marcus, *Autonomy in the Extreme Situation*, 39-60.

31   Michel Foucault, "The Subject and Power," in Hubert L. Dreyfus and Paul Rabinow, *Michel Foucault: Beyond Structuralism and Hermeneutics*, 2d edition (Chicago, IL: University of Chicago Press, 1987, 216).

32   Kunz, *The Paradox of Power and Weakness*, xx. It should be noted that "radical altruism" is a term that Levinas would probably have had difficulty with, in part, because it might obfuscate the fact that responsibility as he uses the term, is prior to, and deeper than altruism as conventionally un-

an ethic is perhaps the best way, at least in general terms, to maintain one's humanity and individuality against the negative aspects of our modern "mass" society."[33] In many ways then, at least ideally, such an existential mode should be integrated into the valuative commitments of any psychoanalytic outlook, especially its conception of a so-called successful analysis.

RESPONSIBILITY FOR-THE-OTHER IN THE CLINICAL ENCOUNTER

In what ways is a Levinasian view of the centrality of responsibility for the Other in human experience implicated in the psychoanalytic understanding of certain kinds of psychopathology and clinical practice? Needless to say, to do justice to this subject would require its own book, though I will take up this question in considerable detail in the last chapter. For now, I will merely suggest what, to the field's detriment, is often either left out, or underemphasized in conventional psychoanalytic discussions of guilt, in particular, neurotic guilt.

First, what I hope is obvious to the reader by now, is that a Levinasian-animated psychoanalysis would embrace a "for-the-Other" attitude on the part of the analyst towards the analysand. This attitude is aptly evoked by Alford in the imaginary words he puts in the mouth of an analyst modeled after D. W. Winnicott. By way of clinical context,

---

derstood; that is, responsibility lies at the foundation of the self. "Egoism and altruism are posterior to responsibility, which makes them possible" (*Otherwise than Being*, 197). Nevertheless, for Levinas, radical altruism, the "stuff" of saints, is a highly desirable form of life.. He writes, for example, "the putting in question of the *I* by the Other is, *ipso facto*, an election, the promotion to a privileged place on which all that is not me depends. This election signifies the most radical commitment there is, total altruism" (*Proper Names*, 73).

33 Samuel P. and Pearl M. Oliner's pathbreaking book *The Altruistic Personality: Rescuers of Jews in Nazi Europe* (New York: The Free Press, 1988) shows that rescuers came from homes in which empathy, care, responsibility for, and to, others and other moral and ethical values pervaded their everyday lives. Moreover, the rescuers' parents acted upon these strongly maintained values. Unlike their neighbors, who were mainly preoccupied with their own survival and decided not to become involved, rescuers felt a more profound sense of responsibility and concern for the fate of their fellow humans. Moreover, they were strengthened by their conviction that their actions could make a life-saving difference.

says Alford, the analysand had the conviction that he had to obliterate the analyst in order to know him, or as I interpret Alford's passage, to get close to him as a separate and individuated person. In Alford's words: "Behold, I am here for you, naked and alone. You may do to me (in fantasy and in words) anything you wish, but in the end you will learn that it does not satisfy. But I will not teach this with words or interpretations, only by remaining other, a mystery to you, as you are to me."[34]

In this seemingly cryptic analytic interchange we sense many of the key aspects of the Levinasian outlook that I wish to put in sharp focus: The absolute responsibility that a person, in this case the analyst, has for the Other, the analysand, a responsibility that is indeclinable, unsubstitutable and, in a certain sense, non-reciprocal; the fact that no matter what the analysand wishes in fantasy and/or says to the analyst, no matter how violent and sadistic his words are as he tries to "murder" the analyst, the Other/analyst retains his absolute integrity, enigmatic strangeness and otherness. That is, the analyst, despite the relentless lethal efforts of the analysand, can never be fully understood, manipulated, coerced or murdered.

And finally, and I am aware that I am extrapolating from Alford, the above interchange hints that the mechanism of change (as analysts sometimes call it) for this analysand is, in part, living a life of responsible engagement with other people. This mainly means creating less self-centric, egoistic and narcissistic ways to give of oneself, that is, creating more authentic and generous ways to serve others. To do so always means respecting the infinitely enigmatic and radical otherness of the other. The analysand must fight his inclination to totalization, the tendency to reduce the other to a rationally intelligible, thematizable and thus manipulable entity. Levinas elsewhere evocatively describes this inclination, as reducing the "saying," the analysand's articulation of something meaningful, to the "said," a theme which is spoken and comprehended. Ethical language, says Levinas, is the saying, that is, it is speech prior to it solidifying into the said, which appropriates otherness into rationalization and thematization.[35] In other words, it is the awesome trace of infinity, that fundamental, never-ending unin-

34 C. Fred Alford, Levinas, the Frankfurt School and Psychoanalysis (Ithaca, NY: Cornell University Press, 2002), 74.

35 Levinas, "Introduction," Is it Righteous To Be? 4.

telligibility that is embodied in the encounter with the Other, that one must not only be mindful of, but reverential towards.

NEUROTIC GUILT

In the remainder of this chapter I want to suggest how certain manifestations of guilt, in particular what analysts call neurotic guilt, can have their origins and motivational power in seriously lapsed responsibility for the Other. I will further suggest that, in certain instances, such a formulation is often more experience-near and clinically helpful to the analysand in that it addresses the ontological[36] basis and significance of those indistinct and amorphous conscious and unconscious "guilt feelings" that analysands frequently complain of. In this context, the psychological is being conceptualized as a point of entry into the ontological.[37] Given the extreme complexity of the concept of guilt, for the sake of clarity and economy of presentation, I will mainly be drawing from the Freudian version of psychoanalysis in my discussion and, secondarily, from some of the other psychoanalytic perspectives mentioned in the previous chapter. Moreover, I will largely be dealing with guilt as it relates to aggressive misconduct rather than guilt over sexual misbehavior such as maternal incest and patricide or child masturbation. I do this, in part, because, as Freud said, "hate has a relation to objects [and] is older than love."[38] That is, after Auschwitz, only an ethical theory that struggles to explain the ultimate ethical problem of all eras, why individuals and groups take great pleasure in murdering, is worth our serious attention.

For Freud, psychoanalysis is less interested in the fact, or reality, of guilt, at least as most ordinary people, including analysands, tend to construct the notion and use the word. Most generally, such guilt can be roughly defined as the unpleasant and deeply troubling feeling

---

36 Ontology, as I indicated earlier, is the theory of being as being. In the current context, therefore, ontological refers to the basic structures of being.

37 To some extent, Levinas might find this claim troubling. He points out, for example, that while the ontological language used in *Totality and Infinity* is not at all a definitive one, its language "is ontological because it wants above all not to be psychological." Levinas seems to be implying that the psychological, including psychoanalysis, does not go deep enough (*Of God Who Comes to Mind*, 82).

38 *S.E.*, Vol. 14. 139.

that occurs from violating a consciously held value or moral principle. Rather, psychoanalysis is mainly concerned with the neurotic sense of guilt, that is, what results from those internal experiences that are not adequately accountable in terms of violating the individual's consciously held values and moral principles. For Freud, the neurotic sense of guilt emanates from an unconscious, intra-psychic conflict between the super-ego and the id, the latter standing for those infantile aggressive and sexual wishes that are the touchstones of clinical psychoanalysis. This conflict is an internalized representation[39] and continuation of early, often so-called "primitive" conflicts between the child and his parents or caretaker. As Rycroft further points out,[40] this internalized scenario is made more complex by the fact that the super-ego is conceptualized as getting its motivating energy from the child's own aggressive wishes. As a consequence of this, says Rycroft, guilt is affected directly by the extent to which the person expresses, via his conscious and unconscious self-narrative, his aggressive wishes and feelings by turning them on himself in the form of severe moral judgment and censure. This moral censure is for example, manifested in the unreasonable blame, disapproval, criticism and the other forms of extreme self-punishment and retribution meant in part, to assuage the sense of guilt, those guilty feelings the analysand, often with great difficulty, grumbles about.

It should also be mentioned that some psychoanalytic writers, for example, Melanie Klein, extend the Freudian formulation in claiming that individuals have an inherent destructive instinct. This hypothesized instinct, Kleinians further argue, automatically leads to assuming the existence of an innate sense of guilt. Such inherent guilt emanates from the mindfulness of the wish to obliterate what is also cherished, to resist what is also capitulated to, namely, the "breast"/mother.

Levinas, who was, as he himself indicated, largely unknowledgeable about, nor a particularly sympathetic reader of psychoanalysis, has, I think, an illuminating perspective on the problem of guilt, in particular, the Freudian notion of neurotic guilt. Of course, Levinas never

---

39 A representation, according to Rycroft, is most elementally, that which permits the psyche "to present to itself" that which is not in reality present. It is a largely reliable replication within the psyche of a perception of a meaningful object or thing (Charles Rycroft, *A Critical Dictionary of Psychoanalysis* (Middlesex, England: Penguin Books, 1968), 141.

40 Ibid., 59-60.

used psychoanalytic language nor systematically wrote about guilt directly, let alone from a sophisticated psychological perspective.

For Levinas, at least as I interpret him, neurotic guilt, that seemingly unrealistic and in a certain sense, undeserved tormented feeling of self-absorption, self-loathing, worthlessness and misery, occurs, as the result of an individual's attempting to avoid the meaningful awareness of the much more painful, threatening and identity-subverting experience of what has been called genuine or real guilt.[41] By genuine guilt I mean the conscious awareness of, or unconscious sense, that one really did, in reality (often elaborated in conscious and/or unconscious fantasy), rupture, if not permanently damage or destroy relations with the Other, especially the positive relations associated with such significant others as a spouse, parent, child or friend. This includes not only the guilty sense that emanates from the blatant acts of physical and emotional violence that we so often hear about or read about in the daily newspaper. It also includes the simple and everyday self-serving inhumanities manifested in our relations with others. These may include, for example, acts of commission, like saying something intentionally mean-spirited to, or about another person, often behind his or her back, and/or, acts of omission, like deliberately and callously looking the other way when one should assist the vulnerable or besieged other.[42]

---

41   Levinas describes his own sense of genuine guilt following his support of Heidegger in the famous 1929 Davos debate between Ernst Cassirer and Heidegger. In a farcical revue satirizing the debate, Levinas played Cassirer and ridiculed his distressed and sorrowful attitude and pacifism. Said Levinas forty years later, "And then when Hitler came to power I couldn't forgive myself for favoring Heidegger at Davos" (*Humanism of the Other*, Introduction by Richard A. Cohen, xv, xvi.) In fact, allegedly, Levinas, on a trip to the United States after World War II, actually tried to locate Cassirer's widow in order to apologize to her (Samuel Moyn, *Origins of the Other: Emmanuel Levinas Between Revelation and Ethics*, Ithaca, NY: Cornell University Press, 2006, 12). It is also worth speculating whether Levinas's emphasis on for example, "responsibility for the Other," "guilt without fault" and "irremissible guilt" in his writings is in part, related to some kind of irrational "survivor's guilt." That is, Levinas, a self-described Holocaust survivor who lost his parents, other family members and his community in the *Shoah*, may have felt, consciously or unconsciously, like so many survivors, unjustifiably guilty for surviving and being unable to rescue those who died.

42   As I mentioned earlier, for Levinas something as simple as saying, "after

As these everyday examples suggest, and what I want to emphasize, is that for Levinas, the person who is genuinely guilty senses, if not knows, at least on some conscious, preconscious or even unconscious level, a hard-to-swallow truth about himself: that his offensive, guilt-inducing behavior was mainly due to putting his transparent egoistic and narcissistic needs and desires before the best interests of the Other. Through neurotic guilt and the self-punishment that always follows in the form of extreme self-condemnation, one is, in effect, barring from one's critical self-consciousness and self-scrutiny a more excruciating awareness: that my neurotic guilt, with its vague fear of retribution and need for punishment, indicates, or at least implies, having committed, in some form, an objectionable real action against an undeserving, often, though not necessarily, cherished or loved, blameless Other. This abhorrent action can be expressed in a number of interrelated conscious (and/or unconscious ways), such as, in an unreasonable hostile thought expressed and directed at one's spouse (e.g., "I could kill you, you are a shit."); a heartless feeling shouted by a teenager to one's parent, or by a friend to a friend (e.g., "You make me sick, I wish you were dead."); or a cruel observable behavior, a public display, aimed at one's child, (e.g., humiliating him by betraying a confidence at a social gathering).

Thus, for Levinas, such genuine guilt as we are calling it, reflects the awareness on some level, that one has in a crucial way let down, if not radically abandoned or betrayed the other person. That is, in the Other's summoning me to responsibility, despite myself as Levinas would argue, I have failed, miserably failed, to adequately respond with empathy and care, to the needy other's call. Most important perhaps, by ignoring or rejecting the other's plea to be responsible, to give help, I feel that my right to exist is, in some sense, profoundly questioned. Such genuine guilt, insinuates Levinas, can become the awful and inescapable feeling, though ultimately, life-affirming "obsession," that inevitably compels me to turn towards the other person with a

---

you, sir," at a doorway is an everyday example of showing respect and responsibility for and to the Other. Conversely, to thoughtlessly go through the doorway before the Other, is in some way, to act selfishly, this being a guilt-inducing and, for Levinas, a guilt-worthy action perpetrated against the other. The Other by his or her very existence, awakens, accuses and judges me.

seemingly impossible to satisfy guilt that I wish I never instigated.[43] Real guilt, says Martin Buber, demands "reconciliation";[44] it demands making what in another context and with a somewhat different emphasis, Melanie Klein famously calls reparation: to make good that which one has injured in reality,[45] though it is almost always made worse via conscious and unconscious fantasy. Psychoanalytically speaking, we can thus say that neurotic guilt is, in part, a bribe to the super-ego to avoid the more painful, humiliating, irrepressible and debilitating experience of genuine guilt. Stated somewhat differently, unfaced, unanalyzed genuine guilt can turn into neurotic guilt. As is well known to analysts, such avoidance of honest self-confrontation can have far-reaching negative, if not dire, consequences for the self-accused perpetrator of the guilt-worthy action.

I have argued that an important aspect of the resolution of one form of neurotic guilt is to uncover its motivational center, to help the analysand recognize that his neurotic guilt is in part, a consequence of not hearing the call to open oneself with the fullness of one's being to the Other, a summons that demands one to be for the Other before oneself. For Levinas, this means relating to the other in the most caring manner, as if he were, for example, responding to the pained pleas for help from an orphan, widow, beggar or an ill person, someone whose vulnerabilities betray their desperate need to be compassion-

---

43   Hutchens, *Levinas*, 90.

44   Martin Buber, *The Knowledge of Man: Selected Essays*. Trans. Ronald Gregor Smith and Maurice S. Friedman. Ed. Maurice Friedman (New York: Harper and Row, 1965), 147. There are some similarities between Buber's formulations of responsibility, guilt and other notions. However, there are also some very serious differences. See Levinas's "Martin Buber and the Theory of Knowledge," in *The Levinas Reader*, 59-74. See also Friedman's appendix, which compares Levinas and Buber, in his *Martin Buber: The Life of Dialogue* (London: Routledge Books, 2002), 4th ed., 337-352. Finally, take a look at Atterton, et al., *Levinas and Buber*.

45   For Klein, reparation is a defense mechanism designed to diminish guilt by action meant to put right or make good the damage imagined to have been perpetrated against an ambivalently cathected object (i.e., "persons, parts of persons, or symbols of one or the other"). Ultimately, according to Klein, what one strives for in this process is the restoration of an internal object that in unconscious fantasy has been obliterated. Reparation is associated with the depressive position in Kleinian terms. See Rycroft, *A Critical Dictionary of Psychoanalysis*, 100, 141.

ately tended to. Such a modality of being is, to some extent, analogous to being a non-judgmental, non-patronizing, unconditionally accepting and loving parent. This parent not only anguishes over the fate, the survival, of her vulnerable, needy and possibly hurt child, but also wants her child to flourish, including becoming the best adult person she can. Following Levinas, such a person is characterized by an unwavering commitment to an impossible to realize goal, but one which one is obligated to nevertheless pursue forever: that is, tending to the best interests of others before oneself and striving to make the world a better, more just and more beautiful place. There is in other words, says Levinas, a demand on us, in a sense before all moral reasonings or normative values, a "primordial"[46] summons to which we must respond else we are fated to feel agonizingly guilty in some form. For Levinas, then, there is an unqualified demand that rises from the radical otherness of the other, a demand that emanates from the direct experience of the other's vulnerability, neediness and inevitable death.

As I pointed out earlier, Levinas's notion of what we are calling genuine guilt, at least as I construe it, is, in his words, an "accusation," an assumed debt without any choice, one that can never be fully satisfied. Levinas says about the face-to-face relation,

> The I suspends its persistence in being, its *conatus essendi*, in its subjugation to the other, as if the I were 'guilty' with respect to the neighbor. This is a new style of accusative guilt without fault, 'indebtedness' without loan. An obligation of responsibility for which no one else can be substituted, a debt that no one can pay in the place of me and thus, for that me, the very concreteness of its uniqueness as an I.[47]

Thus, for Levinas, guilt is a fundamental, if not formative aspect of subjectivity. That is, guilt comes about mainly because one is from the outset, susceptible and vulnerable, responsive to the other's living pres-

---

46   Levinas, *Totality and Infinity*, 199. Levinas assumes there is a primordial facial expression commanding "you shall not commit murder," and elsewhere, he refers to a "primordial responsibility for the other" (*Is It Righteous to Be?* 182). However, he does not demonstrate or "prove" that these so-called primordial expressions and responsibilities are in fact the assumed universal, inherent structures of being, rather than, for example, socially constructed meanings and valuative commitments that he and every good man embraces.

47   Levinas, *Is It Righteous to Be?* 229.

ence, to the summoning call of the self/other relation itself.[48] Indeed,
as social psychologists have pointed out, for example, while there are
individual differences, in general, people seem to be intrinsically empathic: affective empathy is the human tendency to experience emotion
in response to others' emotional experiences; Cognitive empathy is the
human inclination to see things from another person's perspective.[49] In
this sense then, guilt, or rather genuine guilt, is best viewed as a kind
of moral compass pointing us in an other-oriented, other-regarding
direction. Says Todd, "the self is bound to the Other in a relation of
guilt in which the self bears the burden of the Other's subjectivity, the
Other's freedom, and the Other's mortality."[50] Thus, for Levinas we are
guilty because we are susceptible to the Other, his presence moves us.
We sense, if not feel, utterly accused—the Other's anguish causes me
anguish. Most importantly, "guilty self-identification", or rather, embracing genuine guilt, always points to action-guiding responsibility.
Guilt is a "responsible response" towards the Other's pain, a response
that generates pain for the person "who cannot help but feel guilty."[51]

Thus, for Levinas, there is always more that I can give to the Other,
and it is this awareness of my shortcomings and limitations that can
feel like a "persecution," an unending and agonizing sense of guilt and
unfulfilled responsibility. Levinas takes this notion to an extreme when
he says that "I am responsible for the persecutions that I undergo...
since I am responsible for the Other's responsibility."[52] Alford contends
that Levinas is not saying that one is the reason or ultimate cause for
one's persecution, he is not "blaming the victim." Rather, says Alford,
Levinas is saying that the persecuted person nevertheless remains responsible for everyone else in the world.[53] Levinas, continues Alford,
cites at least twelve times in his writings a quote from Dostoyevsky,
one that I too have quoted, and which I think best conveys this point,

48 Sharon Todd, *Levinas, Psychoanalysis, and Ethical Possibilities in Education* (Albany, NY: SUNY Press, 2003), 99, 110. Todd does an excellent job
of explicating Levinas's notion of guilt, mainly using Kleinian sources.

49 Mark H. Davis, *Empathy: A Social Psychological Approach* (Madison,
WI: Brown and Benchmark, 1994).

50 Todd, *Levinas, Psychoanalysis, and Ethical Possibilities in Education*, 109.

51 Ibid., 113, 114.

52 Levinas, *Ethics and Infinity*, 99.

53 Alford, *Levinas*, 84-85.

"we are all guilty [elsewhere translated by Levinas as "responsible"] of all and for all men before all, and I more than the others."[54] Such an "ethical metaphysics," as Edith Wyschogrod has called it, challenges the individualism that is so pervasive in psychoanalysis, an individualism that tends to stress individual needs, desires and rights over individual obligations and responsibilities towards others.

For psychoanalysis this means, following Levinas, that there is a boundless and relentlessly growing sense of individual guilt and responsibility that the analysand feels as he authentically faces himself, one that insinuates the main meaning of his emotional, neurotic suffering.[55] Thus, the analysand feels what can be described as the primordial experience of conscience, perhaps, and I am speculating, emanating in part, from the innate aggression and guilt that Klein so aptly describes; that is, the discovery of having, in some real sense, taken away the other's possibilities of getting on, of flourishing or, even worse, existing. Responsibility, as I have said a number of times, following Levinas, is infinite, and this awareness, this mindfulness, means that I can never rid myself of all my guilt because it is built into the human condition, is ontological, a basic structure of being. Still, implies Levinas, and this is the measure of our humanity, one must keep trying to eradicate one's guilt through making reparations, to empathically understand, serve and sacrifice for the Other.

In this view, neurotic guilt is thus the elaborate system of hideouts that the individual creates in order to keep out of consciousness in a meaningful form, or at least to blunt, the painful awareness that one has freely chosen to be deaf to the cry of the Other, to serve oneself before the Other. Perhaps on the deepest level, the analysand intuits the truth of which his neurotic guilt is a manifestation, and cover for, namely, the sense that one has in some way numbed oneself to keep from realizing, in word and deed, says Levinas, the "holiness" of being a subject who in the very fiber of his being carries responsibilities, not only for one's significant others, but for everyone in the world.

---

54 Levinas, *Ethics and Infinity*, 98, 99.

55 Peperzak, *To the Other*, 192.

GENUINE VERSUS NEUROTIC GUILT

Drawing from a Levinasian view of the human condition, I wish to conclude this chapter by further distinguishing the analysand's soul-destroying experience of neurotic guilt from the soul-redeeming experience of genuine guilt. A clinical vignette will be presented to illustrate some of the crucial differences between these two forms of guilt.

Genuine guilt, as I am using the term, is not the result of internalized conflict as analysts usually describe the origin of neurotic guilt. Rather, genuine guilt is the consequence of injured or spoiled real relations between people of whom the perpetrator is on some level, consciously or unconsciously aware, and feels deeply regretful about. As Buber points out, we can say that genuine or what he calls "existential guilt" is said to occur "when someone injures an order of the human world whose foundations he knows and recognizes as those of his own existence and of all common existence."[56]

Psychoanalysis, as I construe and practice it, attempts to show the analysand the variety of ways in which he tries to avoid the meaningful awareness of his genuine guilt, often preferring to get bogged down in the endless emotional thicket of neurotic guilt, especially its guilt/punishment cycle. The libidinal, aggressive and archetypal interpretations of Freud, Klein and Jung, for example, the analysand may know by heart, and use as an avenue of flight from himself, not as a vehicle for insight and changed behavior. Such an escape from the awareness of being genuinely guilty, at least as I am using the notion, is mainly based on having failed to comprehend and empathically meet the Other's needs before one's own. In this sense, unaccepted, disavowed or repressed genuine guilt can morph into neurotic guilt.[57] In a manner of speaking, the analysand says to himself, "Better such [neurotic] guilt and punishment than facing the awful burden of freedom and responsibility for, and to the Other."[58]

We are now ready to illuminate the key distinction between neurotic guilt and genuine guilt, especially in its clinical context, a distinction that is animated by a Levinasian-inspired ethical sensibility.

---

56   Buber, *The Knowledge of Man: Selected Essays*, 127.

57   Rollo May, ed., "Contributions of Existential Psychotherapy," in *Existence* (New York: Basic Books, 1958), 52-55.

58   Ernest Becker, *The Denial of Death* (New York: The Free Press, 1973), 213. I have paraphrased Becker.

As I have argued, neurotic guilt can be, in part, psychoanalytically understood as a defense, a front for avoiding the confrontation with genuine guilt. It is a centripetal psychic process in that it gets one more deeply enmeshed in oneself, mainly through the self-accusations of worthlessness and the guilt/punishment self-narrative. In other words, neurotic guilt is highly narcissistic: it is self-obsessing as it keeps the self focused on its own center isolated from the real Other, a reflection of the self's tendency to isolation and self-sufficiency. Neurotic guilt also retards, if not stops, any real self-illumination, personal growth and development. By definition, it always has a moribund trajectory, that is, it always leads to clinical symptoms. Neurotic guilt is most evident in the clinical context in that the analysand has both a vague fear of retribution and the need for expiating punishment in some form or another. Moreover, the dialogue that the analysand has with himself, his internal dialogue, is experienced by the analyst as mainly a narcissistic form of monologue.[59] Such a mode of relation to oneself reflects the overall conceptual and behavioral impoverishment, the bogging down of the forward movement of life that characterizes the neurotically guilty analysand. As we shall see, whereas neurotic guilt always wounds and cripples the human animal, genuine guilt heals and sets him free.

In contrast to neurotic guilt, genuine guilt is characterized by authentic self-confrontation and self-understanding. Ironically, and paradoxically, rather than being centripetal in character, genuine guilt is centrifugal and this is a positive and hopeful development. Genuine guilt is a psychic process that moves one away from the interiority of egoistic psychism, away from the ego with its egological accusations of worthlessness and failed conquests. In other words, genuine guilt steers one away from one's inordinate self-centricism and narcissism, towards a more other-directed, other-regarding mode of being in the world. Clinically, this manifests itself in the analysand's not presenting so much as self-obsessive; rather, he is more for-the Other in outlook and behavior. His dialogue with himself is not, like the neurotically guilty, a largely narcissistic form of monologue, but reflects the analysand's willingness to struggle to find the apt words through which to articulate his profoundest fears, wishes and misgivings. Most importantly, the genuinely guilty person seeks out the injured, ag-

59 Lawrence J. Silberstein, *Martin Buber's Social and Religious Thought* (New York: New York University Press, 1989), 143-145.

grieved Other in order to make reparations, real and symbolic, to put things right, to restore the damaged Other to his or her original whole, uncompromised state, at least to the extent that it is possible. Unlike neurotic guilt, genuine guilt that is honestly faced is asymptomatic, always lead to greater freedom and expansiveness. Most importantly, it leads to efforts that reflect the perpetrator's willingness to assume greater responsibility, not only towards the damaged particular Other, but, by extension, all others, everywhere.

Finally, genuine guilt that is confronted leads to other positive developments in the personality, including one's evolving a for-the-Other mode of being in the world. These developments, to some extent nurtured by the psychoanalytic process as I conceive it, include, for example, the analysand's greater sense of humility and forgiveness of himself and of others. Such a consciousness is, in part, rooted in the awareness that it is an aspect of our existential make-up that we hurt others, especially those we love. Says E. Mansell Pattison, a psychiatrist, "Left to our own devices all of us will betray ourselves and our fellow men."[60] In other words, following Levinas, analysands and analysts would benefit from a reduction in their inflated self-importance and destructive narcissism that comes about through a greater mindfulness of the fact that we are all fundamentally flawed, deeply flawed, creatures. Says Kant, there is a smudge of "radical evil" in the human being wherever it emanates. We are frequently selfish, impatient, dishonest, envious, mean-spirited and sometimes downright cruel. Most importantly for this discussion, we are limited and flawed in our capacity to love and in our relations with others, the main area of interest in psychoanalysis.

Unless checked by "moral force",[61] by conscience and moral action—all aspects of responsibility for the Other—we are all prone to everyday "inhumanity" towards others, especially to those dear to us, which is often the basis for our subversion in terms of guilt and other forms of unhappiness. Freud, genius that he was, memorialized a similar insight in his concept of the death instinct, that innate instinct to de-

60   E. Mansell Pattison, "The Holocaust as Sin: Requirements in Psycho-analytic Theory for Human Evil and Mature Morality," in Steven A. Luel and Paul Marcus, eds., *Psychoanalytic Reflections on the Holocaust: Selected Essays* (Hoboken, NJ: University of Denver and KTAV Publishers, 1988), 89.

61   Ibid.

stroy or obliterate not only oneself, but also others. Most later analysts have, however, preferred to speak about the general innate tendency towards aggression toward others. This and other psychoanalytic formulations speak to Freud's awareness of our flawed nature, to our inherent "sinfulness" as St. Augustine would say. Augustine may well be incorrect about original sin, and perhaps it is more reasonable to believe that we are born innocent. Yet, apparently, to most people, it *feels* the other way, as if for as long as one can remember one has been sinning and impure. Moreover, from a psychological perspective, especially a Levinasian-inspired one, it seems good to take account of that feeling.[62] Whichever language, secular or religious, that one prefers, the self or soul-redeeming response to such an awareness of our flawed nature, is the same: the willingness and capacity to experience genuine guilt and make reparations, rooted in a heart, mind and spirit-felt infinite responsibility for, and to, the Other.

CLINICAL VIGNETTE

I want to conclude this chapter with some excerpts from a case study that depict some of the important differences between neurotic and genuine guilt, including the redemptive role of the analysand's embracing a responsibility for the Other calculus in his relation to himself and in his self-other relations. The same analysand, John, will be further discussed in subsequent chapters located at the end of each chapter, as he relates to such themes as anxiety, love, suffering and religiosity.

John, age 28, was a doctor, a Modern Orthodox Jew, who was married with two children, and living in a cosmopolitan religious community of which he felt a meaningful part. He came to me because, he said, he was suffering from largely unintelligible bouts of anxiety and depression, irrational fears of life-threatening illness to both himself and his beloved family, and moribund thoughts of death, meaninglessness and Jewish group catastrophe. He also complained that he had a blunted hedonic potential, that is, he had great difficulty finding pleasure in things that most people usually find pleasurable. When I first met him, John had been married for about two years to his current wife, a pediatrician, and had been married briefly a few years before, to a woman, who, like his current wife, was a daughter of Holocaust survivors. John said that he regarded his current life as "blessed" and

---

62   I am indebted to Phillip Cary, Augustinian scholar, for this point (Personal communication, 3/21/01).

felt that he had no valid reason to complain, but he could not help it, he felt emotional storms of unhappiness.

In general, John was a pleasure to work with in the four times a week analysis that spanned seven years; he was articulate, often beautifully metaphoric, self-conscious and psychologically-minded. He could also be sarcastic, overly critical of others, mistrustful, extremely pessimistic in outlook and painfully self-absorbed. The latter two qualities were the basis for his wife's often repeated complaints when they occasionally bickered. John knew through the analytic process that the disruptive challenges to his infantile narcissism and selfishness, his impoverished self-concept and shaky self-esteem were in the service of his achieving greater self-knowledge, self-mastery and the capacity to love and work. By the end of the analysis, in general, John was able to, less neurotically, give and receive love, at least, in a reciprocal sense. John also achieved a higher level of autonomy, integration and humanity as was mainly reflected in his profound capacity, at least episodically, to care for his family, friends, patients and materially needy others, above and before himself, exhibiting what Levinas calls, the "wisdom of love."

By way of further contextualizing this and subsequent vignettes, John came from a financially well-off, assimilated Jewish suburban home. His father, a scientist/ businessman, was a somewhat emotionally remote, depressive and at times intimidating man who was obsessively concerned with John's education and future stability in life. Despite these hard to live with qualities, during the analysis John gradually came to regard his father as a flawed but supportive father whom he loved. His mother, a high school English teacher, though a rather narcissistic and verbally seductive woman, capable of enjoying herself, was, to him, also adoring, encouraging him when he felt defeated by life. John, the youngest child, had two bothers and one sister, whom he felt close to and got along with nicely. They were all professionals, married, with children and living near-by.

In general, John described his childhood as unhappy for three main reasons: (1) he was seriously injured and ill multiple times as a child, including having had a traumatic bicycle accident at age four leading to some facial disfigurement and permanent scarring. He had also had cancer, which was successfully operated on when he was age ten, though he said the fear of getting cancer again was always with him. This, in part, accounted for John's rigid adherence to a healthy lifestyle, including careful eating and getting up at 4:30 a.m. to exercise and meditate before he prayed and went to work. Through his analysis, John realized that his traumatic medical history accounted in part, for his narcissistic vulnerabilities (e.g., self-esteem fluctuations), depressiveness, fearfulness and anxiety; (2) From the time John started school, he was a very poor student in a highly competitive school system, suffering throughout high school from what seemed to be an emotionally depressed intelligence. Growing up in such a competitive and achievement-oriented neighborhood was devastating to John's self-esteem and self-concept; (3) John's mother had a longstanding affair with a neighbor of which she inappropriately shared some of the details with him, culminating in John's walking in on her and her lover kissing when he once came home from school unexpectedly. Needless to say, this episode, and his mother's affair in general, was also injurious to his self-esteem and masculine identity and created Oedipal havoc that took him years to more or less put right.

As this brief history implies, there were a number of areas in John's personality functioning and behavior that mediated neurotic guilt, such as his tendency to extreme self-criticism, self-absorption and depressiveness. However, perhaps the main issue that he often came back to in his analysis that relates to his guilt, was the fact that although he was first married to a person he described as a lovely and gentle woman, he cheated on her in the first year of marriage while studying abroad, leading to a painful divorce. He then subsequently married the woman he had the affair with, his current wife. I remember in one session, early on in his analysis, John, in his dramatic fashion walked into my office and before he lay down on the couch, he came up to me, nearly eyeball to eyeball and said, "Doctor, look into my eyes, man to man, my marriage, my life is based on moral ruin!"

What John was referring to was the fact that he felt extremely guilty that he had married his first wife, and then after countless lies and deceptions, divorced her, having crushed her hopes and dreams to be happily married and build a family and a future together. What made his behavior even worse, John said, was that his first wife was an only child, a daughter of two of the most decent people he had ever met, both Holocaust survivors. That he severely messed up their daughter's life was bad enough, but that he also caused her parents additional suffering, was too horrible to contemplate and therefore he felt disgusted and ashamed of himself. To make matters worse, John found out through a mutual friend that his first wife had great difficulty finding another husband and that when she did, they were not able to have their own children. John said that he had heard that the fertility problem was mainly the husband's. As a result, the couple decided to adopt a child who, it was later found out, had serious neurological and learning problems.

In a certain sense, I agreed with John's negative characterization of his actions leading to his divorce, but I felt that his guilty suffering had a thinness to it in that it did not get to the heart of what made his actions objectionable to him. John avoided facing the fact that, to some extent, he was, during much of this episode, in his own words, "a self-serving, manipulative bastard from start to finish. I deserve to suffer for this." Hence, John developed some fairly obvious symptoms that were connected to what he regarded as his objectionable behavior, such as intrusive self-denigrating thoughts that he was an imposter, a public saint and a private bastard, and inappropriate anger at his second wife whom he consciously and unconsciously blamed for his "moral ruin," as "she seduced me." John's tendency to brooding self-absorption and withdrawal from his wife were related to this latter factor.

John's neurotic guilt climaxed one Sabbath morning while in his local synagogue. He turned around and thought that he saw his first wife's father sitting a few rows behind him. John pretended that he did not notice the elderly gentleman, but, perspiring heavily, felt mounting anxiety and fear. Fearing an angry confrontation with the man, John suddenly quickly walked out of the sanctuary and ran outside, only returning to the synagogue a half hour later full of anxiety. After the service, John insisted to his wife that they go home quickly because of his intense discomfort about the proximity of his first wife's father. "I felt like a hunted animal," he told me. As he was leaving the crowded synagogue, John found himself only a few feet away from the gentleman, and while nearly fainting from anxiety and fear, glanced into the old man's seemingly accusative eyes, only to realize that the man he feared was in reality someone else.

John reported this story with amazement and horror that his mind could play such tricks on him and that he had fabricated such a frightening scenario. Instead of being able to analyze his internal reaction and behavior, John obsessed over how guilty he must be to have conjured up the whole episode. Absent, however, was any real exploration of the episode and intensely felt regret about his actions towards his ex-wife. Instead his narrative gave the impression that he was talking

for talking's sake and concluded with a highly intellectualized assertion that he must be guilty if he imagined such a punitive situation.

We had already spent a considerable period of the analysis getting to
understand the early roots of these symptoms; the development of the
punitive super-ego based on the image of the scary, accusative Oedipal
father compounded by the severe accidents and illnesses of his young
years; the longing for and rage at his seductive mother; his anxiety
at feeling trapped by her and his wish to destroy her to escape her
clutches. All these elements, in part, constituted his neurotic guilt.

However, despite the work done, many of John's symptoms persist-
ed, and it became clear that the neurotic guilt served the function of
masking John's genuine guilt at what he had actually done to his first
wife. In my view, genuine guilt was an appropriate reaction to having
deeply hurt his wife and her parents by his mainly selfish, narcissis-
tically-driven actions. Largely inadvertently, John had harmed these
good people by putting his infantile needs and self-centered desires
before his ex-wife's inalienable rights and best interests. One of the
least psychoanalytically explored aspects of guilt is the tendency to
avoid taking responsibility for the destructive consequences of even
well-intentioned actions, at least well-intentioned for the actor. Such
a destructive potential is most prevalent and dangerous when one is
lodged in a mainly for-the-self mode of being. That is, "the road to
hell is paved with good intentions" when one's main reference point
and priority is satisfying oneself before the other. Moreover, like all
genuine guilt, there is a pained realization that what has been injured,
damaged or destroyed cannot be healed, undone or fixed, as there is a
self-confrontation with a brutal fact of existence, namely, the irrevers-
ibility of lived time.

There are other aspects of John's thinking and feeling that reflect
the defensive nature of his neurotic guilt in that he avoided or denied
important aspects of reality. For example, John was not able to focus
on the fact that his ex-wife intensely pressured him to marry her; she
threatened that unless he married her in the not too distant future, she
would leave him. John tried to resist her pressure, but his infantile fear
of abandonment was too strong. In addition, John was all too willing
to see himself as the aggressor in the marriage, viewing himself as the
main culprit, but failed to consider that his wife knew that he was
intensely ambivalent about marriage but still decided that it was the
right thing for her to do at the time. Thus, what, in part, generated this

neurotic guilt is that John did not in reality destroy his wife: he hurt her. It was the old omnipotent rage at the early narcissistic mother that drove him to extreme self-blame.

In other words, John was not able to see that his wife was not simply a passive victim to his selfishness and callousness, but rather co-produced the marital trajectory and break-up. John had great difficulty acknowledging that his wife, herself an autonomous adult, made her own decisions all along the way, and that she was, responsible for her own actions, including the unintended negative consequences of her good intentions, at least as she construed them at the time. While it is true that his wife was not aware of the whole story throughout the demise of the marriage, such as the existence of the mistress, she alone must bear the responsibility for the failure of their marriage, which was caused by her acts of commission, including pressuring John into marrying her, and omission, letting John return to Europe alone for a year immediately after they were married to finish his medical training.

As I indicated earlier, one of the key differences between neurotic and genuine guilt is that in the latter there is the wish to make reparations, real and symbolic, that express regret for one's misdeed, and the aim to heal or mend that which has been hurt or damaged. In John's situation this was not easy, as he had no contact with his ex-wife, who avoided his overtures to meet and talk, and from what he had heard from a mutual friend, still appeared to hate him. This situation left John with no real-life alternative but to make reparations in fantasy: acknowledging his selfish, deceitful and callous motivations and behavior, asking his ex-wife for forgiveness, and making a vow never to act similarly again toward anyone. He needed to see his insensitive, self-serving and selfish behavior towards his present wife as both a punishment of her and repetition of his self-centeredness. Through such an internal process of brutally honest self-scrutiny and accountability to the inviolate, indestructible core of his conscience, John's sense of neurotic guilt, with its attendant symptoms, diminished, while his autonomy, integration and sense of responsibility for himself, and toward others, grew more profound. The latter development manifested itself not only in John's improved relations with his wife, he also became less detached and defensively analytical in his attitude towards his patients as well as less inclined to seeing them as mainly "cash cows," as he had once described them. Focusing more holistically on his patients as suffering people, he became a more personally engaged, caring and effective doctor.

3

THE HORROR OF EXISTENCE

This impersonal, anonymous,
yet inextinguishable 'consummation' of being,
which murmurs in the depths of nothingness itself
we shall designate by the term there is.
The rustling of the there is…is horror.

Levinas[1]

Anxiety has long been viewed by psychoanalysts as perhaps the most common presenting symptom among analysands, contributing to many of their worst problems in living. Anxiety, that dreadful self-absorbing feeling of worry or nervousness, in its extreme form, horror and panic, that usually emanates from anticipation of some kind of perceived threat, menace or danger, the basis of which is mainly "unknown or unrecognized."[2] Nearly everyone has had such anxious experiences and it is, in part, for this reason that Freud and others have argued that anxiety is one of the foundational features of human existence. Anxiety, as conventionally understood, has two interrelated aspects. It has a psychological or mental dimension, such as in tension and apprehension, and also a physiological or bodily dimension, such as in breathlessness and sweating. Anxiety, to the analyst, is not the same phenomenon as fear or what is sometimes called realistic anxiety. Whereas anxiety is connected to a danger that is unconscious, fear is a response to a consciously recognized, usually external, realistic danger. In general, most mental health professionals of diverse theoretical persuasions, including analysts, view anxiety as pathological when it seriously diminishes effectiveness in living, impairs the attainment of desired goals or fulfillment, and/or blocks reasonable emotional equanimity and comfort.

Levinas, as far as I can tell from his biography and scholarly writings, was no stranger to anxiety, in part because of his incarceration

---

1 "There is: Existence without Existents," *The Levinas Reader*, 30, 32.

2 *American Psychiatric Glossary*, 7th edition. Ed. Jane E. Edgerton. (Washington, D.C., American Psychiatric Press, 1994), 18.

for five years in a Nazi-administered labor camp for French Jewish soldiers. At the same time, his wife and daughter were in hiding from the Nazis, their fate and the fate of his parents, relatives and community unknown, which must have caused Levinas to experience extreme anxiety as well as loneliness, depressive feelings and fear, worrying about the survival of his loved ones and himself. Moreover, Levinas was a student of Heidegger and steeped in the phenomenological tradition, and it was therefore impossible for him not to be intellectually engaged in the subject of anxiety or dread (angst), the feeling of being on the verge of nothing that informs Heidegger's writings.

In this chapter, I want first to briefly summarize two psychoanalytic views of the nature of psychopathology, anxiety manifestations in particular. My main purpose in doing so is to help contextualize what I think is the intriguing, though generally ignored, contribution of Levinas to the understanding of this important and all-too-common human experience, one that analysands and analysts frequently struggle with in one form or another as they engage in the analytic encounter. It is mainly through unraveling Levinas's forbiddingly opaque notion of the "there is," "the phenomenon of impersonal being," as he calls it,[3] that I hope to provide a complementary angle of vision on the source, expressions and meanings of certain forms of anxiety. Such a Levinasian angle of vision, can, I hope, deepen and expand the psychoanalytic understanding of this complex, multi-faceted and common human phenomenon. Moreover, by beginning to fill in the gap in the psychoanalyst's understanding of the origin, course and phenomenology of "anonymous existence," or "being in general,"[4] I hope to strengthen his ability to empathize with the analysand's "horror and panic"[5] that Levinas says constitutes the "there is," as well as to help the analysand derive some transformational insights from such a dreadful self-experience.

I should stress from the onset that for Levinas the "there is" is not simply a synonym for anxiety as the term is commonly used. In fact, Levinas says the "there is" is neither a psychological problem nor even a subjective experience, at least not as it is usually construed. However, as I hope to suggest, despite what Levinas says, his description of the

---

3 Levinas, *Ethics and Infinity*, 48.

4 Levinas, *Existence and Existents*, 44, 52.

5 Levinas, *Ethics and Infinity*, 49.

"there is" and his interpretation of its meanings (none of which are easy to pin down, as in a certain sense the "there is" is ineffable), all point to a mode of experience that is, for want of a better term, akin to (though not to be reductively equated with) the experience of sudden, massive and decisive anxiety. This is anxiety not as it is psychoanalytically described and understood. The horror and panic of anonymous, impersonal being, the "there is," can be reasonably described as referring to a mode of being in which the individual is so overwhelmed by a unique form of unbearable anxiety, at least phenomenologically speaking, that he has access to a dimension of his being that is characterized by radical insomnia, by a horror of being. In this view, such intense anxiety may be understood as a central part of the psychological context that signals and prepares the way for the awful inevitability of the "there is." This experience of extreme and largely inexplicable generalized anxiety, followed by the even more hellish "there is," followed by a return to normal consciousness, possibly with a degree of self-illumination, is the experiential process that I will be focusing on in this chapter. It is this kind of horror and panic associated with the "there is" that Levinas probably felt at times in the Nazi forced labor camp that may be one of the important reasons that he wrote about the "there is" "for the most part" while a prisoner in the stalag.[6]

Finally, a note of caution and consolation. As Davis points out, Levinas's "there is" is trying to capture something that Levinas describes "as lying beyond any experiential or cognitive measure,"[7] "neither nothingness nor being."[8] That is, continues Davis, like the entire Levinasian oeuvre, Levinas's poetic and evocative description of the "there is" is elliptical and paradoxical. Moreover, it is sated with similes and comparisons meant to block the reader from assimilating the enigmatic "there is" into familiar modes of experience and understanding that, in the reader's mind, have ultimate clarity and explanatory supremacy. Rather, Levinas, like Socrates, is a gadfly. He wants to disrupt his readers' conventional modes of experiencing and thinking, to stimulate their skepticism so that they do not rush to premature closure about something that Levinas says can never really be pinned down. Thus, the "there is" is an open-ended notion, and this fact, along with Levi-

---

6 Levinas, *Existence and Existents*, xxvii.

7 Davis, *Levinas*, 131.

8 Levinas, *Ethics and Infinity*, 48.

nas's obtuse literary style, makes any coherent explication of the "there is" exceedingly difficult for the explicator and rather hard going for the reader. It is less so, however, if one is mindful of the fact that the experience of reading Levinas, similar to being in an analysis, involves going on a long voyage of the mind and spirit.

PSYCHOANALYTIC VIEWS OF ANXIETY: SIGMUND FREUD AND W. R. D. FAIRBAIRN

Freud had three theories of anxiety, though the last one is regarded as definitive.[9] As Rycroft has noted,[10] the first theory asserted that anxiety was a result of repressed libido, the second was that it was a repetition, an analogue of the birth trauma, and the third was that anxiety had two fundamental forms, primary and signal anxiety. Both primary and signal anxieties were regarded by Freud as responses of the ego to the heightening of instinctual pressure and emotional tension. Primary anxiety is the emotion associated with disintegration of the ego. In its extreme, such anxiety, what is called panic, is a feeling of utter helplessness, a transitory functional disorganization of the personality. Signal anxiety was conceived as an early warning system that alerts the ego to an imminent threat to its equilibrium and integrity. The purpose of signal anxiety, a form of self-monitoring, inner watchfulness and vigilance, Rycroft further notes, is to make certain that by allowing the ego to implement defensive safeguards, debilitating primary anxiety is never experienced.[11] Freud conceived anxiety to be related to a series of danger situations that are intrinsic to a child's growth and development.[12] As Moore and Fine succinctly describe it, the first of these threatening situations is the loss of the primary love object, most often the mother, the caregiver on whom the child is utterly dependent for survival.[13] Next, as the child begins to experience the mother as a

---

9 Freud, "Inhibitions, symptoms and anxiety," In *S.E.*, volume. 20: 75-174; "New Introductory Lectures on Psychoanalysis," *S.E.*, volume 22: 1-182.

10 Charles Rycroft, *A Critical Dictionary of Psychoanalysis* (Middlesex: Penguin Books, 1972), 8.

11 Ibid.

12 Burness E. Moore and Bernard D. Fine, eds., *Psychoanalytic Terms and Concepts*. (New Haven: The American Psychoanalytic Association and Yale University Press), 25.

13 Ibid.

separate person with worth and importance, and object constancy has been attained (between ages 24 and 36 months, according to Margaret S. Mahler), the fear of losing the mother's love becomes the child's paramount anxiety. During the Oedipal phase, says Freud, anxiety and fear associated with physical harm, that is, castration, assume center stage. Lastly, in the latency phase (between ages 6 and 12), the child's typical anxiety and fear is that the "internalized parental representations," the super-ego, will stop loving the child and will chastise, punish and abandon him. As Moore and Fine further note, and Freud pointed out, though these particular fears and anxieties are associated with specific phases of psychosexual development, they can and do routinely exist in the adult ego and personality. Most importantly, in a neurotic adult, the main unconscious fear and anxiety is that one of these childhood danger situations will be re-experienced.[14] For the classical analyst, anxiety reactions and neurotic symptoms are the ego's attempts to prevent these traumatizing unconscious anxieties from becoming psychic eventualities. The focus of treatment is to make the unconscious anxieties conscious and thereby strengthen the ego's ability to ward off and control debilitating anxiety, thus protecting the integrity of the personality.

Freud's theory of anxiety has a relational thrust to it; like Levinas, he is, in part, focused on the meaning of the "Other," especially the "m/ other" in human existence, but it was mainly through the emergence of relational and self-psychology that intersubjectivity took center stage. It is for this reason that I have chosen to review, in addition to Freud, one of the seminal British object relational theorist's accounts of the development of psychopathology, including anxiety manifestations and conditions, before I consider Levinas's notion of the "there is."

"Psychology," says W. R. D. Fairbairn is the "study of the relationships of the individual to his objects."[15] Fairbairn's reconceptualization

---

14 Ibid.

15 W. R. D. Fairbairn, "Repression and the return of bad objects (with special references to the 'war neurosis,'" in *Object Relations Theory of the Personality* (New York: Basic Books, 1952), 60. Briefly, as Rycroft points out, for Freud, an "object" refers to "that towards which desire and action is directed." It is that which the person needs in order to obtain instinctual gratification. The object is also "that to which the person relates himself" (usually "persons, parts of persons or symbols of one or the other)." What are called "internal objects" are the "phantoms," images that occur "in phan-

of psychoanalysis deviated from Freudian theory in at least two important ways. First, as Moore and Fine point out, Fairbairn viewed the "ego as a structure" that existed from birth rather than emanating from the id as a consequence of its interactions with reality.[16] The ego was self-energizing; it did not derive its energy "from the id; it was a dynamic structure."[17] Fairbairn's rejection of the notion of a separate id was in part rooted in his view that "libido is a function of the ego" and aggression is a response to real-life neglect, interference, and frustration of the individual's attempt to generate satisfying connections with others.[18] Fairbairn also deviated from Freud in his assertion that "libido is object-seeking, not pleasure-seeking"; its goal was not the discharge of tension but the creation of gratifying relations with others.[19] In other words, for Fairbairn there is a fundamental human striving to relate and to connect to others, and the infant therefore is "hardwired" toward relationships from birth.[20] This relations-seeking and relations-maintenance has adaptive value in terms of biological survival.[21] As James Grotstein notes, for Fairbairn, "the human being was born and lived his lifetime with such an inescapable need for the object, that this object dependence informed all stages of development, from immature to mature dependency."[22] Moreover, for Fairbairn the inevitable frustrations and inadequacies in the mother-infant relationship lead to "the internalization of an object" that is gratifying and un-

---

tasies which are reacted to as 'real'" (Rycroft, *A Critical Dictionary of Psychoanalysis*, 100).

16 Moore and Fine, *Psychoanalytic Terms and Concepts*, 71-73. My summary of Fairbairn's theory is largely taken from a previous publication of mine (Marcus and Rosenberg, *Psychoanalytic Versions of the Human Condition. Philosophies of Life and Their Impact on Practice*, 161-163.

17 Moore and Fine, *Psychoanalytic Terms and Concepts*, 71.

18 Ibid.

19 Ibid.

20 Ibid.

21 Ibid.

22 James S. Grotstein, "W.R.D. Fairbairn and His Growing Significance for Current Psychoanalysis and Psychotherapy. In Marcus and Rosenberg's *Psychoanalytic Versions of the Human condition: Philosophies of Life and Their Impact on Practice*, 162.

gratifying.[23] Anxiety, insecurity and ambivalence are stimulated in the infant leading to the activation of defenses, especially splitting, which Fairbairn viewed as a "universal mental phenomenon necessary" to manage frustration, dissatisfaction, and over-stimulation in early relationships.[24] Says Grotstein, "the human condition predicates man as having a schizoid nature by virtue of the splitting disassociations that inevitably characterize the formation of the endopsychic structure"[25] (the unitary all-embracing psychic structure Fairbairn called the ego). For Fairbairn, schizoid persons desire loving connections and affectionate attachments to objects; however, their internal worlds are so animated by violent assaults from split-off, destructive objects, that real life interpersonal relationships are nearly impossible.

For Fairbairn, psychopathology, including anxiety manifestations and conditions, is the "study of the relationships of the ego to its internalized objects."[26] The internalized objects within Fairbairn's perspective are by definition, by their very nature, psychopathological structures. Psychopathology for Fairbairn, unlike Freud (who mainly saw it as a consequence of conflict over pleasure-seeking impulses), was rooted in disturbances and interferences in relationships to others. Understanding the infant's real-life experiences with his early significant others was thus crucial for understanding healthy and unhealthy development. For Fairbairn, intimates Grotstein, maternal deprivation in particular was the basis for psychopathology. Fairbairn believed that psychopathology, including anxiety and panic, was best conceptualized as the ego's efforts to maintain old connections and yearnings represented by internal objects. The main problematic that undergirds all psychopathology for Fairbairn is between the developmental inclination toward mature dependence and more differentiated and satisfying relations, and the childish refusal to relinquish infantile dependence and connections to undifferentiated objects, emanating from the terror of losing connection of any kind. As we will soon see, Levinas's first inkling of the "there is" was when he was a child separated from his parents in a common, seemingly non-traumatic familial context. Says

---

23 Moore and Fine, *Psychoanalytic Terms and Concepts*, 72.

24 Ibid.

25 James S. Grotstein, "W.R.D. Fairbairn and His Growing Significance for Current Psychoanalysis and Psychotherapy," 162.

26 Fairbairn, "Repression and the return of bad objects," 60.

Grotstein, "In his emphasis on the importance of introjective over projective identification," Fairbairn "formulated object relations theory as being fundamentally traumatic, that is, objects are internalized only when they are felt to be endangering. Thus, strictly speaking, the term 'object relations' constitutes a default category of failed interpersonal relation where the responsibility lies with the external parental objects."[27] Thus, for Fairbairn, "only bad objects are internalized; good objects do not have to be because they are satisfying."[28] Psychopathology, such as anxiety and panic, for Fairbairn, emanates from the ego's self-fragmentation as it tries to maintain the connection to the object (e.g., a significant other) and control its unsatisfying elements.

Finally, it is worth noting that psychoanalytic therapy for Fairbairn is best understood in terms of how it differs from Freud. Unlike Freud, who believed that the analytic experience is mainly constituted by the working through of unconscious conflict about one's id impulses, Fairbairn thought it should aim at reconstituting the individual's capacity to form and maintain authentic, real relationships with others. "Mature dependence," Fairbairn's term for the theoretically possible but practically unreachable ideal state of emotional health, is manifested in terms of the individual's ability to sustain intimate, mutual connections to other people. Moreover, says Grotstein, the individual no longer has the need to introject and identify with the realistic badness of one's early and later objects so as to preserve his needed goodness. In the healthy person, there is no need to self-fragment in order to sustain connection and loyalty to the contradictory and irreconcilable aspects of significant objects, that is, of valued, cherished others.

Thus, we have two psychoanalytic ways of describing and formulating the experience of anxiety. For Freud, anxiety reactions and neurotic symptoms are compromise formations, the ego's feeble efforts to safeguard the person from re-experiencing childhood traumatizing unconscious threats to its integrity. For Fairbairn, anxiety reflects the ego's inadequate efforts to maintain old connections and yearnings represented by internal objects. Both of these formulations of anxiety, correctly I think, describe it as an impossible-to-ignore disruption of comfortable consciousness by extremely unpleasant affect, or worse, by horror and panic. What I hope to suggest is that Levinas's notion

27   Grotstein, "W.R.D. Fairbairn and His Growing Significance for Current Psychoanalysis and Psychotherapy," 162-163.

28   Ibid., 163.

of the "there is," impersonal being, gives psychoanalysis a point of entry into a complementary understanding of a primal human anxiety, with its diverse manifestations, that can blunt the development of authentic self-identity and the capacity to love. Like Freud, Levinas seems cognizant of the inevitability of anxiety, that is, the inevitability of traumatic disruptions of consciousness emanating from both within the person (e.g., guilt for a real or imagined misdeed), and/or from the outside world (e.g., the death of a loved one). While Freud focuses on anxiety as it relates to conflict over the sexual and aggressive drives, and Fairbairn, to the disturbance and interference of relationships with significant others, Levinas posits that it is only from a radical otherness, something that can neither emanate from nor be assimilated into the conventional ego of Freudian and other forms of psychoanalysis,[29] that authentic self-identity and the capacity to love, mainly construed as a responsibility for the Other mode of being, can develop.

THE "THERE IS"

The "there is" is one of Levinas's most enigmatic philosophical abstractions, a kind of hypothetical construct, a "thought experiment" meant to evoke a dimension of being, of deeply internal experience, that is central to the Levinasian project. The notion of the "there is" is "elemental," a key notion that helps animate Levinas's efforts to further his project of describing and explicating "how our encounter with the Other enters into the drama of consciousness."[30] Levinas's notion of the "there is" attempts to describe the relationship between the burden of existing and the human Other that demands an ethical response.

Finally, the "there is" gives us an inkling of what Alford surmises is Levinas's greatest fear, and indeed, many peoples' fear to one degree or another, "that love for the being of another will trap the human in being."[31] This fear of entrapment within oneself, without escape, points to what Levinas is getting at, though not only this, not nearly this. Such a mode of experience, with its attendant hellish anxiety,

---

29   Edwin E. Gantt and Richard N. Williams, "Pursuing Psychology as Science of the Ethical," in Gantt and Williams, *Psychology For The Other*, 8.

30   Davis, *Levinas*, 23.

31   C. Fred Alford, *Levinas, the Frankfurt School and Psychoanalysis* (Ithaca, NY: Cornell University Press, 2002), 57. Alford provides a most interesting rendering of the "there is" mainly through the work of the English object relations theorist D. W. Winnicott.

horror and panic, and its "egocentric interiority"[32] and imprisoning
narcissistic self-absorption, is what I believe Levinas views as the main
obstacle preventing the individual being from loving, from embracing
a "responsibility for the Other" existential orientation. For Levinas,
"love," a word he deeply distrusts and thinks is compromised, what
he prefers to call "being-for-the-Other," is in fact the "escape" from the
"there is," the only way "to stop the anonymous and senseless rumbling
of being."[33]

Let us begin with Levinas's descriptions of the "there is":

> My reflection on this subject starts with childhood memories. One
> sleeps alone, the adults continue life; the child feels the silence of his
> bedroom as 'rumbling.' It is something resembling what one hears
> when one puts an empty shell close to the ear, as if the emptiness
> were full, as if the silence were a noise. It is something one can also
> feel when one thinks that even if there were nothing, the fact that
> 'there is' is undeniable. Not that there is this or that; but the very
> scene of being is open: there is. In the absolute emptiness that one
> can imagine before creation—there is...neither nothingness nor
> being. I sometimes use the expression: the excluded middle. One
> cannot neither say of this 'there is' which persists that it is an event
> of being. One can say that it is nothingness, even though there is
> nothing. *Existence and Existents* tries to describe this horrible thing,
> and moreover describes it as horror and panic.[34]

Elsewhere Levinas further describes the "there is," again reminiscing
about his childhood:

> The "there is" is unbearable in its indifference. Not anguish [as in
> Heidegger's *es gibt*], but horror, the horror of the unceasing, of a
> monotony deprived of meaning. Horrible insomnia. When you
> were a child and someone tore you away from the life of the adults
> and put you to bed a bit too early, isolated in the silence, you heard
> the absurd tie in its monotony as if the curtains rustled without
> moving. My efforts...consist in investigating the experience of the
> exit from this anonymous 'nonsense.'[35]

Finally, Levinas, draws from Blanchot to describe the "there is":

---

32 Levinas, *Time and the Other*, 101.

33 Levinas, *Ethics and Infinity*, 52.

34 Ibid., 48-49.

35 Levinas, *Is It Righteous to Be?* 45-46.

He has a number of very suggestive formulas; he speaks of the 'hustle-bustle' of being, of its 'clamor,' its 'murmur,' of a night in a hotel room where, behind the partition, 'it does not stop stirring'; 'one does not know what they are doing next door.' This is something very close to the 'there is.'[36]

For now, I want to emphasize what is striking about Levinas's descriptions. In two of three instances, he refers to experiences of separation from adults, probably his parents, and the lonely and pained experience of being excluded from their palpably bountiful, pleasurable and meaningful lives. The third instance also speaks to being excluded from the stirrings of life and pleasure that Levinas fantasizes are occurring behind the partition, next door. Thus, according to Levinas's descriptions, the "there is" emerges within the psychological context of felt radical disconnection, distance and loneliness, the opposite of the phenomenology of love, with its strong feelings of connection, closeness and togetherness.

Levinas points out that the "there is" refers to no identifiable subject, but rather it describes what he calls "existing without existents"[37] (roughly the difference, following Heidegger, between Being and being). By this is meant an anonymous modality of existing prior to the emergence of the individual human subject. Levinas's concern is how the self emerges out of the "there is," that is, roughly, how personal identity evolves into a self-determining, self-actualizing "for the Other" person. However, such individuation is only authentic and worthwhile to the extent that it resists subjugating its "concrete subjectivity," its individuality, to the violence done to it by two sources: by the philosophical paradigm of rationality, with its tendency to "metaphysical reductionism" and totalization, and by the violence done by the developing self to itself.[38] This discussion of the "there is" mainly pertains to the second form of violence (the first I have already discussed in earlier chapters), for instance, how individuals avoid responsibility for and to the Other, how they truncate their ties to empathy and blunt their capacity to love.

Levinas, according to Peperzak, indicates that the "there is" is "a treacherous semblance of nothingness, a hiding place of mythical

---

36 Levinas, *Ethics and Infinity*, 50.

37 Levinas, *Time and the Other*, 44.

38 Hutchens, *Levinas*, 36-38.

powers without face, an indeterminate and opaque density without orientation or meaning, a senseless and therefore terrifying chaos."[39] The "there is," says Levinas, pre-exists nothingness, it is evoked in the terrifying silence facing the "vigilant insomniac."[40] The vigilant insomniac "is and is not an I" who cannot manage to fall asleep.[41] As we have seen, for Levinas, the child who in his bed senses the night dragging on has an experience of horror that "is not an anxiety,"[42] at least not as conceived by psychoanalysts. Rather, it is something even more terrifying and menacing, though Levinas only hints at this difference:

> The impossibility of escaping wakefulness is something 'objective,' independent of my initiative. This impersonality absorbs my consciousness; consciousness is depersonalized. I do not stay awake; 'it' stays awake. Perhaps death is an absolute negation wherein 'the music ends.... But in the maddening 'experience' of the 'there is' one has the impression of a total impossibility of escaping, of 'stopping the music.'[43]

The "there is," says Levinas, thus signifies the end of objectivizing consciousness, as it is not an object of perception or conscious thought (though Levinas's childhood examples seem to suggest otherwise), and cannot be comprehended or intentionally created. According to him, it is impossible to avoid the experience of the "there is" because one is immersed and inundated in it. This inescapability, experienced as dread and panic, suggests Levinas, signifies "the impossibility of death...the impossibility of escaping from an anonymous and uncorruptible [sic] existence."[44] For Levinas, says Alford, the "there is" is not a psychological experience (it is not a question of "states of the soul")[45] as usually construed, because "it is subjectivity itself which has fled." This is because all that constitutes an experience as psychological, that is subjectively knowable and intelligible, is besieged with the horror and panic of mere existence. Consciousness in other words, has been

---

39 Peperzak, To the Other, 163.

40 Hand, The Levinas Reader, 29.

41 Ibid.

42 Levinas, Ethics and Infinity, 49.

43 Ibid., 49.

44 "There is: Existence without Existents," in The Levinas Reader, 33.

45 Levinas, Ethics and Infinity, 50.

objectified, it has become a thing, an it, and personal identity has become swamped, swallowed up by it.[46]

What Levinas is getting at is a reversal of the way in which Heidegger conceptualizes this type of subjective experience, the "es gibt" (the "there is"). The Heideggerian "es gibt" is generosity and abundance, it refers to "the donation by Being to beings of light, freedom and truth."[47] In contrast to the "there is" as abundance and diffuse goodness, the "there is" is unbearable in its indifference. Before the generosity of Being, says Levinas, there is a "chaotic indeterminacy" to being that comes before all giving, "creativity and goodness."[48] Heidegger's "es gibt," arguing from beings to Being, is mainly rooted in the fear of pure nothingness, of death. In contrast, for Levinas the experience of the "there is" is a terrifying feeling that there is no way of escaping from mere being, there is "no exit" from existence, not even suicide, as I shall shortly explain. In other words, says Levinas, in contrast to Heidegger's use of the term "there is," the horror of the night of the vigilant insomniac is not merely anxiety about nothingness and the fear of death. Rather, "there is horror of…the fact that tomorrow one still has to live, a tomorrow contained in the infinity of today. There is horror of immortality, perpetuity of the drama of existence, necessity of forever taking on his burden."[49] Levinas says elsewhere, "Anxiety, according to Heidegger, is the experience of nothingness. Is it not, on the contrary—if by death one means nothingness—the fact that it is impossible to die?"[50]

What Levinas is contrasting is the horror of the night to Heideggerian anxiety, fear of being to Heideggerian fear of nothingness. The primordial anxiety and fear for Levinas is mere being, existing forever, with no escape, to be trapped in the nocturnal horror of existence that is prior to the emergence of consciousness, into, perhaps, a kind of terrifying, persecutory psychotic-like regression into a pre-verbal autistic-like primary narcissism.

46 Alford, Levinas, The Frankfurt School and Psychoanalysis, 57-58.

47 Davis, Levinas. 129; Levinas, Ethics and Infinity, 4-48 and Is It Righteous to Be? 45.

48 Adriann Peperzack, Beyond: The Philosophy of Levinas. (Evanston: Northwestern University, 1997) 3.

49 Levinas, "There is: Existence without Existents," 34-35.

50 Levinas, Time and the Other, 51.

Before further explicating Levinas's notion of the "there is" and showing how it can enhance psychoanalytic theory and practice, I want to
elucidate another unwieldy term, "hypostasis" of the self[51] (coming into
existence), a process that is an essential part of Levinas's description
of the "there is." Hypostasis of the self is Levinas's attempt to explain
how "the self assumes a self-reflective and self-determining form."[52] It
is as close to a developmental theory accounting for the birth of personal identity, the self, as there is in Levinas, though as we shall see, he
does not avail himself of the insights of psychoanalytic developmental
theory or the research literature on child development, and thus some
of what he describes is not congruent with this received knowledge
about the birth and development of human identity.[53]

THE "THERE IS" AND THE EMERGENCE OF THE SELF

For Levinas, as Hutchens points out,[54] in the beginning there is the
"there is," that is, "the self is anonymous and indeterminate…without
being anything," and motivated "to become conscious and present to
itself." Neither "subjective nor substantive," says Hutchens, the self
then withdraws and shrinks back from this "there is" state as it strives
for definition, identity and constancy. This dynamic process of hypostasis entails "becoming something," in Levinas's language that means
evolving into an existent (being) from simple, plain, "mere existence"
(Being).

However, the hypostasizing self struggles to become an existent and
more than simply an existent. It struggles, it "works to exist,"[55] says

---

51   Ibid., 51-57; Levinas, *Existence and Existents*, 61-100. Hypostasis was
     a term that Levinas used mainly in his early writings. It can be defined,
     Wyschogrod further says, as "the appearance of something that arises from
     anonymous being and that now carries being as its attribute" (Wyschogrod,
     Emmanuel Levinas, 244).

52   Hutchens, *Levinas*, 43.

53   A critique of Levinas's developmental theory, as I have loosely called it,
     from the point of view of psychoanalytic and other developmental theories
     and findings is beyond the scope of this discussion. I only mention this
     point as a cautionary note.

54   Hutchens, *Levinas*, 43. I have liberally drawn from Hutchens' excellent
     summary and analysis of "the hypostasis of the self," as he calls it, in this
     section.

55   Ibid., 44.

Hutchens, as if existing were an effort necessary of any self. Originally in a state of isolation and solitude, there is something in its anonymous striving and impersonal work of existing that prompts its existence as a self. Exactly what this "something" is Levinas does not say. It is this work to exist, he says, that allows the self to depart from the "there is," its anonymous existence, and become a determinative, separate and present self. "Hypostasis is the emergence of the uniqueness of the self," the self-empowerment that permits an avenue of flight from the dreaded impersonality and anonymity of the "there is."[56] The self thus evolves and appropriates consciousness that reflects specificity and "localization."[57] It is by the fact of being consciousness that the self views itself as disengaged, as separate from impersonal existence. The self, in other words, comes to existence out of itself. It relinquishes its objectivity and develops itself through the subjective processes and procedures of consciousness. However, and this is critical to this discussion, the self is still aware of the "incessant murmur" and "rustling" of anonymous existence and can never totally relinquish the ominous "rumbling" of "there is."[58] The self must declare and affirm itself in this anonymity, assuming determination by being watchful over, and mindful of, itself. Although, continues Hutchens, the self never stops being unique and a lone being "in this process of self-determination," it never completely inoculates itself to the dread of being within the terrifying "rustling" of impersonal existence. As the self creates a space for itself and situates itself in that space as a singular and developing self, it is, says Hutchens, burdened with an "I," a fleshy body, including a brain capable of feeling and perception, Moreover, such an acquisition involves "hosting a guest entrusted to it, which is conscience."[59]

Conscience, for Levinas, at least on the level of knowing, is what mainly constitutes consciousness.[60] It is the recognition of our obligations to the Other, to all Others. It is the mindfulness of the fact that

---

56   Ibid.; Levinas, *Ethics and Infinity*, 48.

57   Levinas, *Existence and Existents*, 66.

58   Levinas, *Otherwise Than Being: Or Beyond Essence*, 164.

59   Hutchens, *Levinas*, 44.

60   George Kunz, "Simplicity, Humility, Patience," in Gantt and Williams, *Psychology For The Other*, 127; Levinas, "Bad Conscience and the Inexorable," in *Of God Who Comes to Mind*, 172-177; Levinas, *Time and the Other*, 109, 110, 114, 117, 118; Levinas, *Totality and Infinity*, 261.

my responsibilities are allocated to me, for example, as wife to husband, parent to child, as a neighbor, a colleague, a countryman and a fellow human being.[61] It is, in its adult expression, the mindfulness of my obligation to embrace "*menschlichkeit*," to be a compassionate and kind person, and the awareness of the guilt of not having been so, or not nearly enough. "The interiority of mental life is, perhaps, originally this," what Levinas calls "bad conscience." Bad conscience is, in part, ignoring the obligation not to leave the other man alone in the face of his suffering and death. More generally, it is denying the "possibility of dreading injustice more than death, of preferring the injustice undergone to the injustice committed and which justifies being by that which assures it."[62] And finally, Levinas proclaims, "The true inner life is…the obligation to lodge the whole of humankind in the shelter—exposed to all the winds—of conscience."[63]

As Hutchens points out, for Levinas the next sub-phase of the hypostasis of the self, of self-development, is that the self becomes split into two, a divided self:

> The self then divides itself into a subject of thinking and a 'psyche' upon which it reflects consciously. Hypostasis 'doubles up' the self: on the one hand, it is always reflecting upon itself in an unchanging way, that is it 'remains the same in its very alterations' and on the other hand, what it is conscious of undergoes alterations. Identity is always being changed by the processes of being self-conscious and yet what does the identifying does not change. The self is in flux, but never loses itself in flux. Repulsed by the changes it necessarily undergoes, the self retreats into itself, away from the world to which it is exposed as it changes. It withdraws into an insular self-sufficiency in order to be at peace with itself.[64]

For Levinas, while the self strives to be safe, self-sustaining and self-sufficient within its narcissistic fortress, within its protective cocoon, the reality is that it can never be completely self-determined. This is because the body, mind and spirit are vulnerable to assaults from within, such as from ontological anxiety and guilt, and from without, such

---

61   Kunz, "Simplicity, Humility, Patience," 127.

62   Levinas, "Bad Conscience and the Inexorable," in *Of God Who Comes to Mind*, 175, 177.

63   Levinas, *Proper Names*, 122.

64   Hutchens, *Levinas*, 44.

as from the demanding, challenging and often harsh external world. Despite all of its feeble, neurotic and absurd efforts at self-determination and self-sufficiency, those forms of pathological narcissism that are meant to sustain the analysand's weak, fragmentation-prone self, the self is, in Levinas's language, still plagued, haunted by the rumbling of the horror of being, the "there is." It is only through engaging that which is strange, alien and external to this narcissistic self, that one is able to diminish the toxic effects of the empowering, though normalizing, homogenizing and totalizing rational procedures described earlier. Most importantly, however, it is through the ethical response to the human face, responsibility to the Other, that one can blunt, if not avoid, the "there is" and achieve a modicum of what analysands call peace of mind.

THE "THERE IS" AND PSYCHOANALYSIS

I am aware that this discussion of the "there is" has been a long and complex one that the reader may feel has, as the saying goes, generated a lot of heat but little light. Indeed, some of what Levinas is talking about has similarities to familiar psychoanalytic notions such as depersonalization, the feelings and thoughts of unreality and/or weirdness pertaining either to the self or the outside world, or both; derealization, the feelings and thoughts of alienation or detachment from one's environment that often occur simultaneously with depersonalization; or loneliness, that awful feeling of being companionless and solitary. All seem to capture something of the "there is." Moreover, certain descriptions of ontological insecurity, for example, the feeling that one is threatened by non-being, also call to mind aspects of the "there is," as does Sartre's "nausea."[65] Indeed, Rollo May's contribution,[66] and R. D.

65 Jean-Paul Sartre, *Nausea*, trans. Lloyd Alexander (New York: New Directions, 1949). Levinas discusses nausea in his slim volume, *On Escape*. Sartre's first version of his novel goes back to 1931; while Levinas's essay was written in 1935, it is not clear if either author influenced the other in their formulation of the "there is." It is worth noting that Sartre's and Levinas's uses of the term nausea are quite different. For Sartre, nausea emanated from the horror of nothingness that threatened the autonomous self, whereas for Levinas, nausea depicted the failure to escape from the bounty and plenitude of being. The real-life implications of these differing viewpoints however, are not so clear.

66 Rollo May, "Contributions of Existential Psychotherapy," in *Existence: A New Dimension in Psychiatry and Psychology*, eds. Rollo May, Ernest Angel

Laing's brilliant descriptions of engulfment, with its subversion, if not eradication of identity, implosion, the apprehension that at any instant the outside world will overwhelmingly pour in and "obliterate all identity as a gas will rush in and obliterate a vacuum," and petrifaction, a version of fear and horror that one will be transformed into an inanimate object like a rock, or changed into a automaton or contraption devoid of feelings, subjectivity and self-awareness, all to some extent resonate with Levinas's concept of the "there is."[67]

While phenomenological purists will continue to debate the nature of the "there is" and attempt to discern its differences from and similarities to certain forms of anxiety, depersonalization and the like, for our purposes it is the connection between the experience of the "there is" and the development of authentic self-identity and the deep capacity to love that I want to make clear. The fact that Levinas lacks any kind of psychologically sophisticated developmental theory, appreciation of dynamic unconscious processes and internalized object relations, makes mining his insights about personal identity and the capacity to love, difficult to discern and explain, at least psychoanalytically speaking.

Most striking about Levinas's descriptions of the "there is" in his childhood and hotel examples is the fact that they seem to be associated with feelings of extreme abandonment and aloneness, a painful narcissistic, autistic-like, frozen mode of self-experience. Such a state, a kind of free fall into the void, is rooted in the profound despair of not having one's imagined life-sustaining needs and wishes satisfied by the outside world (and internalized object world), usually one's significant other(s). The "there is" experience is characterized by feelings of internal loss, emptiness and rage for not having one's infantile, narcissistic wishes to possess, control and feed-off the loved object gratified, regardless of its impact on the object, the other. As Melanie Klein has described, such wishes to ruthlessly and aggressively obtain what one desires and needs lead to a depressive feeling that one has annihilated one's own good object.[68] The imagined loss of one's life-sustaining external and internal objects leads to the feelings of pain, loss and guilt

---

and Henri F. Ellenberger (New York: Clarion Books, 1958), 37-91.

67 R.D. Laing, *The Divided Self* (Baltimore, MD: Penguin Books, 1959), 44-48.

68 Melanie Klein, *Contributions to Psychoanalysis, 1921-45* (London: The Hogarth Press, 1948).

associated with Klein's depressive position, and, in my view, also to some extent with the "there is." In this formulation, the love and concern for others is mainly driven by the anxiety of being abandoned and alone and, secondarily, by guilt for one's aggression towards one's ambivalently loved object, as in "I have destroyed those who care for and love me; how will I survive?"[69] The "there is" is being "without there being any objects. The being in every silence, every non-thought, every way of withdrawing from existence."[70]

The "there is" can be viewed as a primitive defense, a last ditch attempt to sustain oneself psychically by retreating into a solipsistic enclosure.[71] Such an enclosure, a narcissistic web of being, is both a tomb and a womb-like place. On the one hand, it reflects the horror and panic of feeling radically abandoned and trapped in being, that is, trapped in an endless, solitary, linguistically deprived, and Godless awfulness. On the other hand, the enclosure is a closed system in which, paradoxically, night, ambiguity and indeterminateness shield oneself from the even more threatening and painful demands of relatedness, intersubjective engagement and active partaking in life, giving and receiving love conceived as responsibility for and to the Other.

There is a second "higher level" aspect of the "there is" that I want to put into sharper focus that also has direct bearing on psychoanalysis. The "there is," says Levinas is "the consciousness of having no way out,"[72] of being riveted, chained to existence, in horror and panic. Not even suicide is viewed as an escape from the dread and pain of existence. It is hard to imagine falling into such a dire state in which not even death is viewed as a desirable option or a form of relief. As I have

---

69   C. Fred Alford, "Melanie Klein and the Nature of Good and Evil," in *Psychoanalytic Versions of the Human Condition*, Marcus and Rosenberg, 123-124.

70   Levinas, *Alterity and Transcendence*, 98.

71   Levinas is not entirely clear whether the "there is" mainly a retreat, "a hiding place" (Peperzak), a "withdrawing from existence" (Alford), or the origin, the beginning of existence.

72   Levinas, *On Escape*, 2. As Samuel Moyn suggests, Heidegger's influence is evident here. While Levinas ultimately rejected Heidegger, he never discarded the view that "man's essence...lies in a kind of bondage." Moyn is quoting from Levinas's essay "Quelques réflexions sur la philosophie de l'Hitlerisme." (See Moyn, *Origins of the Other: Emmanuel Levinas Between Revelation and Ethics*, Ithaca, NY: Cornell University Press, 2006, 103).

observed in analysands, there are certain subjective states that not even the fantasized womb-like shielding feeling of being anesthetized or asleep appears as a way out of the pain. Levinas is thus claiming that built into the human condition is the proclivity to experience a form of existential pain that is so bad, so inescapable, that even suicide does not feel like a plausible way to stop the pain. Psychoanalytically speaking, the "there is" as horror and panic, is a trauma for consciousness and an impossibility for symbolization. It cannot be avoided in the same way as being cannot be avoided.[73]

In most people, such a distressing state is largely ineffable, never consciously experienced, at least not in a "pure" form. Perhaps, rephrasing psychoanalyst Joseph Sandler, we can say that the "there is" is something of a "background of unsafety." For others, the "there is" comes over them like an emotional storm, and still for others, it is only the derivatives of the "there is" that are felt, such as in the form of extreme anxiety and panic, as conventionally expressed and understood. Fatigue, indolence and insomnia, says Levinas, also contain the shadow of the "there is."[74] For Levinas, suicide is not a viable avenue of escape. The nature of the experience is that it is "impossible to die."[75] Levinas does not tell us why, though, as Alford points out, suicide assumes a pained subjectivity revolting against an absurd and meaningless existence.[76]

Of course, in a certain sense, Levinas is wrong. Death, so far as we know, does end the pain. However, to the person amidst the "there is," there is the deeply felt sense that even if one were to die, palpable life would not end, the music would not stop. Perhaps we can say, following Levinas, that such a person feels that even if one were to die, the dire consequences of one's selfishness and malignant narcissism, callousness, misdeeds and other shortcomings, especially towards those we think we care about and love, will continue to ripple negatively through the lives of those whom we leave behind. The conscious and/or unconscious awareness of our realistic or genuine guilt for having denied and ignored our responsibilities for and to the Other is in a

---

73 John Lechte, "Levinas," *Fifty Key Contemporary Thinkers; From Structuralism to Postmodernity* (New York: Routledge Books, 1994), 116.

74 Levinas, *Existence and Existents.*

75 Levinas, *Time and the Other*, 50-51.

76 Alford, *Levinas*, 63.

certain sense felt as an inescapable self-accusation that not even death can obliterate. Moreover, sometimes such a state of mind includes a notion that after one dies one is still held accountable to God or some other cosmic judge, or as Hamlet said, "perchance to Dreame." Thus, the circle of fire is closed, there is no exit from the horror of being, of My being Me. Insomnia, Levinas calls it, the seemingly without-end, self-shattering, anxious and panicked awareness that I have irrevocably inflicted injury on those I love and, even worse, there is no way of making reparations, no way of putting things right.

Thus, I am claiming that while phenomenologically speaking, the "there is" experience resembles feeling trapped in the horror and panic of mere being, its potential meaning and significance after one re-enters into normal, self-reflective, self-critical consciousness includes a feeling of bad conscience, of culpability.

This is not the conscience of Freud's superego, the internalizaton of parental and societal values, demands and prohibitions. Levinas's conscience goes deeper, as it is based on the experience that the face of the Other calls my selfish, egotistical and generally self-centric way of being into ultimate question. The "there is" is burning into the soul of the individual who experiences the accusation and the warning that unless one breaks free from one's ego-centeredness and destructive narcissistic desires, one is doomed to the hellish solitary confinement, the horror and panic, of being trapped in a maze of grotesque happenings of guilt without escape. One feels, in other words, hugely blameworthy and accountable, condemned to a life sentence without parole.

For Levinas, and this is crucial to his conceptualization of the "there is," the possibility of escape from the horror of the "there is," means embracing a different mode of being in the world, what he calls "otherwise than being."[77] "Otherwise than being" is Levinas's way of describing love, understood as "responsibility for the Other," "being-for-the-Other." It is through love, "in the form of such a relation that the deliverance from 'there is' appeared to me."[78] "The true bearer of being, the true exit from the 'there is' is in obligation, in the 'for the Other,' which introduces a meaning into the nonsense of the 'there is.' The I subor-

---

77   In this context, embracing otherwise than being implies that it is something that one can in a certain sense choose. However, for Levinas any "choice" is a "second order" choice as we are all subject to the otherwise (*autrement*); it is a condition of possibility for any encounter with another.

78   Levinas, *Ethics and Infinity*, 52.

dinated to the other. In the ethical event, someone appears who is the subject par excellence. That is the kernel of all I would say later."[79]

Love, then, understood first and foremost as "for the Other," before oneself, is the antidote to the horror and panic of the "there is," and to the wide range of anxieties and other forms of suffering that are manifestations of, and emanate from, the "there is." The redemptive value of love is phenomenologically evident when one contrasts its adjectival differences with the "there is." The "there is," compared to love, is experienced as anonymous versus individuating; imprisoning/entrapping versus free/wandering; near psychic-death versus psychic rebirth; heaviness of being versus lightness of being; self-centric/self-interested versus fiercely Other-related/Other-regarding; and finally, amidst the "there is," the world is experienced as a wall, whereas in love it is experienced as an open gate.

Levinas's dialectical formulation between the "there is" and "love" is easily linked to Freud's and Fairbairn's conceptualizations about anxiety and psychopathology that we discussed earlier. For Levinas, Freud and Fairbairn, and other psychoanalytic theorists, authentic self-identity, maturity and health in psychoanalytic language, are best manifested and expressed in the deep capacity to love widely. This capacity is, in part, rooted in ridding oneself of one's self-absorbing internalized unconscious childhood conflicts over one's sexual and aggressive drives (Freud), as well as the self deficits (e.g., in self-coherence, self-continuity and self-esteem), mainly emanating from inadequate early parenting and caretaking (Fairbairn). Only through "working through" these life, pleasure, relationship and meaning-denying conflicts, and repairing the developmental deficits that often underlie them, is it likely that one can evolve into the kind of person capable of being "otherwise than being," in Levinas's terms, a person capable of "leaving oneself…being occupied with the other, that is with his suffering and death, before being occupied with one's own death."[80] Exactly how Levinas understands this extraordinary form of being in the world, the inter-human relations in which one embraces the "ethical order," what he calls the "order of love," the "order of compassion,"[81] will be the subject of the next chapter.

---

79 Levinas, *Is It Righteous to Be?* 45-46.

80 Ibid., 46.

81 Ibid., 50.

CLINICAL VIGNETTE

John came into his session the morning after he had had a terrible nightmare. He said that this nightmare forcefully awakened him, and he found himself "unable to breathe," in a "panic" that was "beyond words" it was so "horrible" (the "there is?"). John presented his dream as follows:

> I was in a Greek discotheque/restaurant located in a place I once went to with my wife and teenage son. It was called The Greek Cave, in Astoria [Queens, New York] where all the Greeks live. It was called The Cave because to access the disco you have to descend about three flights of stairs before entering this underground cavernous, dazzling spectacle of boisterous people, lively music and dancing and sumptuous, plentiful food. As I was enjoying myself, I suddenly sensed something bad was going to happen, I scanned the room and noted that there were no windows or escape exits except the stairway by which we had come down. In a nervous voice I told my wife and son to run up the stairs with me though they looked at me like I was out of my mind. Suddenly, the ceiling began to crack and I started to scream, 'the ceiling is collapsing, run with me for your lives.' I reached out and grabbed my wife's hands, but my son was somehow somewhere out of my reach, I think he was walking back from the bathroom behind the dance floor. I saw myself running up the stairs with my wife, and my son was trapped in the falling rubble, trying to escape while holding two wounded people on his back. I felt a pain I could not even begin to describe, I shouted 'Oh, my God, is he dead? I awakened in a sweat, feeling unbelievable anxiety and fear...

John's associations to his dream were crucial to unraveling its meanings and its significance for his current life. He indicated that he had had the dream the day after his son's twentieth birthday. John noted that his son had come into the world with great difficulty, having been prematurely born twelve weeks early. His viability was in serious question. John remembered the long drives he had made to the hospital for many months following his son's birth, often after work at dusk. He remembered one rainy afternoon in particular in which he was so overwrought for his son that he noticed the rain on his windshield and imagined for a moment, as if it were real, that it was not rain but embryonic fluid that was drenching his windows. In John's mind, this embryonic fluid was the life source for his unborn son and it was leaking on to his windshield in the same way that his wife's waters had once leaked out, causing his son's premature birth. John said that he was so upset that he pulled off the highway and cried. Such extreme despair and anxiety at that moment, and throughout his son's premature birth and its aftermath, characterized his experience of the four months of hospital visits to his son while he grew in his incubator.

John's next association was to his own childhood, of being in the hospital at ages five and nine with serious illnesses. He remembered the terrible feelings of fear and annihilation anxiety, especially while in an oxygen tent, a basis of his intense identification with his son in his incubator. John also remembered the loneliness he felt at night after his parents left to go home after visiting hours. Moreover, he described one incident when he had to be restrained by a nurse because he chased his mother to the elevator door trying to hold on to her. To this day, John claims that his parents never stayed with him through the night, though his mother's recollections indicated otherwise. In other words, it was the presence of his mother's absence that was most troubling to John while he lay alone in his hospital bed. He remembered rocking himself to sleep with the words, "home, home," that being the only way he could escape the feeling of abject loneliness, vulnerability and despair.

Finally, John's associations went to an experience he had had about three or four months before his son was born. He described his fear and panic about having been threatened for a number of months by a man he had testified against in court in a child abuse case in which he had been the attending emergency room doctor. In his testimony John had accused the perpetrator of neglecting and endangering his children as well as physically and psychologically mistreating them. Based largely on John's testimony, the judge ordered that the perpetrator not see his children for the foreseeable future.

That afternoon, after testifying, John had a message on his answering machine from some man, probably the perpetrator, "Dr. Schwartz, I'm coming to get you real soon." At first, John played down the risk of this threat, but when it was repeated four or five more times, each time with more threatening language, "I'm going to hunt you down like an animal," John began to feel extremely anxious and frightened. In fact, after being told by the police that there was nothing they could do because there was no hard evidence that it was the perpetrator (the voice was probably one of his associates), John decided to secure an illegal handgun (he could not legally buy one quickly) for protection as well as a bullet proof vest which he wore to work. After a few months of harassing and intimidating telephone messages, the calls finally stopped. John further noted, however, that a few months before this episode, a "crazy patient" accused him of criminal malpractice and was suing him for seven million dollars, another threat to his survival. John had to pay for an expensive lawyer, as his malpractice policy did not cover criminal allegations. The case was ultimately dismissed but John felt overwhelmed by the whole experience.

Before trying to make some sense out of all of this, I should remind the reader that after John had his nightmare he awakened in a frenzied state, full of utter panic. In fact, he said he was shaking and shivering uncontrollably. Unable to calm himself down after about a half hour he had the thought that he should awaken his wife for comfort, though, strangely, he decided not to disturb her. As the feeling of horror and panic mounted, John reached for some anti-anxiety medication that he had. He took one pill but it did not take effect as fast or as effectively as it was supposed to. John says that he had the urge to take another one, "no," he said, "I wanted to take the whole bottle, to sleep, to die, to do anything to make the pain go away." When I asked him why he didn't finish himself off, he replied, "My wife would be sad for a while but she would manage, but my kids would be fucked up forever and that I couldn't bear." Eventually, after about three more hours of this anguish, trying to rock himself to sleep in his easy chair, John finally fell asleep for a few minutes, only to be awakened by the morning sun coming into his room. Feeling relieved that it was finally day, he dragged his exhausted and battered body and soul to the bathroom to begin his day.

After weeks of analyzing his nightmare and the frenzied state that followed, John co-produced with me the following interpretation of these events that he found illuminating and which, as often occurs in analysis, led to further questions. John felt that the dream reflected the disturbing phase of life he was going through, namely, that his two beloved children were separating from him and his wife, both going off to college. He had indicated many times that while he welcomed his children's growth and development, he felt that their separation and individuation raised troubling questions about what he was going to do with his life. What would act as a replacement world of meaning for his background role, the increasingly marginal significance that he now had to his children's lives? He was worried that with an "empty nest" he and his wife would have boring and purposeless lives.

John felt that it was significant that in the dream he was with his son and wife, all three of them enjoying themselves at the disco/restaurant, for it depicted the self-perception that he was capable of providing pleasure and knowledge to his children, such as exposing them to different cultures. John also said that the sudden collapsing of the ceiling in the dream reflected his depressive feeling that no matter how good things are, they can, without warning, be taken away from you, or even worse, that you can, often violently, lose that which you cherish the most, lose your connection to the people you love. John indicated that it was noteworthy that his daughter was not in the dream. He said that he had invited his daughter to come with them to the disco but that she had refused, saying that she "had better things to do" and that it would "be embarrassing" for her to go with him, her mother and brother. John said that during the day of the dream, what Freud called the "day residue," the harmless aspects of everyday life that contribute to the formation of the dream, he had seen a performance of *The Merchant of Venice*. He said that he felt irrational, incessant annoyance at Jessica, Shylock's daughter. If you recall, Jessica is noteworthy for her contempt for her father and her Jewish heritage. John believed that Jessica's betrayal of her father, in marrying Lorenzo, a Christian, and by stealing her father's money when she eloped with Lorenzo, depicted an ungrateful daughter. When I pointed out to John, that the text insinuates that for Jessica living in Shylock's house was oppressive because of his miserliness and his frowning upon such pleasures in life as music and merriment, as well as Shylock's forbidding Jessica to enjoy the masque even from the security of her window, John ignored my point. He said that Jessica wanted to be Christian because of her opportunistic social aspirations to be part of Venetian society, rather than a Jewish pariah, and also because of her long-maintained, unjustified hatred of her father.

From the point of view of understanding why his daughter was not with him at the disco, John concluded that he was angry at her for rejecting him, for not allowing him to be important to her as she was moving on in her life. I indicated that this was only part of the reason he felt so angry at her; he was also angry because she would not allow him to control her and make her do what he thought would be good for her. Thus, John's associations suggest that he irrationally viewed his daughter's emancipation from him, her going to college, as a form of rejection, defiance and abandonment, just as she said to him in real life that she had "better things to do" and would be "embarrassed" to go with him to the discotheque.

John felt that there was another important thread in the dream, the most important. He said that running through the nightmare and its associations, and the panic attack afterwards, were feelings of deep guilt and shame. He felt guilty for not being able to protect his son from the collapsing ceiling, just as he was not able to shield his son from his traumatic birth and near death; he was not able to raise his daughter properly so that she loved him; instead she felt, as he saw it, that she viewed him as emotionally miserly and incapable of giving her joy or anything worthwhile. Moreover, said John, such an understanding of the nightmare explained to him why his associations went back to being in a hospital as a sick, abandoned child. He said that he was unconsciously relating to his children as if they were meant to nurture and parent him, rather than the other way around. He felt that the associations with testifying in court, with his own "accusations" of the perpetrator's "neglecting" and "abusing" the children, reflected his own sense that he did not live up to his responsibilities to love and care for his children. He felt accused by his children, he had let them down and made them "crazy," that is, neurotic. Finally, John noted that the references to the death "threats" made to him by the perpetrator reflected that he somehow knew that he had done wrong as a parent and deserved to be punished, perhaps even to die. The repetitive threatening telephone calls, the accusations of wrongdoing, were, in his view, his own conscience accusing him of failing his children, of shirking his responsibilities and refusing to be anything else but a needy, dependent, narcissistically-absorbed child, more concerned with his own survival than his children's.

Finally, John said that the seemingly inescapable panic and fear that he felt after the nightmare, which lasted into the early morning, was a form of punishment for his guilt over his selfishness and other limitations of character, but also that it reflected perhaps his greatest fear. He felt that as a result of ignoring his obligations to the face of the Other, in his case as a parent to his children, that he was destined to suffer. He would forever be in a state of forced separation from everyone and everything that he loved and felt connected to in the world, just as he felt that fateful night: hence, he never awakened his wife for help. Such abject aloneness, the experience of radical abandonment, a near "death-in-life" experience, was a consequence, he felt, of his profound sense that through his narcissistic excesses, inordinate egotistical needs and characterological shortcomings, he inflicted irreparable acts of violence on those who, along with his wife, he loved most, his children. John indicated that he felt ashamed of himself.

After such painful realizations, emanating, in part, from a confrontation with the "there is," John was ready to begin to do the heavy lifting of profoundly changing his outlook on himself and others, as well as his behavior, embracing the interpersonal virtues of compassion, gratitude and love. He was now, as Levinas said in another context, better able to use his intellectual, moral and personal resources to pursue more deeply and selflessly, his ethical obligation, service to, and responsibility for-the-Other. Levinas calls this development, using wisdom in the service of love.

4

LOVE WITHOUT LUST

"I would say this quite plainly," says Levinas,
"what is truly human is—and don't be afraid of this word—love. And I
mean it even with everything that burdens love or,
I could say it better, responsibility.
And responsibility is actually love, as Pascal said:
'without concupiscence' [without lust]…
love exists without worrying about being loved."[1]

Levinas

Though Levinas does not omit eroticism from his account of love,[2] he seems to be most interested in positing a love "in which the ethical aspect dominates the passionate aspect."[3] It is thus not altogether surprising that Levinas mentions that the most perfected form of love, of "disinterested love, without concupiscence," of "responsibility for the other man," is depicted in the "for-the-Other of saintliness." "I'm not saying that men are saints, or moving towards saintliness. I'm only saying that the vocation of saintliness is recognized by all human beings as a value, and that this recognition defines the human…. Man is the being who recognizes saintliness and the forgetting of self."[4]

Holding up such a selfless form of love as an ideal mode of being in the world, let alone an ideal for the average analysand, is far-fetched

---

1 Levinas, *Is It Righteous to Be?* 143. For Pascal, says Levinas, concupiscence, powerful feelings of physical desire, is "an assumption and an investment by the I." (*Of God Who Comes to Mind*, 68).

2 This subject will be discussed in the following chapter, "Eroticism and Family Relations."

3 Levinas, *Is It Righteous to Be?* 165.

4 Levinas, *Alterity and Transcendence*, 171, 175, 180. Levinas also says in the same interview that he does not "affirm saintliness…[though] man cannot question the supreme value of saintliness," 180.

and uncomfortable for most analysts. Analysts can, of course, appreciate the psychic achievement and social benefit of such a magnanimous altruistic orientation. However, from a more cynical psychoanalytic point of view, such a pervasive "for-the-Other" mode of being is fundamentally flawed in that it is unrealistic and flies in the face of human nature, at least human nature as conceived by Freud and others as inherently narcissistic, egotistical, pleasure-seeking, aggressive and selfish in its outlook. That is, as W. W. Meissner has pointed out, altruism is "maladaptive...without egoistic restraints." For the psychoanalyst altruism is sometimes a cover for aggressive and narcissistic motives and actions depending on the context and criteria we use for judging morality (remember that the Nazis thought they were doing God's work by ridding the world of Jews). But, psychoanalytically speaking, the human project is mainly about finding a balance between what analysts call "healthy narcissism" or appropriate self-investment and self-regard, and care, concern and affection for others.[5] For the psychoanalyst healthy altruism requires a high degree of self-esteem to allow an individual to maturely love another person. For example, a modicum of self-constancy and secondary narcissism are necessary in order to feel loved. In order to affirm the other's goodness as the other loves me, I need to be able to let myself be loved by the other. According to psychoanalysis, such reciprocity is a profound act of affirmation of the other, characteristic of mature love relations. Moreover, to believe that the love one has to give, or is obligated to give for the sake of the other, as Levinas might say, is worth giving, requires that one believe that what one has inside is "good" in the first place.

I say all of this by way of orienting the reader to the fact that Levinas's ethically- infused notion of love, conceived mainly as asymmetrical, non-reciprocal responsibility for and to the Other, is not a formulation that is central to any psychoanalytic theory of love and intimacy that I am aware of. Nor is such a formulation generally regarded as a goal or a central characteristic of a successful psychoanalysis. As Freud

---

5 W.W. Meissner, *The Ethical Dimension of Psychoanalysis* (Albany, NY: SUNY, 2003), 163,166, 151. As Thomas Hobbes pointed out in his great work of social engineering, *Levianthan*. Ed. Richard Tuck (Cambridge: Cambridge University Press, 1991), altruism can be a manifestation of self-interest and self-preservation. It can, for example, emanate from a desire for recognition and respect, for God's blessing and eternal reward or the fear of retaliation.

asked, "Why should analyzed people be altogether better than others?" His response, "Analysis makes for integration, but does not of itself make for goodness."[6]

In this chapter I want to pick up where Freud's troubling observation leaves off. I want to suggest the possible benefit to psychoanalytic theory and practice of embracing the evocative metaphor of the "cultivation of goodness" as central to "mature," "healthy," and/or "authentic" love relations.[7] Levinas says that "to think the other as other, to think him or her straightaway before affirming oneself, signifies concretely to have goodness." Elsewhere he notes that "responsibility for the other is the experience of the good, the very meaning of the good, goodness. Only goodness is good."[8]

Put more straightforwardly, I want to suggest that Levinas's notion of love, and to a considerably lesser extent his analysis of eroticism and family relations, radically challenges psychoanalysis to develop further the ethical realm in its account(s) of love and intimacy. Indeed, as Rubin points out, there has been a "failure" by psychoanalytic writers "to articulate a workable theory of intimacy." Moreover, he claims, "Despite love's extraordinary importance in the lives of individuals, it has been a curiously neglected topic in the psychoanalytic literature," a view that Meissner, who has recently reviewed the pertinent literature, tends to agree with as far as I can tell.[9]

---

6 Letter to J. J. Putnam, 6/17/15, in Nathan G. Hale, editor, *James Jackson Putnam and Psychoanalysis* (Cambridge: Harvard University Press, 1971), 188.

7 I put all of these words in quotation marks to indicate to the reader that they are radically philosophical, that is, they are open to multiple definitions and meanings and interpretations depending on what theoretical or, in this case, what psychoanalytic and linguistic framework one is using. Needless to say, it is beyond the scope of this volume and my expertise to unravel all of this.

8 Levinas, *Is It Righteous to Be?* 106, 135. Levinas from time to time quotes Plato's words, the "Good beyond Being" to strengthen this claim. As Cohen points out, by quoting Plato Levinas gives "philosophical dignity" to the notion of a "thought beyond being and truth" (Richard A. Cohen, translator's introduction, in *Time and the Other*, 14). For Plato the ultimate good was conceptualized as an effective transcendental principle animating the world. In his theory, the highest good was the supreme Idea, roughly equated with the totality of being.

9 Jeffrey B. Rubin. *Psychotherapy and Buddhism. Toward an Integration* (New

This is surprising given the fact that Freud wrote that "Truth is only the absolute good of science, but love is a goal of life quite independent of it..."[10] Moreover, as is well known, Freud viewed the capacity "to love and to work" as the best indication of mental health and probably the soundest basis for having a meaningful life.[11] As Fine pointed out, in his early years Freud even suggested setting up an Academy of Love. Fine further notes that "Psychoanalysis should be looked upon as theory of love. The psychoanalyst may be defined as a person who teaches others how to love."[12] All of this fits in well with Levinas's understanding of the function of philosophy. "Philosophy is the wisdom of love at the service of love."[13]

As I review a few of the important psychoanalytic contributions to understanding the many facets of love, followed by a further explication of Levinas's account of love, I hope to persuade the reader that perhaps one of the reasons that mainstream psychoanalysis has had such difficulty developing an adequate, let alone a compelling account of love and eroticism is because it has mainly embraced a self-centric, "in itself" and "for itself" conception of the human condition while underplaying man's primordial sociality, conceived by Levinas as "for the Other," as responsibility for, and obligation to the Other. Such a Levinasian-inspired account of love relations is not meant to replace current psychoanalytic views of love and intimacy, for such views are in many ways apt and extremely useful. Rather, my contention is that such accounts need some widening and deepening to more centrally include the under-explored and crucial ethical realm of love. In this way, psychoanalysis can provide a more empathic and comprehensive account of the human condition.

York: Plenum, 1996), 176; Rubin, The Good Life. Psychoanalytic reflections on love, ethics, creativity, and spirituality (Albany, NY: State University of New York Press, 2004), 46-47; Meissner, The Ethical Dimension of Psychoanalysis, 151-175.

10   Freud, letter to S. Ferenczi, 1/10/10, in Ernest Jones, Life and Work of Sigmund Freud (New York: Basic Books, 1955), Volume 2: 446.

11   Erik H. Erikson, Childhood and Society (New York: W.W. Norton, 1950), 264.

12   Reuben Fine, History of Psychoanalysis (New York: Columbia University Press, 1979), 576.

13   Levinas, Otherwise Than Being, 162.

Perhaps most importantly, such a Levinasian outlook on love can stimulate what I believe is the analysand's inherent, often unconscious desire to transform his self-centric and egotistical interiority, that is, his selfish cravings and infantile narcissism, into "goodness," best expressed as radical altruism. Such radical altruism, scientists tell us, is possibly innate,[14] reflecting an inherent desire for self-subversiveness, for what the *Bhagavad Gita* beautifully describes as a liberation from the finite self, ego consciousness, and self-centeredness. In more analytic terms, this means liberation from the self-destructive narcissism of the ego, that which often prevents us from achieving what perhaps we really want in life: self-transformation on the way to self-transcendence. Such a mode of transcendent being is a kind of spirituality. However, for Levinas the "spiritual" is profoundly anchored in everyday social reality and ethical human relations, in living a life that is characterized by an extreme, deep-seated, far-reaching responsibility for the Other, before oneself, that is, "otherwise than being."[15]

PSYCHOANALYTIC NOTES ON LOVE

Levinas did not trust the word love: "I don't very much like the word love, which is worn out...debased...[and] ambiguous." While Levinas preferred to speak "of the taking upon oneself of the fate of the other" [16] as roughly synonymous with love, he was emphasizing a crucial problem in the psychoanalytic and other scholarly literature on love. That is, what is love anyway? I have no intention of entering deeply into the problems of the definitions and meanings of love for it would require many volumes even to scrape the surface. However, it is important that the reader understand that there is no consensus with

---

14 Biologists and ethologists have for many years asserted that there is "a biological basis to helping and altruism." For example, it is more or less agreed upon that empathy plays a crucial "role in helping and altruism" and that the limbic system "gives humans the capacity to empathize with other persons." Moreover, it would appear that this brain structure was probably existent "in the earliest mammals over 180 million years ago." In other words, empathy is most likely innate (see John F. Dovidio and Louis A. Penner, "Helping and Altruism." In G. Fletcher and Margaret S. Clark, eds, *Blackwell Handbook of Social Psychology. Interpersonal Processes.* Oxford: Blackwell Publishing, Inc., 2002, 176, 177).

15 Levinas, *Is It Righteous to Be?* 236, 201.

16 Ibid., 165, 169.

regards to defining and understanding the term and the experience(s) it allegedly refers to. Thus, the straightforward, though clearly limited, *The Concise Oxford Dictionary*'s definition of love is probably the best place to begin our discussion: "an intense feeling of deep affection or fondness for a person or thing; great liking."[17]

To make matters even more complicated, there are many forms of love, each with its own phenomenology and psychodynamics. For example, there is love of wife/husband/significant other, child, parent, God, knowledge, beauty, country, a cause, humanity, brotherly love, and, according to Freud, possibly the purest of all love relations love for our pet! Says Freud, "It really explains why we can love an animal... with such extraordinary intensity; affection without ambivalence, the simplicity of a life free from the almost unbearable conflict of civilization, the beauty of an existence complete in itself...Often when stroking Jo-fi [his dog] I have caught myself humming a melody which, unmusical as I am, I can't help recognizing as the aria from *Don Giovanni*: 'a bond of friendship unites us both.'"[18]

---

17   *The Concise Oxford Dictionary*, ed. by R.E. Allen (Oxford: Clarendon Press, 1990), 708.

18   From a letter to Princess Maria Bonaparte in 1934, quoted in Ralph Steadman, *Sigmund Freud* (New York: Paddington Press, 1979) 108. It is little known, let alone cited, that Freud made the odd comment that only "the relation of the mother to her son, which is based on narcissism" is truly free of "aversion and hostility," that is, is not ambivalent. Such a claim as any honest-talking, "good enough" mother would tell you, is preposterous (*Group Psychology and the Analysis of the Ego*, in S.E. vol. 18, 101).
      It is also interesting to note that Levinas, like Freud, mentions his experience with a dog as deeply meaningful in his life. When Levinas was incarcerated in a Nazi-administered forestry commando unit, and he was marched to and from his work through the French streets under the hateful, anti-Semitic stares of the onlookers, it was [a dog] Bobby (as the prisoners named him), who would appear at morning assembly and was waiting for them as they returned, jumping up and down and barking in delight. Says Levinas, while the onlookers "stripped us of our human skin...[and we felt] no longer part of the world,...for him [Bobby], there was no doubt that we were men." For Levinas, it was this dog, not the human onlookers who attested to the dignity of the person. "There is transcendence in the animal" (*Difficult Freedom*, 152-153). Interestingly, in Jewish tradition, it is the dog that will merit leading the singing of praises to God in the World-To-Come. See my "I'm Just Wild About Harry. A Psychoanalyst Reflects On His Relationship With His Dog," (*The Psychoanalytic Review*, 94(4),

Whether Freud meant exactly what he said is not clear, but he was pointing to strong friendship as one of the clearest expressions of a "higher level" form of love, of what Aristotle called "perfected" love. Aristotle indicated that friendships [i.e., love] are shaped and sustained on different bases. There are those who sustain friendship mainly for the sensual gratification it provides; others sustain friendship for reasons of usefulness, and finally, there are friendships that are lodged in virtue. That is, one wants for one's friend what is most beneficial for one's friend. Such friendship is "perfected," says Aristotle, *telia philia*, in that its goals and aspirations, its objective, does not go beyond the friendship itself. It facilitates the good. Needless to say, such friendships are neither easily created nor common.[19] Roughly speaking, Levinas's notion of love seems most in harmony with *telia philia*, while the Freudian construal of love most resonates with the first two forms of Aristotle's friendship, though obviously the matter is hardly so clear or simple. Our focus in this chapter will be on the ideal form of love between two adults, at least as psychoanalytic perspectives tend to construe it, that is, what analysts sometimes call "healthy," "mature" or "authentic" "object love." Briefly, object love depicts the self's cluster of emotions and attitudes towards "integrated whole objects" (e.g., significant others) that is the basis, the source of its gratification and pleasure.[20]

For Freud, as for all subsequent psychoanalysts, love has been approached mainly from the point of view of describing and understanding that which interferes and corrupts the capacity to love. Indeed, there is no body of knowledge that better depicts what St. Augustine called "disordered love," a lack of psychological fit between various human needs and wishes and the objects that can gratify them.[21] While

August, 20007, 639-656).

19 Aristotle. "Nicomachean Ethics" and "Eudemonian Ethics" in *The Complete Works of Aristotle*, 2 volumes, ed. J. Barnes (Princeton, NJ: Princeton University Press, 1984). I have based my summarizing comments on Daniel N. Robinson's *The Great Ideas of Philosophy*, Part 2 (Chantilly, Virginia: The Teaching Company, 1997), Course Outline, 12-15.

20 Burness E. Moore and Bernard D. Fine, (eds.), *Psychoanalytic Terms and Concepts* (New Haven, CT: American Psychoanalytic Association and Yale University Press), 129.

21 Paul Marcus, *Ancient Religious Wisdom, Spirituality and Psychoanalysis* (Westport, CT: Praeger, 2003), 142-145.

psychoanalysis has in general been unsurpassable in explicating that which subverts mature love, it has been much weaker in depicting what constitutes and sustains it. What follows are some of the most interesting contributions of psychoanalysis to understanding what constitutes healthy/mature love relations.

For Freud, all love relations are a "refinding of the object," roughly analogous to the emotional experience of symbiotic togetherness with the mother or caregiver.[22] What this means in terms of establishing love relations is that to some extent the choice of our significant other repeats or calls to mind aspects of our childhood caregivers. Love, says Freud, "consists of new editions of old traits and it repeats infantile reactions."[23] That is, all love is based on infantile templates, is fundamentally a fixation on the parents, what Freud calls transference love. According to Reuben Fine, transference love and ordinary love only differ in terms of degree.[24] The problem with this is that if we refind that which is "bad" from our childhood experiences, it usually leads to impoverished and/or destructive intimate relationships. The trick, then, is to refind in the significant other that which is consciously and unconsciously "good" from our childhood caregivers, so that I and my partner have a better chance of being happy in our love relation.

For Freud, however, to accomplish this seemingly straightforward task is not at all simple for it requires resolving at a higher level of personality integration at least three aspects of love: "narcissistic versus object love, infantile versus mature love, and love versus hate."[25] To the extent that love is dominated by inordinate, unhealthy and pathological narcissism (e.g., self-centeredness and selfishness), infantile and dependent wishes and behavior (e.g., the other exists mainly to gratify one's needs and wishes on demand) and hate (e.g. heightened ambivalence), one's love relation is doomed to failure. To the extent that it is animated by altruistic concerns (e.g., enhancing the other), is mature (e.g., the recognition that the separate other has needs and wishes worthy of gratifying) and is mainly affectionate (e.g., not corrupted by aggression) it is likely to succeed. For Freud, and this needs to be emphasized, all relationships are ambivalent, at least to some

---

22 Moore and Fine, *Psychoanalytic Terms and Concepts*, 113.

23 Freud, "Observations on Transference-Love," *S.E.*, 12: 168.

24 Fine, *History of Psychoanalysis*, 48.

25 Moore and Fine, *Psychoanalytic Terms and Concepts*, 113.

extent. However, ultimately, the pre-condition to maintain a stable, healthy, mature love relation is that affectionate sentiments towards one's significant other are in general, much stronger and pervasive than the aggressive ones.

For Freud, love is understood within his closed energy-driven model and instinct-dominated outlook. All forms of love are seen as derivatives of instinct and their function is to give instinctual gratification. In a sense then, for Freud all love is love of a need-satisfying object. Mature object love, in contrast to infantile, dependent, need-satisfying love, is love that recognizes the reality of the other, his otherness, that he is a separate person with needs and wishes requiring and deserving gratification. Perhaps most importantly, for Freud the capacity for mature love requires object constancy, the capability to maintain an enduring relationship with a specific, single, separate other. This in turn presupposes the development of both a stable, structurally sound, coherent self and secure internalized object relations. Normal love, says Freud, thus results from the blending of caring, affectionate and sexual feelings toward a person of the opposite sex. Its accomplishment is characterized by genital primacy in sexuality and by object love in relationships with others.[26]

For Freud, love relations, actually all human relations, largely reflect a utilitarian motive, that of using the other to gratify biologically-endowed drives as means to one's end. As Kleinian analyst Donald Meltzer points out, for Freud, love is like opening up a factory, of making a kind of capital investment bent on generating a profit. One does not invest one's libido unless one feels fairly sure that one will get back more than one gives.[27] For Klein, on the other hand, and to some extent for Levinas, love is conceptualized more in terms of bequeathing a charity.[28] That is, says Alford, "love gets from the very act of giving. It gets the opportunity to repair the self by repairing and restoring the

26 Freud, "Three Essays in Sexuality" in S.E., vol. 7. Freud's heterosexual bias is here exemplified. The term "significant other" could be used as a replacement for "opposite sex."

27 Donald Meltzer, The Kleinian Development: Books I, II and III in One Volume (Perthshire, Scotland: Clunie Press, 1978), volume 1, 84, as paraphrased in C. Fred Alford, "Melanie Klein and the Nature of Good and Evil." In Marcus and Rosenberg, eds., Psychoanalytic Versions of the Human Condition, 128.

28 Ibid.

world, or at least a little part of it."[29] For Klein, love emanates from
the infant's sense of gratitude toward the "good" mother, in Kleinian
language, toward the satisfying, "good breast." This feeling is the basis
for the infant's and later the adult's "appreciation of all goodness in the
self and in others."[30]

It is crucial, however, to briefly contextualize Freud's views on love
in terms of his broader version of the human condition. As Wallwork
points out,[31] for Freud the supreme moral criterion, what he took to be
the "good" that reflected what humans strive for was "happiness."

> [W]hat [do] men themselves show by their behavior to be the pur-
> pose and intention of their lives? What do they demand of life and
> wish to achieve in it? The answer to this can hardly be in doubt.
> They strive after happiness; they want to become happy and to re-
> main so.[32]

Wallwork further points out that for Freud, as was the case with
Aristotle and other great humanist moral philosophers, happiness was
in part conceptualized as "eudaimonia." However, eudaimonia is not
simply a moment or experience of pleasure alone, but a "veritable form
of life, a flourishing form of life capable of realizing the full range of
possibilities for rational beings."[33] As Wallwork puts it, happiness for

---

29   Ibid.

30   Martin S. Bergmann, *The Anatomy of Loving: The Story of Man's Quest
     to Know What Love Is* (New York: Fawcett Columbine, 1987), 248.

31   Ernest Wallwork, "Ethics in Psychoanalysis," in *Textbook of Psychoanaly-
     sis*. Eds. Ethel S. Person, Arnold M. Cooper and Glen O. Gabbard (Wash-
     ington D. C: American Psychiatric Publishing, 2005), 287. I have liberally
     drawn from Wallwork's useful overview in this section of this chapter.

32   Freud, *Civilization and Its Discontents*, S.E., vol. 21, 76.

33   Daniel N. Robinson, *The Great Ideas of Philosophy*, Part 2, Course Out-
     line, 17. Aristotle's influence on Freud's view of happiness is considerable
     and thus the former's view of happiness deserves a brief clarifying note. For
     Aristotle, says Robinson (Ibid., 12-19), to achieve happiness one required
     excellence of character, that is, habits of virtue (the capacity of discerning
     and choosing the middle path between the extremes of excess and deficien-
     cy in one's behavior and emotions, including personal friendships and pub-
     lic life). The highest form of happiness for Aristotle was the contemplative
     life. Also worth noting is that for Aristotle happiness was the foundation
     for ethics whereas for Freud ethics was based on the essential requirements
     of human cohabitation and survival. For Levinas, in contrast, unchosen

Freud is rather a matter of *functioning well* than feeling good. The mentally healthy person's happiness consists in the well-being that comes with certain forms of sublimation: loving and being loved, creative work, the pursuit of knowledge, freedom and aesthetic appreciation. These goods of life that make happiness possible are not instrumental means to functioning well, but constituent aspects of happiness.[34]

For Freud, love was perhaps the most important way of obtaining happiness, giving and receiving love; the "union of mental and bodily satisfaction in the enjoyment of love is one of its [life's] culminating peaks."[35] Love is also, says Freud, crucial because it underpins other extremely important aspects of life and civilization. For instance, it libidinally binds and animates ones ties to family, friends, community and to the world at large. Without the force of Eros, Freud's poetic metaphor for the life-force and sexual instincts, civilization is doomed to be overwhelmed by the inherent aggressiveness and destructiveness that constitutes Thanatos, the Death Instinct.

Psychoanalysis has of course developed its theories of love since Freud in interesting ways and I want to briefly touch upon some of these contributions. This mini-survey is meant to be illustrative not comprehensive.

Erik H. Erikson, the great ego psychologist, describes love as the key virtue, as the ego strength that emerges after successful resolution of the intimacy versus isolation ego crisis, the sixth stage of human development of the life cycle. Erikson defines love as "mutuality of devotion forever subduing the antagonisms inherent in divided function."[36] Love thus involves a complementarity of identities, having both the ego strength to share identity for "mutual verification" of selected identity, and drawing from the supportive and nurturing other "the strength to be 'self-ish.'"[37]

---

and indeclinable responsibility for the Other was the basis for ethics.

34 Wallwork, *Ethics in Psychoanalysis*, 287.

35 Freud, Observations on transference love: further recommendations in the technique of psycho-analysis, S.E., vol. 12, 169.

36 Erik H. Erikson, *Insight and Responsibility*, (New York: Norton, 1964), 129.

37 Christopher F. Monte, *Beneath the Mask. An Introduction to Theories of Personality*. 2d. edition (New York: Holt, Rinehart and Winston, 1980, 256.

Heinz Kohut's psychoanalytic self-psychology claims that love is fundamentally establishing a "selfobject." A selfobject is someone who strengthens and sustains the sense of self, the self's cohesion, firmness and harmony.[38] In infantile love the significant other, the selfobject, mainly functions for my benefit and survival, a template rooted in early childhood experience of the empathic, supportive, reassuring and approving "good" mother or caregiver. In mature love the self is better grounded, sustained and strengthened and thus capable of a more intense experience of receiving and giving love. In other words, for Kohut, in the love relationship one refinds the good mother, the selfobject, the one who calls to mind, sustains, and strengthens structural self-coherence, energic vigor, aliveness and integration and balance among the diverse elements of the self. For the love relationship to work, both people need to refind the self-selfobject relationships they had in their parent/caregiver-to-child relationships. For Kohut, the sense of comfort, healing and happiness that characterizes the best of love is precisely the byproduct of this mutual self-selfobject refinding.

Finally, Jacques Lacan says it is "impossible to say anything meaningful" or intelligible about love.[39] For Lacan, love must be understood in terms of what he views as the larger ethical goal of psychoanalysis, namely, the discovery of the reality and truth of the Unconscious and its powerful interpretive grip over the subject.[40] Thus, as Evans points out, Lacan says love is situated as a "purely imaginary phenomenon" although it has an impact in the symbolic register.[41] Love for Lacan, "is autoerotic" and mainly has a "narcissistic structure" since "its one's own ego that one loves in love, one's own ego made real on the imaginary

---

38   Heinz Kohut, How Does Analysis Cure? (Chicago, IL: University of Chicago Press, 1984), 49. See also Heinz Kohut, Analysis of Self (New York: International University Press, 1971).

39   Dylan Evans, An Introductory Dictionary of Lacanian Psychoanalysis (London: Routledge Books, 1996), 103. I have liberally drawn from Evans for my summary of Lacan's theory, including using his Lacan quotations.

40   Fryer, The Intervention of the Other, 190.

41   Evans, An Introductory Dictionary of Lacanian Psychoanalysis, 103. Briefly, according to Malcom Bowie, the Imaginary is the realm "of mirror images, identifications and reciprocities." The Symbolic "is the realm of language, the unconscious and the otherness" that stays other (Lacan, London: Fontana Press, 1991, 92).

level."[42] Lacan further notes that "to love is, essentially, to wish to be loved."[43] For Lacan love entails only "an imaginary reciprocity" and mutuality, the "reciprocity between 'loving' and 'being loved'" that, along with the "fantasy of fusion" with the loved other mainly comprises the compelling illusion of love.[44] Lacan rejects Freud and most other analysts who claim that love is the central clinical goal in psychoanalysis and, for that matter, the goal of life. Rather, he says that the aim of analysis is to reclaim the voice for one's desire by clarifying and making intelligible the familial experiences and knots, the governing signifiers, that have had such a powerful interpretive hold on one's way of being in the world. As far as I can tell, this may or may not lead to a greater capacity and actualization of love in one's way of being in the world.

Thus, as I will discuss in more detail at the conclusion of this chapter, one of the limitations in the theorizing on love in Freud, Klein, Erikson, Kohut and Lacan, at least from a Levinasian point of view, is that all of these theorists to some extent, treat the significant other reductively as a depersonalized love object, as a thing to be used for one's satisfaction. Even sophisticated relational theorists, like Jessica Benjamin, tend to view the other mainly as a source of reciprocal gratification of one's relational needs, which from a Levinasian point of view, frequently results in two people in a doomed arrangement of mutually instrumental use.[45]

---

42   Ibid., 103. Jacques Lacan, *The Seminar, Book I. Freud's Papers on Technique, 1953-54, trans. with notes by John Forrester*, New York: Norton; Cambridge: Cambridge University Press, 1988, 142. Sartre, too, claims that love can never really be other than the demand to be loved. This view follows from his questionable assumption that originally I am for-myself rather than for-the-Other.

43   Ibid., Jacques Lacan, *The Seminar, Book II. The Ego in Freud's Theory and in the Technique of Psychoanalysis, 1954-55, trans. Sylvana Tomselli, notes by John Forrester*, New York: Norton; Cambridge University Press, 1988, 253.

44   Ibid.

45   Jessica Benjamin, "An Outline of Intersubjectivity: The Development of Mutual Recognition." *Psychoanalytic Psychology* 7 (Supplement, 1990): 33-46. See also *Like Subjects, Love Objects* (New Haven, CT: Yale University Press, 1995).

LEVINAS ON LOVE

Throughout his work, including that on love, Levinas aims for the transformation of the form of subjectivity that underlies many psychoanalytic theories. The egological subject is mainly characterized by its "spontaneous free power"[46] and autonomy, which emanates from its own existence and is largely "for itself" in nature. For such a subject, the world is approached as a grand spectacle laid out before him to enjoy.[47] In contrast, Levinas puts forward an ethical subject, one that he describes as responsible for the Other, a responsibility that emanates from the Other.[48] For this subject, the world is a precious burden with which we are "entrusted," or better yet, a world we are commanded to hallow.[49] Heteronomy (from the Greek *hetero-nomos*, meaning "other ruling") is here more powerful than autonomy (from the Greek *autonomos*, meaning "self-ruling"). While Levinas appreciates the human inclination to seek out pleasure and enjoyment, including love relations, as these strivings are constituent aspects of existence, his focus is on service for, and to the other, not to be confused with servitude or bondage.

In a number of interviews[50] Levinas tells us what he thinks the nature of love is, including its "essence" and its "perfection":

1. "The responsibility for the other is the grounding moment of love. It is not really a state of mind; it is not a sentiment, but rather an obligation. The human is first of all obligation." (133)

2. "In the otherness of the other lies the beginning of all love." (134); "I think that when the other is 'always other', there is the essence of love…. The more other the other, the more he is loved, or rather, the more he is loved, the more he is other."[51] (58)

---

46   Rudolf Bernet, "Levinas's critique of Husserl." In Critchley and Bernasconi, *Cambridge Companion to Levinas*, 90.

47   Alphonso Lingis, "II. The Sensuality and the Sensitivity," in *Face to Face with Levinas*, 226.

48   Rudolf Bernet, "Levinas's critique of Husserl," 90.

49   Alphonso Lingis, "II. The Sensuality and the Sensitivity," 226.

50   Levinas, *Is It Righteous to Be?*

51   Franz Rosenzweig, a Jewish philosopher who greatly influenced Levinas, beautifully makes a similar point about love: "The highest love does not identify itself with its objects but instead loves what it knows as different…. The gap and the feeling of a gap first extracts from love its full force

3. "To approach someone as unique to the world is to love him. Affective warmth, feeling, and goodness constitute the proper mode of this approach to the unique, the thinking of the unique." (108); "It is proper to the principle of love that the other, loved, is for me unique in the world. Not because in being in love I have the illusion that the other is unique. It is because there is the possibility of thinking someone as unique that there is love." (50)

4. "Here in language there is the possibility of expressing in a didactic manner this paradoxical relation of love, which is not simply the fact that I know someone—it is not knowing—but the sociality irreducible to knowledge which is the essential moment of love. Practically, this goodness, this nonindifference to the death of the other, this kindness, is precisely the very perfection of love." (58)

For Levinas then, love is conceived as responsibility for the Other, such that the other's being and death are more important than one's own. This, he suggests, may be "the human vocation in being." Such responsibility for the Other, says Levinas, is a kind of "madness,"[52] it is "an absurd thesis."[53] Absurd or not, Levinas's thesis is one that the best philosophical minds of our time have been engaging, one that I hope mainstream psychoanalysis will begin seriously to engage.

How does Levinas's heady notion of love as fundamental responsibility for the Other actually play out in everyday relations between adults? To answer this important question I ask the reader to keep in mind the above list of Levinas's key terms that describe his notion of love: love is not merely a strong feeling, it is an obligation; authentic love does not mainly strive after union and fusion, it always respects the other's radical otherness and cherishes the other as unique; love is not primarily characterized by mere mutual pleasure giving and reciprocal affirmation,[54] rather, it is expressed as acts of goodness for the sake of the other's best interests, often requiring self-sacrifice.

---

and gives it wings that can beat most strongly" (Quotation from Samuel Moyn, *Origins Of The Other: Emmanuel Levinas Between Revelation and Ethics*, Ithaca, NY: Cornell University Press, 2006, 113).

52 Ibid., 250.

53 Ibid., 108.

54 This is not to say that a degree of reciprocity is not essential to a flourishing intimate relationship. For example, social psychologist's have found that intimacy is largely an evolving process of an increasing reciprocity of self-disclosure in which each individual feels his or her most private self

112 BEING FOR THE OTHER

For Levinas, to participate authentically, meaningfully and lovingly in the life of another person involves positive feelings and warmth, but most importantly, responsibility. On this point, he is in full agreement with that great intersubjective Jewish philosopher, Martin Buber. Said Buber, feelings merely "accompany the metaphysical fact of love, but they do not constitute it...Feelings one 'has,' love occurs. Feelings dwell in man, but man dwells in love...Love is responsibility of an *I* for a You."[55]

There are two figures in the real world who perhaps best depict the inner attitude and outer behavior of persons capable of living their love as responsibility for the Other. The first, the devoted mother, or caregiver, Levinas actually describes in his discussions of maternity.[56] The second, the master teacher, he only makes passing reference to. I want to describe briefly how the ideal mother and master teacher manifest the form of Levinasian love that I am referring to. I mainly leave it to the reader to extrapolate these metaphors to the details of everyday adult love relations.

For Levinas, "maternity in the complete being 'for the other' which characterizes it, which is the very signifyingness of signification, is the ultimate sense of this vulnerability."[57] Alphonso Lingis, in his translator's introduction to *Otherwise Than Being*, says "Concretely the acts by which one recognizes the other are acts of exposing, giving, of one's very substance to another. Responsibility is enacted not only in offering one's properties or one's possessions to the other, but in giving one's

---

affirmed, comprehended, and taken care of by the other (H.T. Reis and P. Shaver, "Intimacy as interpersonal process," in S. Duck (ed.), *Handbook of Personal Relationships; Theory, Research and Interventions*, ed. Steve Duck (Chichester, England: Wiley, 1988, 367-389).

55 Martin Buber, *I and Thou*, trans. Walter Kauffmann (New York: Charles Scribner's Sons, 1970), 66. Says Levinas, "And love means, before all else, the welcoming of the other as *thou*" (i.e., welcoming the unique other, one whom I am responsible for). *Proper Names*, 5-6.

56 Levinas's work on women, the feminine as he calls it, has been severely criticized, sometimes for good reason. I will touch on some of this later in this chapter when I discuss his observations and formulations on eroticism. However, for now, I am simply using the word mother as a signifier for selfless-like love for the other. The word "caregiver" would be a gender-neutral term.

57 Levinas, *Otherwise Than Being*, 108.

own substance for the other. The figure of maternity is an authentic figure of responsibility."[58]

Writing in one of his Talmudic commentaries, Levinas develops one of the core aspects of maternity, the quality I want to focus on. "*Rakhamim* (Mercy), which the Aramaic term *Rakhmana* evokes, goes back to the word *Rekhem*, which means uterus. *Rakhamim* is the relation of the uterus to the *other*, whose gestation takes place within it. *Rakhamim* is maternity itself. God as merciful is God defined by maternity.... Perhaps maternity is sensitivity itself..."[59]

In other words, the existential stance that best exemplifies one's responsibility for the other is one that is characterized by mercy or, in less religious language, compassion. Compassion is a notion that is grossly under-explored in the psychoanalytic literature. Moreover, it is hardly ever a term that analysts use in describing a successful analysis. Meissner, for example, a Jesuit priest/analyst, in his recent book on the ethical dimension of psychoanalysis does not even list compassion in his index, while Wallwork, in his review article on "Ethics in Psychoanalysis," also does not discuss compassion as part of the deep ethical theory informing the practice of psychoanalysis.[60] In contrast, compassion, sometimes called mercy or lovingkindness (e.g., in Buddhism) is a core virtue of all major wisdom religions of the world.[61]

Compassion, defined straightforwardly as sympathy for the suffering of the other, including a desire to help, especially as manifested in the ideal mother, can be viewed as having at least two dimensions. First, compassion involves the ceaseless, abundant unconditional love for the other. Second, it expresses a love devoted to helping and at times, steering the other in a new direction. This requires abiding patience, empathy and understanding, and forgiveness. These two dimensions of compassion constitute, in part, the engaged love that Levinas seems to be pointing to in his notion of responsibility for the Other. Adult love relations then, are based on a fundamental obligation to make ourselves fully available, with boundless compassion, to the neediness (in the non-neurotic sense), especially the suffering, of the beloved.

---

58 Ibid., xix.

59 Levinas, *Nine Talmudic Readings*, 183.

60 Meissner, *The Ethical Dimension of Psychoanalysis*; Wallwork, "Ethics in Psychoanalysis."

61 Marcus, *Ancient Religious Wisdom, Spirituality and Psychoanalysis*.

Forgiveness is the second term I want to mention as characteristic of the "good enough mother," and, by extension, the responsible subjectivity that is equated with the capacity to love, as Levinas construes it. For the secularist, including the secular psychoanalyst, the word forgiveness, like compassion, is saturated with religious connotations and meanings, and therefore is generally not a crucial part of the dialogue between the typical secular analyst and analysand, nor is it usually part of scholarly psychoanalytic discourse.[62]

Like compassion, forgiveness, the act of pardoning somebody for a mistake or wrongdoing, requires a profound psychological capacity, as well as considerable autonomy, integration and self-esteem. Not only is the capacity to forgive a pre-requisite for being a "good enough," responsible mother or caregiver, it is also necessary for maintaining the integrity and continuity of any love relation.

Levinas seems to be circling the same insight when he boldly and provocatively claims that one is responsible for the persecutor, including one's own, by embracing the responsibilities of the persecutor that are not discerned and manifested.[63] Says Levinas, "In maternity what signifies is a responsibility for others, to the point of substitution for others and suffering both from the effect of persecution and from the persecuting itself in which the persecutor sinks. Maternity, which is bearing par excellence, bears even responsibility for the persecuting by the persecutor."[64] In other words, for example, when my lover says something offensive and unkind to me, it is my responsibility to help him see how he has pained me, and to help steer him back on track. It is my responsibility to demand justice from my lover, and, in so doing, I encourage him towards greater critical self-reflection, sensitivity and compassion. Moreover, by pointing out his culpability, I mobilize

---

62 Ethel Spector Person, "Forgiveness and its Limits: A Psychological and Psychoanalytic Perspective." *Psychoanalytic Review*. 94(3), June 2007, 389-408.

63 Hutchens, *Levinas*, 24-25.

64 Levinas, *Otherwise Than Being*, 75, 112, 113. Levinas acknowledges that, philosophically, to hold a person culpable for the transgressions he did not do is "simply demented." Yet, he also claims that "the uniqueness of the self is the very fact of bearing the fault of another." I am obligated to substitute myself for the Other, including to be responsible for his transgressions (Ibid., 113, 112.).

greater responsibility for himself, in terms of self-control, remorse and making reparations.

Suffice it to say, that forgiveness, a core aspect of responsibility for the other, can foster favorable modifications in one's emotional life and in one's love relation: As Richards and Bergin point out, it can reduce one's anger, resentment and retaliatory wishes; it can renew a person's sense of self-efficacy, control, and power in that one is taking a more active and compassionate role in changing how one views one's sense of being mistreated or having done the mistreatment; and of course, forgiveness can possibly lead to the reconciliation between the perpetrator and the offended. In addition, by forgiving, individuals enlarge their options, autonomy and freedom to develop, grow and flourish. Forgiveness also encourages people to take responsibility for their wrongdoing, which makes it somewhat easier for the offended to reduce his hurt and perhaps begin the healing process.[65] Finally, perhaps, forgiveness also includes transforming one's rage, resentment and animosity. By forgiving someone who has mistreated you, you, in effect, give up the right to hit it back at the offender, this being one of the main reasons it is so hard to forgive.

The second real-life figure who best expresses love as responsibility for the Other is the master teacher.[66] As Levinas points out, the Other is one's teacher: "The other is…the first rational teaching, the condition of all teaching."[67] Moreover, for Levinas the teacher-student relationship initiates the messianic in that the teacher redeems and comforts the student, and points him in the direction of living a life of peace, justice and compassion.[68]

Being a master teacher involves bringing all of oneself to the student (i.e., the loved other), as opposed to partially attending to the

---

65 P. Scott Richards and Allen E. Bergin, *A Spiritual Strategy for Counseling and Psychotherapy* (Washington D. C: American Psychological Association, 1997), 212. See also E. L. Worthington, Jr., *Forgiving and Reconciling: Bridges to Wholeness and Hope* (Downers Grove, IL: InterVarsity Press, 2003).

66 Aslaug Kristiansen, "The Interhuman Dimension of Teaching: Some Ethical Aspects." In Maurice S. Friedman, *Martin Buber and the Human Sciences* (Albany, NY: SUNY, 1996), 221.

67 Levinas, *Totality and Infinity*, 171, 203.

68 Levinas, *Difficult Freedom*, 85-87; Wyschogrod, *Emmanuel Levinas*, 204.

student's words. It involves taking great care of what is given to him. It demands that one be willing and able to do all he can in order to find the best solution to the problem of the student, to ease that which troubles him. In the adult-to-adult love relation this includes the everyday "hands on" problems in living associated with, for example, a significant other's work difficulties or raising children. It also involve responsibly responding to the "big" problems of existence that characterize the vicissitudes of the life cycle, including those situations that Freud thought reflected what he called the "harshness" of life.

Responsibility towards one's student also involves attempting, with great gentleness and care, and within the context of profound trust, to disrupt the student, to undermine the security-maintaining walls around him that constitute his taken-for-granted assumptions about himself and the world. The purpose of such disruption is to create the conditions of possibility for the student to think differently. This means encouraging him to create the space inside himself to imagine a wider horizon, and if he chooses, to expand, deepen and change his perspective on a particular issue, and/or to shift his perspective on life. In an educational context, this can be accomplished by the teacher's listening to the student with the fullness of his whole being and responding with the maximum of his intellectual and emotional resources.

The application of this existential orientation of the master teacher to his student is easily recast to the adult-to-adult love relation and for that matter to most forms of love. In the adult love relation genuine responsibility means helping the significant other to actualize his human potential. For a teacher this means acting like a midwife to the soul, facilitating the birth of a new self, a better self, a self capable of actualizing the best of its intellectual, emotional and moral capacity, especially for love, compassion and forgiveness, among other human virtues.

RETURN TO THE "OTHER" FREUD

I am well aware that all of this talk about responsibility for and to the Other, the obligation to give to the other before oneself, and the cultivation of goodness as a general existential orientation in the world is perhaps troubling to the mainstream psychoanalyst for a number of reasons. In his view, not only is such an expectation naïve and unrealistic for most people, it flies in the face of human nature as usually psychoanalytically conceived: man is inherently egoistic and narcissistic, tending to put himself first, and is inclined to insensitivity and indifference to the Other.[69] Moreover, a Levinasian approach also seems to cultivate a kind of masochistic outlook, a masochistic submission to the other's needs and desires. I want to respond briefly to these criticisms with the hope that the analyst will perhaps be more inclined to make some space for Levinas in his outlook, that is, to consider incorporating a Levinasian perspective on love, and for that matter, on the human condition.

Thomas Aquinas famously wrote, "If our natures were different our duties would be different." How one conceptualizes human nature will to some extent, determine how one formulates what it is reasonable to expect from people, especially in terms of their moral life. To the extent that one views the human condition mainly in terms of its dark side—conflict, deficit and psychopathology—then one is likely to obscure seeing and working with other dimensions of being. This includes the individual's yearnings for self-transformation and self-transcendence, for radically ethical living, what Levinas calls, "otherwise than being."

The received wisdom about Freud is that he did not have a very positive attitude about most human beings and what was possible in terms of enhancing their moral life. For example, he wrote that

> I don't cudgel my brains much about good and evil, but I have not found much 'good' in the average human being. Most of them are in my experience riff-raff, whether they loudly proclaim this or that ethical doctrine or none at all.[70]

> The unworthiness of human beings, including analysts, has always impressed me deeply, but why should analyzed men and women in fact be better. Analysis makes for integration but does not of itself make for goodness.[71]

While Freud's view by no means depicts how all analysts view such things, I do believe that his fundamental cynicism and pessimism have to some extent tainted how analysts conceptualize the human condition and the human capacity for self-transformation and self-

---

69 One hears the echo of Thomas Hobbes in this characterization.

70 Letter to Oscar Pfister, 10/9/18, in Jones, *The Life and Work of Sigmund Freud*, 2: 457.

71 Letter to J.J. Putnam, 6/17/15, in *James Jackson Putnam and Psychoanalysis*, 188.

transcendence. This is especially the case when it comes to articulating what is possible in terms of improving, enhancing and elevating human moral life.

However, this is only one side of Freud. He also believed, though this is much less known, that human beings were capable of living somewhat less selfishly and self-centrically than his theory and severe and gloomy comments suggested. For example, as Wallwork points out, Freud quietly urged people to strive to live according to the commandment, "thou shalt love thy neighbor as thyself."[72] Freud believed that such an ideal was a worthwhile personal goal, and not one that was utterly unobtainable. In *Civilization and its Discontents*, while Freud challenged the extreme demands for self-denial and selflessness of the Christian interpretation of the commandment to love thy neighbor as thyself, says Wallwork, he actually reinterpreted it along more moderate, broadly humanistic lines. "I myself have always advocated the love of mankind," he wrote to Romain Rolland.[73] Freud also noted in his essay "Why War" that the commandment to love was the best cure for the human proclivity to violence, hatred and war:

> Our mythological theory of instincts makes it easy for us to find a formula for indirect methods of combating war. If willingness to engage in war is an effect of the destructive instinct, the most obvious plan will be to bring Eros, its antagonist, into play against it. Anything that encourages the growth of emotional ties between men must operate against the instinct for war. These ties may be of two kinds. In the first place they may be relations resembling those towards a loved object, though without having a sexual aim. There is no need for psychoanalysis to be ashamed to speak of love in this connection, for religion itself uses the same words: 'Thou shalt love thy neighbor as thyself.' This, however, is more easily said than done.[74]

My point is that there is an "other" Freud, one that is less dour than received wisdom would have him. This Freud admiringly intuits another form of subjectivity, one that imagines the human person as fundamentally an ethical subject. Such a subjectivity goes beyond the

72 Wallwork, "Ethics in Psychoanalysis," 287. I am indebted to Wallwork for the Freud quotations.

73 In *The Letters of Sigmund Freud*, ed. E. L. Freud (New York: Basic Books, 1975), Letter 218, 374.

74 Freud, "Why War?" in *S.E.*, vol. 22, 212.

egological, self-centric one that dominated Freud's published writings, and to some extent, animates, and limits, psychoanalytic views of the human condition and what humans are capable of. I agree with the "other" Freud, that an outlook that has the love commandment as one of its guiding metaphors raises the bar in terms of what we imagine our analysands can achieve in their moral lives. It nudges them in the direction of a Levinasian sensibility, of thinking of themselves as ethical subjects. Levinas, of course, takes the matter even further. He notes that the love commandment "still assumes the prototype of love to be love of oneself," that is, "self-love is accepted as the very definition of a person." Rather, Levinas's ethic is one that asserts, "be responsible for the other as you are responsible for yourself."[75] Levinas thus invites us to consider the cultivation of "goodness" as our guiding metaphor. "Goodness," he says, "consists in taking up a position such that the Other counts more than myself."[76] Such an ethical ideal goes beyond the commandment to love, in that it demands an even greater transformation of one's narcissism towards a responsibility for the Other calculus. This leads me to the second criticism of Levinas.

The typical psychoanalyst might claim that Levinas's notion of love as roughly equated to the cultivation of goodness is a viewpoint that smacks of masochism, or at least inordinate self-denial and self-sacrifice. This form of self-negation is precisely what Freud was criticizing in *Civilization and its Discontents* in his discussion of the love commandment.

As Wyschogrod has pointed out, such a charge does not adequately appreciate to what extent Levinas is advocating a "remarkable transvaluation of values."[77] Like Nietzsche and, later, Foucault, Levinas is proposing revolutionizing the dominating tendencies, sentiments, the ways of thinking and being of our age. Levinas, says Wyschogrod, is not advocating submissiveness as analysts usually construe the term, as merely giving in to the demands or the authority of the other.

---

75   Levinas, *The Levinas Reader*, 225.

76   Levinas, *Totality and Infinity*, 224. Goodness for Levinas is his only "absolute value" (*Is It Righteous to Be?* 170). Compare this highest good with Greek conceptions: happiness (Aristotle), pleasure (Epicurus), resignation without despair (Aurelius), and quasi-mystical apprehension of the forms, that is, knowledge (Plato).

77   Wyschogrod, *Emmanuel Levinas*, xvi.

Rather, for Levinas "submissiveness is reinstated as self-donation."[78] With Levinas we are dealing with a radically different notion of the self, of the I, one that I think needs to be included in any psychoanalytic version of the human condition, for it locates the person first and foremost, as an ethical subject seeking out the "Good." Such an ethical subject is struggling to transform the very conditions, the form of his life, such that his capacity to love the Other is deepened, expanded and, finally, is his ultimate concern: "the self is a *sub-jectum*; it is under the weight of the universe, responsible for everything."[79] "Perhaps the possibility of a point of the universe where such an overflow of responsibility is produced ultimately defines the I."[80]

Such an appreciation of the "other" Freud, of love relations and, more generally, the human condition as Levinas describes it, has not been entirely neglected by psychoanalysts, though it has been an extremely marginal inadequately formulated theme. For example, Erich Fromm, the psychoanalytic social psychologist, who is surely one of the greatest, though I think enormously under-appreciated psychoanalytic codifiers and theoreticians on love since Freud, is the exception. In his small gem, *The Art of Loving, An Enquiry into the Nature of Love*, he challenges Freud's physiological instinct-dominated view that human capabilities and inclinations for love and aggression are merely biological potentials. Rather, Fromm reconceptualizes all interpersonal relationships in terms of specific kinds of "being-with," modes of relatedness. In this context, love is one of the key characteristics of the "productive type." The productive person has achieved a high level of autonomy and personality integration: he is capable of being spontaneous, creative, positively related to others, transcendent, grounded, he has a developed sense of personal identity, and he has a stable though flexible frame of orientation toward living. Most importantly, following Freud, the productive person can love and work. "Mature love" says Fromm, "is union under the condition of preserving one's integrity; one's individuality." That is, "love is an active power in man; a power which breaks through the walls which separate man from his fellow men, which unites him with others; loves makes him

---

78   Ibid.

79   Levinas, *Otherwise Than Being*, 116.

80   Levinas, *Totality and Infinity*, 244.

overcome the sense of isolation and separateness, yet it permits him to be himself, to retain his integrity."[81]

For Fromm, sounding similar to Levinas, love, at least the active character of love, can be described as "primarily giving, not receiving." Love is characterized by "care, responsibility, respect and knowledge." In essence, for Fromm, "to love means to commit oneself without guarantee, to give oneself completely in the hope that our love will produce love in the loved person. Love is an act of faith...."[82]

CONCLUDING COMMENT

As I have said earlier, the Levinasian view of love challenges the psychoanalytic theorizing of Freud, Klein, Erikson, Kohut and Lacan, as well as most relational thinkers. It does so in two ways. First, a Levinasian outlook challenges the notion of selfhood that underlies these theories, man as first and foremost egocentric and selfcentric in outlook and behavior.[83] Instead, as Atterton and Calarco point out, Levinas claims that "the relationship of responsibility for the Other is just as early, if not earlier than egoism."[84] Levinas's main objective has been to create "a metaphysics upon ethical foundations by showing man's being in the world to be moral being," a "moral self."[85]

Second, in part as a consequence of this ego-centered version of self, love relations tend to be viewed in terms of two related forms of questionable approaches towards the Other.

---

81 Erich Fromm. *The Art of Loving: An Enquiry into the Nature of Love* (New York: Harper Colophon Books, 1956), 20-21.

82 Ibid., 22, 26, 128.

83 Lacan of course vigorously rejected ego psychology. However, his view of the "I" as a distorting, alienating screen, a mirage, that conceals the divided, conflicted and fractured nature of unconscious desire, still retains a selfcentric bias. For example, Lacan insinuates that all desire is doomed to be a desire to consume the other, to make the other the same. Lacan, a man "in constant need of admiration and power" as one author described him, seems unable or unwilling to consider a more selfless "for-the-Other" mode of being in the world as an authentic non-neurotic human striving (Dominique Scarfone, "Psychoanalysis in the French Community," in *Textbook of Psychoanalysis*, 425).

84 Atterton and Calarco, *On Levinas*, 72.

85 Wyschogrod, *Emmanuel Levinas*, 228, 229.

First, love relations are conceptualized essentially as hedonistic and utilitarian with the other viewed mainly as a need-satisfying object: how can the other pleasure me, what can the other do for me? In an improved variation on this conceptualization, for example, in the work of Rubin and Benjamin,[86] love relations are viewed largely in terms of a mutual instrumental calculus of two equal subjects who appreciate the uniqueness of each other, and give each other satisfaction. This surely goes further than the strict hedonistic-utilitarian view in that it acknowledges the other as unique in terms of desires, goals, values and needs, and it makes satisfying those needs as important: "I am for you, you are for me."[87] This is the love relation as symmetrically conceived. It is perfectly what social psychologists and sociologists tell us is cross-culturally essential and fundamental to human social relations, namely, the "norm of reciprocity": people should assist those who have assisted them, and they should not assist those who have denied them assistance for no sound reason.[88] Levinas's formulation of an ethical self challenges this conventional social science wisdom.

For Levinas, while such a reciprocal approach moves in the direction of relating to the other as Other, this view still subtly retains the wish to make the other the same, to totalize the Other, and thus to open him or her to disrespect, disregard, de-individuation and other forms of intersubjective violence. Such an ontologically based approach seeks to comprehend the otherness of the Other by including him under a notion "that is thought within *me*, and thus is in some sense *the same* as me."[89] To the extent that the Other is mainly construed in terms of his or her Being, is comprehended and thematized on the basis of what he or she has in common with other beings, the Other becomes conceptually the same as others, and therefore loses his uniqueness and individuality.[90] According to Levinas, to comprehend the Other

86   Rubin, *The Good Life*, 49; Benjamin, *Like Subjects, Love Objects*, 29.

87   Levinas, *Is It Righteous to Be?* 193.

88   A. Gouldner, "The Norm of Reciprocity: A Preliminary Statement." *American Sociological Review* (1960): 25, 161-178.

89   Atterton and Calarco, *On Levinas*, 10. I have drawn liberally from Atterton and Calarco's clear exposition to develop this point.

90   In a certain sense, social psychological findings do not support such a sweeping conclusion. For example, in newly married couples it was reported that partners were strongly motivated to monitor each other closely and to attempt to attain a "shared cognitive focus" (William Ickes and Jeffry A.

in this way, is roughly equivalent "to predicting, manipulating, controlling, even dominating the Other."[91]

Instead of approaching the other in terms of ontology, of knowing and comprehension, Levinas offers an ethical approach that always strives to respects the radical alterity of the Other. The consequences of this Levinasian viewpoint are profound for understanding the limitations of the above psychoanalytic theories of love and point us in the direction that I think psychoanalytic theory should go.

Psychoanalytic theory tends to assume that from birth the self is concerned only, and later, mainly, with itself. This is the form of self-love that Freud called primary narcissism. Given this assumption about the human condition, one would therefore require a rationale, a compelling reason to be moral; that is, to love, conceived mainly as responsibility for the Other. This is precisely the assumption and formulation that Levinas rejects. Instead, he vigorously claims that the question of "am I first and foremost responsible for the Other," is a question that makes sense only within a version of the human condition that is lodged in a philosophy of ontology and human reason. In contrast, for Levinas, the self has no such freedom to choose with regards to responsibility for the Other. The Levinasian self does not need an elaborate, or any rationale to be moral: "Responsibility is what is incumbent on me exclusively, and what *humanly*, I cannot refuse."[92]

Perhaps most importantly, at least as it relates to the reciprocity-mutuality assumption lodged in certain relational views of love, I am

Simpson, "Empathic Accuracy Close Relationships," in *Empathic Accuracy*, ed. William Ickes (New York: Guilford Press 1997), 194-217). That is, more generally, says Aron et al, "the self is expanded through including the other in the self, a process which in a close relationship becomes so mutual that each person is including the other in his or her self." Moreover, these authors cite Schutz who describes this intersubjective process as "living in each other's subjective context of meaning." Aron et al also note that Neuberg, an evolutionary theorist, suggests "that interpersonal closeness, experienced as including" the other in the self, may be the method we use to "recognize those with whom we share genes...in the interest of knowing with whom one should share resources" to increase "collective fitness" (Arthur Aron, Elaine N. Aron and Christina Norman, "Self-expansion Model of Motivation and Cognition in Close Relationships and Beyond," in *Blackwell Handbook of Social Psychology: Interpersonal Processes*, 484, 485).

91 Atterton and Calarco, *On Levinas*, 15, 16.

92 Levinas, *Ethics and Infinity*, 101. Atterton and Calarco, *On Levinas*, 71.

responsible for the Other without the Other being responsible for me in return. It may well be reasonable to assume that the Other has responsibilities toward me, but I can never discern this for sure: "Reciprocity is *his* affair."[93] Thus, the other's actions towards you must not be the criterion of your conduct towards him. I am obligated to tend to the Other's needs without expecting emotional and/or other forms of payback. This is asymmetrical love. Says Levinas, "We are all guilty [responsible for] of all and for all men before all, and I more than the others."[94]

The Clinical Vignette for this chapter will be included at the end of the next chapter on "Eroticism and Family Relations" for they are interrelated themes.

---

93   Levinas, *Ethics and Infinity*, 98. Atterton and Calcarco, 30.

94   Ibid., 98.

5

EROTICISM AND FAMILY LOVE

"Love remains a relation with the Other that turns into need,
and this need still presupposes the total,
transcendent exteriority of the other, of the beloved.
But love goes beyond the beloved....
The possibility of the Other appearing as an object of a need
while retaining his alterity, or again,
the possibility of enjoying the Other.... this simultaneity of need and
desire, or concupiscence and transcendence,...
constitutes the originality of the erotic which,
in this sense, is the equivocal par excellence."[1]

Levinas

L evinas was aware that love without concupiscence, without
sexual passion, is an incomplete picture of the love relation.
Like Freud, Levinas believes that love is characterized by its
"ambiguity"; it is both need and desire, physicality and spirituality,
immanence and transcendence, ontology and ethics.[2] Martin Buber
captured something of this point when he wrote, "This, however, is the
sublime melancholy of our lot, that every Thou must become an It in
our world."[3] The unique, present, fully-engaged Other of the direct, reciprocal I-Thou relation inevitably becomes an object among objects,
though the I-Thou relation always remains a transient, transcendent
possibility.[4]

1 Levinas, *Totality and Infinity*, 254-255.

2 Ibid.

3 Martin Buber, *I and Thou.*, 68.

4 Levinas has criticized Buber's notion of intersubjectivity, especially as it
relates to the role of reciprocity in the love relation, the "I-Thou" (i.e., says
Hand (*The Levinas Reader*, 59) it is too formal, exclusive, and not asymmetrical; that is, Buber's I-Thou does not adequately reflect the "height,"
the transcendence of the Other and God). These and other differences,
or rather as Robert Bernasconi says, "failures of communication" and mis-
understandings, are thoughtfully discussed in Atterton et al., *Levinas and
Buber: Dialogue and Difference*.

For both Levinas and Freud, sexuality was extremely puzzling, with Levinas believing "that sexuality at the rigorously sexual level is in essence tragic and ambiguous by which I mean enigmatic."[5] It is the erotic relationship, mainly between a man and a woman, that is the template of the face-to-face encounter with the radical alterity of the Other. The amorous encounter puts into sharp focus important questions about the interhuman relation, for example, how are we to construe and respond to the Other's otherness? In what way does the erotic relationship summon us to responsibility for and to the Other?[6] Is there a self-transcendence "possible in erotic love," a self-transformation "through love in the birth of a child"?[7]

Levinas is here raising some intriguing questions, though his work on eroticism and gender is generally regarded as the least impressive of his oeuvre. As Fryer has pointed out, Levinas's theorizing on "the erotic body" was mainly limited to his early work such as *Time and the Other* and *Totality and Infinity*. Once he more or less relinquished "the metaphysical language of his early work for the 'ethical language'" contained in *Otherwise Than Being*, a thought-provoking analysis of the erotic body vanished.[8] Moreover, perhaps the intense criticism Levinas received about his notion of the feminine contributed to his leaving the theme of the erotic body more or less behind.

Levinas has been criticized for his singularly masculine outlook, in which he characterizes "the female as the other and the feminine as the Other."[9] Simone de Beauvoir vigorously criticized his conception of the erotic relationship as severely sexist,[10] while Luce Irigaray has claimed that Woman in Levinas is reduced to a mere derivative, "underside or reverse side," the negative version of Man.[11] Edith

---

5 Levinas, *Difficult Freedom*, 287-288.

6 Fryer, *The Intervention of the Other*, 72.

7 Wyschogrod, *Emmanuel Levinas*, 131.

8 Fryer, *The Intervention of the Other*, 232. Fryer does not regard Levinas's discussions of the maternal in *Otherwise Than Being* as having an erotic sensibility, though other scholars have disagreed with him on this point.

9 Hutchens, *Levinas*, 146.

10 Simone de Beauvoir, *The Second Sex* (Hardmondsworth: Penguin Books, 1984).

11 Luce Irigaray, "Questions to Emmanuel Levinas: On the Dignity of Love," in *Re-Reading Levinas*, eds. Bernasconi and Critchley, 109-118;

Wyschogrod has described Levinas's "troping of woman as seductive materiality and man as rational discursivity" as fostering "lamentable cultural stereotypes."[12] Stella Sandford, like Wyschogrod, a most sympathetic interpreter of Levinas has nevertheless concluded, "If, therefore, one were to ask whether the thinking of the feminine in Levinas's philosophy could provide resources for feminism, I think the answer would have to be 'no.'"[13] The list of critics of this aspect of Levinas's work is long and contains powerful critiques, especially Irigaray's claim that Levinas is a patriarchal thinker. There are, however, other feminist scholars who find something useful in Levinas's views on gender and erotic relationships.[14]

I have no intention of acting as a defender of Levinas's work on eroticism, gender and family relations. However, while I am sympathetic to the critics of Levinas, I do believe that there are some insights about these subjects, and more generally about erotic love relations, that are worthwhile to highlight as it relates to psychoanalysis. As Davis has pointed out, "whatever the complexities of his conception of the feminine, it still acts as a focus for a set of remarkably deep-rooted, conventional and unproblematized views." That is, Levinas's largely unsuccessful attempt to understand "alterity without appropriating it to the same"[15] paradoxically forces us to think about the Other as the not-same, providing some interesting "food for thought" for the psychoanalyst. I will now discuss Levinas's work on eroticism, gender and family relations through the following sequence of concepts: the feminine Beloved, the caress, fecundity, paternity, and the infinity of time.

"The Fecundity of the Caress: A Reading of Levinas, Totality and Infinity, section IV, B, 'The Phenomenology of Eros,'" in Face to Face with Levinas, 231-256.

12 Wyschogrod, Emmanuel Levinas, xxv.

13 Stella Sandford, "Levinas, Feminism and the Feminine," in The Cambridge Companion to Levinas, 139-160.

14 Lisa Walsh, "Between Maternity and Paternity: Figuring Ethical Subjectivity, Differences 12 (Spring), 2001; 79-111; Catherine Chalier, "Ethics and the Feminine," in Re-Reading Levinas, eds. Bernasconi and Critchley, 119-129; Susan A. Handelman, Fragments of Redemption (Bloomington, IN: Indiana University Press, 1991).

15 Davis, Levinas, 60, 140.

THE FEMININE BELOVED

Levinas would probably have appreciated Freud's declared bewilderment, if not ignorance, about female psychology. In his 1932 essay *Psychology of Women* he wrote, "Throughout the ages the problem of women has puzzled people of every kind.... You too will have pondered over this question insofar as you are men; from the women among you that is not to be expected, for you are the riddle yourselves."[16] In his *Three Essays on Sexuality* he also noted that the "erotic life...of women...is still veiled in an impenetrable obscurity."[17] And finally, he famously wrote to Marie Bonaparte: "The great question that has never been answered and which I have not yet been able to answer, despite my thirty years of research into the feminine soul, is 'What does a woman want?'"[18]

Like Freud, Levinas was a man of his time, and this included having a certain notion of woman as Mystery. However, unlike Freud, Levinas's notion of woman as mysterious is a deliberate rhetorical strategy to help illuminate erotic relations between a male and female and to link it to his wider project of bringing "to light what being-in-the-world must be to be moral being."[19]

Following Catherine Chalier's sympathetic and insightful reading of Levinas, I approach Levinas's concept of the feminine Beloved in terms of his central goal, that we try and think "otherwise than being." That is, "to free a space for transcendence which will enable us to understand the meaning of the word 'ethics.'" The feminine plays a key role for Levinas for suggesting how man's natural life, sexuality, which is mainly for and in itself, can become for the Other. Chalier asks, how can "the virility of being," [i.e., Man], be converted into the "gentleness of a being that is for the Other" [i.e., Woman]?[20]

It should be understood that, for Levinas, the feminine and the masculine do not refer to biological or other real, empirical differences between the sexes, but rather are modalities of being in the world that are accessible to both women and men. "All these allusions to the on-

16   S.E., vol. 22, 113.

17   Ibid., vol. 7, 151.

18   Quotation in Ernest Jones, *The Life and Work of Sigmund Freud* (New York: Basic Books, 1955), vol. 2, 421.

19   Wyschogrod, *Emmanuel Levinas*, 140.

20   Chalier, "Ethics and the Feminine," 119.

tological differences between the masculine and the feminine would appear less archaic if, instead of dividing humanity into two species (or into two genders), they would signify that the participation in the masculine and in the feminine were the attributes of every human being."[21]

Though this strikes me as a reasonable statement, as Atterton and Calarco point out, it does not adequately explain why Levinas uses the term "feminine" to refer to one cluster of qualities and characteristics that are allegedly common to both sexes.[22] Perhaps, Levinas believed that in our current *episteme*,[23] our structure of thought or socio-intellectual reality, the feminine, more than the masculine, has taken on the meanings and significations that he gives the term and thus best assists him and his readership in attempting to think "otherwise than being." Thus, following Peperzak and others, I use the terms feminine and masculine and woman and man, mainly as metaphors for modes of being in the world.[24] Taking her lead from Levinas, Chalier's above question of how "the virility of being," Man, can be transformed into the "gentleness of a being that is for the Other," Woman, makes a startling assumption. The question assumes that Woman is, at least in a certain sense, the superior ethical mode of being compared to Man. Indeed, Levinas makes this point in *Totality and Infinity*, that the feminine signifies that which is "…superiorly intelligent, so often dominating men in the masculine civilization it has entered…"[25] Moreover, he says, in his collection of essays on Judaism, that "Biblical events would not have progressed as they did had it not been for their [women's] watchful lucidity, the firmness of their determination, and their cunning and spirit of sacrifice."[26] The feminine also personifies perhaps Levinas's most highly regarded virtues, she is "goodness" and "the original manifestation of gentleness [kindness] itself, the origin of all gentleness on earth."[27] It should also be remembered that throughout

---

21 *Ethics and Infinity*, 68.

22 Atterton and Calarco, *On Levinas*, 44.

23 Michel Foucault, *The Archaeology of Knowledge and the Discourse on Language*, trans. A. M. Sheridan Smith (New York: Pantheon, 1972), 191.

24 Peperzak, *To the Other*, 158, 195.

25 Levinas, *Totality and Infinity*, 264.

26 Levinas, *Difficult Freedom*, 31.

27 Ibid., 33.

Levinas's writings, the Other, in this case Woman, always has priority over the subject, Man, this being another expression of Levinas's characterizing Woman as the superior ethical mode of being compared to Man.[28] This assumed superiority of women is in many ways similar to Freud's view. Nicholi writes that Freud's letters "indicated he thought of women as more noble and more ethical than men, but his ideas of their role in life and in marriage left much to be desired."[29]

What about Man's "virile persistence in being," as Chalier describes him? For Levinas, claims Chalier, man is viewed as the mode of being that is mainly characterized by self-sufficiency, self-satisfaction and self-conceit, with an overuse of rational discursivity in his approach to the other and to the world at large, and a preoccupation with exploiting, manipulating and conquering the world.[30] Man, says Levinas,

---

28 Levinas, *Time and the Other*, 85. I am paraphrasing Richard A. Cohen's footnote in which he challenges de Beauvoir's criticism that Levinas is sexist. For Cohen, de Beauvoir oversimplifies Levinas when she claims that he assigns "a secondary, derivative status to women: subject (he) as absolute," and "woman as other." However, for Levinas the other always takes precedence over the subject. Says Katz, Levinas "ultimately names the feminine, defined as maternal body, as the paradigm for the ethical relationship itself" (Claire Katz, "Educating the Solitary Man: Levinas, Rousseau, and the Return to Jewish Wisdom." Jeffrey Bloechl, ed., *Levinas Studies. An Annual Review*. Volume 2, Pittsburgh: Duquesne University Press, 2007, 142).

29 Armand M. Nicholi, *The Question of God: C.S. Lewis and Sigmund Freud Debate God, Love, Sex, and the Meaning of Life* (New York: The Free Press, 2002), 145. While Levinas and Freud believed that woman was the superior ethical mode compared to men, scientific research has found that man is "the weaker sex." For example, from the instant "of conception on, men are less likely to survive than woman"; while "there are more male than female embryos, there are more miscarriages of male fetuses"; boys "are three to four times more likely than girls to have developmental disorders like autism and dyslexia"; boys acquire language later, develop less extensive vocabularies and also hear worse than girls; boys show "insight and judgment" later in adolescence than girls who are less impulsive and take less risks than their brothers; "teenage boys are more likely to commit suicide than girls and are more likely to die violent deaths before adulthood" (Marianne J. Legato, "The Weaker Sex," *New York Times*, 6/17/06, A13).

30 Chalier, "Ethics and the Feminine," 120-123. Chalier supports her characterization of Levinas's picture of man with numerous quotations that I have not reiterated for the sake of brevity.

depicts "an alienation which ultimately results from the very virility of the universal and all-conquering *logos*."[31] In a word, for Levinas Man personifies a mode of being in the world that typifies selfishness, egoistic interiority and insufficiently modulated narcissism.

In the bedroom, at his extreme, such a man is aggressively focused on obtaining his own erotic pleasure and more or less disregards his partner, or at least regards her pleasure as secondary, if not incidental. Indeed, Balzac's pithy statement that for a woman to give herself to a man is like giving a violin to a gorilla, might capture something of what Levinas was getting at when he discussed erotic relations between men and women. One can, as I do, read Levinas's work on male/female relations as an attempt to try to help men, or at least the mode of being we often though not exclusively associate with men in our culture, to become more like women at their best,[32] that is, to develop a feminine interiority, one that is more capable of loving at a "higher" and "deeper" level, of goodness and kindness, of being for the Other before oneself. It is the "ontological function of the feminine" to help man overcome his alienation.[33] The feminine or woman "saves the human being," she is a condition of possibility for Man to cultivate an authentic ethical way of being in his relations with the Other and the world at large.[34]

As I have said, for Levinas the feminine signifies the "absolutely other," "alterity is accomplished in the feminine."[35] "The simultaneity or the equivocation of this fragility and this weight of non-signifyingness [non-significance], heavier than the weight of the formless real, we shall term feminine."[36] Levinas does not clearly tell us why the feminine signifies radical otherness, the "event of alterity" as he calls it, the

---

31 Levinas, *Difficult Freedom*, 33.

32 This discussion demands, of course, a certain number of generalizations about men and women. Obviously, there are many exceptions to these generalizations or stereotyping. Moreover, I am aware that what we take to constitute man and masculine and woman and feminine is to a large extent culture specific and part of the individual's project of self-definition and self-constitution.

33 Levinas, *Difficult Freedom*, 33.

34 Chalier, "Ethics and the Feminine," 123.

35 Levinas, *Time and the Other*, 85, 88.

36 Levinas, *Totality and Infinity*, 257.

event that allows the subject, mainly the man in this case, to conquer and transcend death. "Vanquishing death is to maintain, with the alterity of the event, a relationship that must still be personal."[37]

From Levinas's male perspective, the feminine mode of being is personified in the woman's gracious and gentle welcoming of the man, and others, into her "dwelling," as he refers to it.[38] It is the home that is the place where one can feel relaxed and safe from the harsh and demanding outside world. It is the woman's capacity to provide this intimate refuge for rest and contemplation that Levinas regards as characteristic of her goodness. "And the other whose presence is discreetly an absence, with which is accomplished the primary hospitable welcome which describes the field of intimacy, is the Woman. The woman is the condition for recollection [greater attention to oneself and one's possibilities], the interiority of the Home, and inhabitation."[39]

While the above characterization may sound somewhat like a stereotyped version of women as homemaker to some, it is important to be mindful of the fact that for Levinas, this capacity to facilitate security and peace for the man, the Other, is to bring about for him an extraordinary human possibility. It is the woman, in her ability to create this emotionally safe and comfortable space, that man can forget his practical obligations and doings, his need to conquer the world, and his desperate autistic-like quest for transcendence. He can, in a word, play. As Aristotle said, "play is the thing we do when we are free." The point is, that to the extent that one can create the psychological and concrete context for the other to play, the other is most able to realize a key liberating human potential, one that is both a desire and a need. Indeed, Schiller was right when he wrote that "Man is never so

37 Levinas, *Time and the Other*, 87, 81. Levinas, an Orthodox Jew, may have been influenced in his conceptualization of woman as Other (and as mysterious) in part because in Judaism there is a thematics in which women are characterized as Other not merely in the synagogue or within Orthodox circles but also within fundamental "Jewish teachings, symbols and language." Susannah Heschel further says that "Women stand as Other while men are the Subjects in the liturgy, in *halakhah*, and even in Judaism's theological formulations of God as father and king" (see "Feminism," in Arthur A. Cohen and Paul Mendes-Flohr (eds.), *Contemporary Jewish Thought* (New York: Charles Scribner's Sons, 1987, 257).

38 Levinas, *Totality and Infinity*, 158.

39 Ibid., 155.

authentically himself as when at play,"[40] and this includes in his sexual relations. As Levinas says in his discussion of the female body, though I think the observation can also be applied to the male, "The relations with the Other are enacted in play; one plays with the Other as with a young animal."[41] The "caress," which I will shortly be discussing, is also described by Levinas as "a game."[42]

I want to mention one other aspect of Levinas's characterization of the feminine, conceived as radical otherness: woman is essentially unknowable and elusive and works to keep herself that way:

> What matters to me in this notion of the feminine is not merely the unknowable, but a mode of being that consists in slipping away from the light. The feminine in existence is an event different from that of spatial transcendence or of expression that goes toward light. It is a flight before light, hiding away is the way of existing of the feminine, and this fact of hiding is precisely modesty.[43] [He also says elsewhere,] Modesty, insurmountable in love, constitutes its pathos.[44]

What Levinas is getting at here is that woman, the template of otherness, forever remains in a certain sense, concealed from illumination, from reason and analytic intelligibility. Woman resists "signification,"[45] she resists becoming a Said. Modesty is Levinas's term signifying this equivocal, never-to-be fully revealed nature of woman and the phenomenon of love. The pathos of love is precisely the impossibility of fully overcoming love's hiddenness.[46] The point is that for a man to approach a woman, the Other, as if she were capable of being fully

---

40 The Aristotle and Schiller quotes are from a lecture given by Daniel N. Robinson, "The Idea in Freedom." In *The Great Ideas of Philosophy*, part IV (Springfield: The Teaching Company, 1997), Course Outline, 36.

41 Levinas, *Totality and Infinity*, 263.

42 Levinas, *Time and the Other*, 89.

43 Ibid., 87.

44 Levinas, *Totality and Infinity*, 257.

45 Ibid., 256.

46 As Wyschogrod points out, Levinas did not, as some psychoanalysts would tend to do, understand modesty as fundamentally related to repression to the debilitating consequences of "coercive inhibitions" forced by culture upon a "suffering libido." Rather, modesty is viewed "as an absolutely primordial expression of corporeality in the erotic" (*Emmanuel Levinas*, 128.)

comprehended and known, at least in a sustained manner, is an act that comes perilously close to intersubjective violence.[47] Such a mode of engagement betrays the wish to control and dominate, to make the Other the same. Rather, insinuates Levinas, Woman, the Other, must be approached in a way similar to the way the faithful approach their God, with great respect, with wonder, curiosity and enchantment, approached, as Stanislas Breton has said, as "irreducible mystery and radicality," as "passage not possession."[48] Such a mode of engagement is epitomized in the loving physical contact that Levinas calls the caress.

THE CARESS

The caress, conceived as actual physical touch, with all of the erotic fantasies that the word tends to call to mind, is not alone what Levinas wants to evoke by using the word. The caress is not merely the loving physical contact that one initiates with one's feminine Beloved. Rather, in addition, and more profoundly, it is a term that describes a mode of engagement, a "movement toward the Other."[49] Levinas says,

> The caress is a mode of the subject's being, where the subject who is in contact with another goes beyond this contact. Contact as sensations is part of the world of light. But what is caressed is not touched, properly speaking. It is not the softness or warmth of the hand given in contact that the caress seeks. This seeking of the caress constitutes its essence by the fact that the caress does not know what it seeks. This 'not knowing,' this fundamental disorder, is the essential. It is like a game with something slipping away, a game absolutely without project or plan, not with what can become ours,

47 This is perhaps an overstatement. As is well known from social psychology and other research, for an intimate love relation to work, let alone flourish over time, it is necessary for lovers to successfully synchronize and harmonize "their individual and shared motives and actions." Such synchronization and harmonization requires "that they must be relatively accurate," most of the time, "when inferring the specific content of each other's" feelings and thoughts (William Ickes and Jeffry A. Simpson, "Motivational Aspects of Empathic Accuracy." In Garth J. O. Fletcher and Margaret S. Clark, eds., *Blackwell Handbook of Social Psychology. Interpersonal Processes*, Oxford: Blackwell Publishing, Inc., 2002, 229).

48 Stanislas Breton, in Richard Kearney, *Debates in Continental Philosophy: Conversations with Contemporary Thinkers* (New York: Fordham University Press, 2004), 135, 134.

49 Fryer, *The Intervention of the Other*, 75.

but with something other, always other, always inaccessible, and always still to come. The caress is the anticipation of this pure future, without content. It is made up of this increase of hunger, of ever-richer promises, opening up new perspectives onto the ungraspable. It feeds on countless hungers.[50]

The above description of the caress is part of Levinas's attempt to put into sharp focus two different modes of erotic relation towards the feminine, the Other, that also imply a self-relation. The first is rooted in need, it is "a want capable of satisfaction," it can be called the sexual urge. It is "for itself" and "for oneself." The second is rooted in desire, "a want that remains insatiable"[51]: it can be called love. It is "for the Other." Paraphrasing Theodore Reik, Freud's early disciple, the sexual urge hunts for lustful pleasure, while love searches for joy and happiness.

The sexual urge, the first kind of caress, aims at conquering the subjectivity of the Other. For Levinas, "Possessing, knowing, and grasping are synonyms of power."[52] Such an attitude is personified in its extreme, for example, in most heterosexual pornography marketed to men. Themes of domination and bondage, sadomasochism and denigration of the woman are paramount. Moreover, and this is important, the pornographic attitude leaves almost nothing hidden about the woman; it is a clinical-like encounter with her body that is often what makes porno films boring after a few minutes. Levinas does say, however, that "profanation is not a negation of mystery, but one of the possible relationships with it." "Voluptuosity profanes; it does not see."[53] Thus, in the first form of caress, domination is its leitmotif, actually its foundation. It emanates from the realm of freedom, "the structure of the self as egoity."[54] This form of caress is an expression of self-centered, self-interested lust.

An extreme example of this mode of erotic relation was conveyed to me by a pathologically promiscuous, hard drinking, Mafia-associated male psychotherapy patient, who had by the time I met him, slept with about three thousand women over a twenty-five year period. He

50   Levinas, *Time and the Other*, 89.

51   Wyschogrod, *Levinas*, 245, 243.

52   Ibid., 90 and *Totality and Being*, 260.

53   Ibid., 86.

54   Wyschogrod, *Emmanuel Levinas*, 129.

described an encounter with a "gorgeous, hot woman" he met in an up-scale Manhattan singles pick-up bar who became a famous singer. They went to a hotel room and "for three days and nights I drank, she did coke, we ate pizza, and we fucked." When I asked him what it was like to have sex with this gorgeous woman he replied, "she fucked like a man." "What do you mean," I asked. He replied, "She was very aggressive. All she cared about was 'to come.' I could have been a vibrator, it was like I wasn't there." The crude words like "tits," "ass," "cunt," "pussy" and "fucking" are the objectifying, denigrating and aggressive "part-object" language of this first mode of relation to the feminine.

The second form of relation with the feminine, the Other, as expressed in the caress has a very different "feel" to it compared to the caress rooted strictly in the sexual urge and return to the self. In this second form, there is a rearrangement, a repositioning of the sexual urge and its "egoistical forces into a new field,"[55] as well as a "reversal of its system of direction."[56] Man now enters into communion, not fusion,[57] and not with the woman as "part object," but with the whole woman in her concrete presentness. This relation is personified by responsibility for her "as an allotted and entrusted realm of life."[58] Tender words like "darling," "beloved," "sweety" and "making love" are the language of this second form of relating to the feminine. Within the erotic context, how does the woman, conceived as the Other as teacher, bring about in the man a movement from compulsive need for carnal gratification and self-preoccupation, to a gentleness of a being that is for the Other?

For Levinas, this is in part accomplished by the woman's working hard at being mysterious, especially in her assuming numerous "roles" in bed, until such time that she senses that the man is willing and able to relate to her as more than a physical body to caress and use for

---

55   Ibid., 229.

56   Martin Buber, *Between Man and Man*, trans. Maurice S. Friedman (New York: Macmillan Company, 1965), 96.

57   Buber's use of the word communion suggests sharing and fellowship, a relation of love. It is not quite fusion, a melting or blending into each other, a common erotic wish/fantasy and reported experience within the psychoanalytic dialogue. For Levinas, fusion does not constitute a relation with the other through Eros. In fact, he says that it constitutes its failure (*Time and the Other*, 90).

58   Buber, *Between Man and Man*, 98.

carnal gratification, as someone to covenant with, as someone she can reveal her frailty, vulnerability and suffering to, trusting that the man will responsibly respond to her opening up with gentleness, compassion and goodness. Thus, we have the range of female presentations in the bedroom, revelations that are in fact concealments that mesh with typical male fantasies: whore, virgin, master and slave and the like. For the man "The beloved, returned to the stage of infancy without responsibility—this coquettish head, this youth, this pure life 'a bit silly'—has quit her status as a person. The face fades, and in its impersonal and inexpressive neutrality is prolonged, in ambiguity, into animality."[59]

Through such an animalistic presentation the woman gets the man to believe that she has given her whole self over, that she has capitulated to the masculine will to possess her. The reality, or rather the woman's unconscious inner reality is otherwise. While she has given her body up so to speak, her soul, her feminine being and otherness remain hidden and intact. Says Levinas, "the discovered does not lose its mystery in the discovery, the hidden is not disclosed, the night is not dispersed."[60] Exactly how these intersubjective dynamics are enacted is not entirely clear. Perhaps they can be viewed as a kind of power play, both conscious and unconscious, somewhat akin to the play of wills that Sartre has so brilliantly portrayed in his descriptions of romantic encounters.[61]

It is only when the man has demonstrated that he is willing and able to authentically meet the woman in a manner that reflects utter respect for her alterity, responsibility and being for the Other, that she reveals her most intimate self, and then only fleetingly and in a surprising and impossible-to- fully-grasp way. For as Levinas suggests there is

---

59 Levinas, *Totality and Infinity*, 258.

60 Ibid., 260.

61 Jean-Paul Sartre, *Being and Nothingness*, trans. Hazel E. Barnes (New York: Washington Square Press), 1953, 96-97. As Atterton and Calarco point out (*On Levinas*, 62), Levinas has a very different way of understanding the love relation as compared to Sartre, "for whom all relations with the Other are a freely chosen project of the I." Says Sartre, "To will to love and to love are one since to love is to choose oneself as loving by assuming consciousness of loving" (*Being and Nothingness*, 462). Strikingly different, Levinas says that "the Good is not presented to freedom; it has chosen me before I have chosen it" (*Otherwise Than Being*, 111).

"always something more to see, something more to come, another veil to lift,"[62] what he calls "not yet."[63] Such poignant moments of a being-to being-encounter call to mind Buber's I-Thou relation.

As I pointed out in a previous chapter, Levinas has described the ethical moment as personified in such everyday behavior as opening the door for someone and letting them enter first. Saying the words, "*aprez-vous*," reveals the existential respect for the dignity of the Other that she deserves, before oneself. I believe the same is true in the bedroom. To the extent that the man makes giving the woman pleasure, satisfaction and comfort his priority, before he seeks and concentrates on his own, he insinuates responsibility and being for the Other.[64] This moment signifies to the woman that it is safe both to give herself to the man with the fullness of her whole being, at least to the extent possible as she conceives it, and let herself be overwhelmed by his love for her. For some women and men, such "letting go," such radical transparency and encounter, is extremely difficult to allow, for it can feel like a free fall into a void.

In this context the caress is no longer simply an attempt on the part of the man to satiate his lustful sexual urge. Rather, it takes on a very different meaning, as a way to bring about the presence of the one to

---

62   Atterton and Calarco, *On Levinas*, 45.

63   Levinas, *Totality and Infinity*, 258.

64   This is not as straightforward as it may seem, at least at first glance. Suppose that a woman's wish is to allow her to give the man pleasure before he gives pleasure to her? This would mean that the man has to take a more passive role in the erotic encounter. The issue I am raising here, one that Levinas does not adequately take up, is that what constitutes being for the other before oneself, but also love, goodness and the like, is context dependent. What instantiates these so-called ethical moments depends on the intersubjective meaning to the partners. An act can be said to be a loving act, a good act, for the Other, only to the extent that the Other experiences and designates it as such. This is because there is no universally accepted expression and absolute meaning of such actions. The meaning of a loving act is emergent and processive: it can only be said to be loving within the context of how the two people understand and interpret such acts. In other words, within the context of the bedroom, it is a loving act for a man to tie a woman to a radiator and beat her with a whip, if that is what she desires. Likewise, a gentle, passionate and lingering kiss on the lips of a woman who does not like to be kissed that way, could be said to be a hostile act.

the other, as a constant responsibility for the other's soul. Buber beautifully captures this form of caress:

> A man caresses a woman, who lets herself be caressed. Then let us assume that he feels the contact from two sides—with the palm of his hand still, and also with the woman's skin. The twofold nature of the gesture, as one that takes place between two persons, thrills through the depth of enjoyment in his heart and stirs it. If he does not deafen his heart he will have—not to renounce the enjoyment but—to love.[65]

Buber is here making a crucial point that Levinas misses, or at least underplays about the ethically transformative potential of the erotic encounter: the need for a man or a woman to be able to "experience the other side."[66] Unfortunately, unlike Buber and much more so the intersubjective schools of psychoanalysis, Levinas was not much interested in mapping the subtle, nuanced, co-created interaction of two subjectivities,[67] the sharing of worlds of subjective experience.

"Experiencing the other side," says Maurice S. Friedman, Buber's preeminent interpreter, "means to feel an event from the side of the person one meets as well as from one's own side."[68] Most importantly, it involves what Buber calls "inclusiveness," which realizes the other person in the actuality and presentness of his being.[69] For Buber, inclusiveness should not be confused with the psychoanalytic notion of "empathy," the defining means by which the data of psychoanalysis is collected according to self-psychologists. For the psychoanalyst empathy is "the imagining of another's subjective experience through the use of one's own subjective experience."[70] Empathy, say Buber and Friedman, implies the capacity to "transpose oneself over there and in there," into the dynamic structure of an object, to "the exclusion of one's own concreteness, the extinguishing of the actual situation of life, the ab-

---

65 Buber, *Between Man and Man*, 96.

66 Ibid.,

67 Wyschogrod, *Emmanuel Levinas*, 131.

68 Maurice S Friedman, *Martin Buber. The Life of Dialogue*. 4th edition. (London: Routledge Books, 2002), 102.

69 Buber, *Between Man and Man*, 97.

70 Ethel S. Person, Arnold M. Cooper and Glen O. Gabbard, eds., *Textbook of Psychoanalysis* (Washington, D. C.: American Psychiatric Association, 2005), 551.

sorption in pure aestheticism of the reality in which one participates."[71] Inclusion, says Buber, is the opposite of this. "It is the extension of one's own concreteness, the fulfillment of the actual situation in life, the complete presence of the reality in which one participates."[72] Put in more conventional psychological language, following Levinas, we can roughly say that empathy involves both being able to put your self inside the other, without losing yourself, while at the same time, being able to put the other in your self, without eradicating the other's difference and otherness. Exactly how a self's ego is supple enough to incorporate or, more aptly, embrace the other into its experience without necessarily having to project anything upon or into the other, is not clear, nor agreed upon by most psychoanalytic and social psychological theoreticians on empathy.[73]

The point is that the capacity to experience the other side is the bedrock of all authentic love, erotic or otherwise. As Friedman explains the eros of monologue, similar to what I have described as the sexual urge hunting for lustful pleasure, is geared to "display" or mere "enjoyment" of subjective sensations and feelings. The eros of dialogue, what I have called love searching for joy and happiness "means the turning of the lover to the beloved,"[74] says Buber, "in his otherness, his independence, his self-reality," and "with all the power of intention"[75] of his own soul. He does not appropriate into his own being what encounters and faces him, but promises "it faithfully to himself and himself to

---

71   Buber, *Between Man and Man*, 97; Friedman *The Life of Dialogue*, 102

72   Ibid.

73   Sharon Todd. *Levinas, Psychoanalysis, and Ethical Possibilities in Education* (Albany, NY: SUNY Press, 2003). I have drawn from Todd's interesting discussion of empathy as it relates to Levinasian ethicality, though her work is limited, in part, because she has not considered the huge experimental social psychological literature on empathy that in many ways, challenges, if not contradicts both Levinasian and psychoanalytic formulations. For example, sometimes, motivated empathic accuracy (i.e., "partners must effectively coordinate their individual shared motives and actions" to flourish) can actually harm a relationship (William Ickes and Jeffry A. Simpson, "Motivational Aspects of Empathic Accuracy," in Fletcher and Clark, eds, *Blackwell Handbook of Social Psychology: Interpersonal Processes*, 229-249).

74   Friedman, *Martin Buber. The Life of Dialogue*, 102.

75   Buber, *Between Man and Man*, 29.

it."[76] "Love without dialogic, without real outgoing to the other, reaching to the other, and companying with the other, the love remaining with itself—this is called Lucifer."[77] This love is evil in nature because it is monological, or selfish and self-centered. It is not mindful and respectful of the otherness of the other, but instead tries to make the other the same, to possess the other.

For Levinas, at least in my reading of him, it is the man's capacity to communicate to the woman his responsible commitment and ability to experience the other side, perhaps best expressed in trying to satisfy the beloved's need and wish for pleasure and nurturance, before his own, that signifies to the woman that it is time for her to open the gates to her feminine center, to reveal herself with the fullness of her whole being, soul to soul, at least as much as she is capable of in the moment. However, the beloved's transitory revelation of her being is not, for Levinas, in and of itself, the most moving aspect of the erotic encounter. Rather, what is most meaningful is the compassion for her inherent vulnerability, fragility and suffering that such a revelation evokes in the man. It is this compassion and the wish to comfort and nurture, with its transformative and humanizing ripple effect, that signifies the ethical disruption of man's virile being by goodness. As Chalier says, man has been converted, if only briefly, "from the hardness of the being which is for himself to the gentleness of the being which is for the Other."[78]

FECUNDITY, PATERNITY AND THE INFINITY OF TIME

Earlier I noted that for Levinas "sexuality at the rigorously sexual level is in essence tragic." It is tragic for a number of reasons. For example, during foreplay, up until one finishes orgasm, the other is the center of one's universe as it were, the focus of one's near total emotional and cognitive concentration and concern. After orgasm, the other's centrality and importance, at least in some rudimentary sense, is radically diminished to the lover.[79] The pathos of love is that it is a relationship with what is always "slipping away."

---

76 Friedman, *Martin Buber. The Life of Dialogue*, 102.

77 Buber, *Between Man and Man*, 21.

78 Chalier, "Ethics and the Feminine," 123.

79 I am grateful to Helaine Helmreich for further clarifying this point to me.

More importantly, for Levinas, what makes all erotic love tragic is that by its very nature, at least to some degree, it "...becomes self-love...since it is loving the other's love of oneself."[80] Says Levinas, "I love fully only if the other person loves me.... If to love is to love the love the Beloved bears me, to love is also to love oneself in love, and thus to return to oneself," a kind of "pleasure and dual egoism."[81]

While this dyadic pleasure and dual egoism is hugely narcissistically satisfying, it frequently gives way to a profound longing for something more, a movement away from the self and the insular dyad. This "new category," which "goes beyond the possible," Levinas calls "fecundity," the ability to produce offspring.[82] It is through fecundity that the erotic takes on a radically different meaning as does one's self- and self-world relation. The self is profoundly changed through bringing about the birth of a son or daughter within the context of a loving relationship. It is through the child that there is a degree of self-transcendence. Perhaps most importantly, the birth of a child summons the parent to a form of responsibility for the Other that in certain ways, as most parents will tell you, requires considerably more selflessness, sacrifice and being for the Other before oneself, than does one's relationship to one's significant other.

Paternity, then, is the metaphor that Levinas uses to describe a certain kind of relationship to the Other, one that is self-transformative and self-transcendent, and a summoning call to goodness.

> The fact of seeing the possibilities of the other as your own possibilities, of being able to escape the closure of your identity and what is bestowed on you and which nevertheless is yours—this is paternity. This future beyond my own being, this dimension constitutive of time, takes on a concrete content in paternity.[83]

Levinas states categorically that those people who do not have children are not lesser as a result, nor is he mainly referring to paternity as a relationship in the strictly biological and empirical sense with a son or daughter.[84] Rather, what he is getting at is "a parental attitude

---

80   Wyschogrod, *Emmanuel Levinas*, 131.

81   Levinas, *Totality and Infinity*, 266.

82   Ibid., 266, 281, 267. Atterton and Calarco, *Levinas*, 44-45.

83   Levinas, *Ethics and Infinity*, 70.

84   Ibid. and Levinas, *Totality and Infinity*, 277.

with regard to the Other."[85] It is these parental relations without biological bases, such as in filiation and fraternity, that Levinas believes
bring about a degree of going beyond oneself. However, even more
important in my view, it is through this relation with the child that
there emerges a form of responsibility for the Other that is, at its best,
unparalleled in its call to selflessness.

For Levinas, the son and daughter represent alterity, but somewhat
differently than the feminine beloved. The child has the added feature
of being both other and one's self all wrapped up in one. Says Levinas,

> The son is not only my work, like a poem or an object, nor is he
> my property. Neither the categories of power nor those of knowl-
> edge describe my relation with the child. The fecundity of the I is
> neither a cause [n]or a determination. I do not have my child; I am
> my child. Paternity is a relation with a stranger who while being
> Other...is me, a relation of the I with a self which yet is not me.
> In this 'I am' being is no longer Eleatic unity. In existing itself there
> is multiplicity and a transcendence. In this transcendence the I is
> not swept away, since the son is not me; and yet I am my son. The
> fecundity of the I is its very transcendence. The biological origin
> of this concept nowise neutralizes the paradox of its meaning, and
> delineates a structure that goes beyond the biologically empirical.[86]

Thus, the future that we attempt to clutch, to caress in erotic love,
the "not yet" that resides "outside the world of possibles," is in a certain
sense, the future of the son or daughter.[87] The relation with the child
puts us into relation with a new structure of time, what Levinas calls
"infinite time." "The relation with the child—that is, the relation with
the other that is not a power, but fecundity—establishes relationship
with the absolute future, or infinite time."[88]

Infinite time "is the time in which the I exists without the finite limits of mortality."[89] "The time in which being and infinitum is produced
goes beyond the possible."[90] Infinite time, in a certain sense, is the pos-

85 Levinas, *Ethics and Infinity*, 71.
86 Levinas, *Totality and Infinity*, 277.
87 Wyschogrod, *Emmanuel Levinas*, 134.
88 Levinas, *Totality and Infinity*, 268.
89 Atterton and Calarco, *On Levinas*, 48.
90 Levinas, *Totality and Infinity*, 281.

sibility of a kind of everlasting youth, of newness, of eternal spring and hopefulness; it frees, or nearly frees, the self from the past in that, for example, one's mistakes, one's guilt-inducing omissions and commissions, take on new, more life-affirming meaning and purpose. I am reminded of a convicted felon I interviewed in a maximum-security prison who wanted court-ordered visitation with his four-year-old daughter whom he saw only once or twice before he was incarcerated. He told me, "The only thing that makes me want to survive in this jungle is the thought of reunion with 'my baby.' I am finished with a life of crime, all I want is to get out of this hell hole and be a good father to her, to let her know I did not forget her."

Infinite time also frees us, or at least lessens the frightening awareness of growing old and dying. Our good works, such as the goodness that we foster in our children, manifested in their living their lives in a manner that makes the world a better and more beautiful place, means, in a certain sense, that we live on. Fecundity thus brings about goodness in that it is through our children that we transmit important memories and insights and instantiate obligations and responsibilities to those who come after us.[91] Levinas calls this release from the past, or at least, this easing of the burdens of the past, and more generally, the release from the mainly egological interiority that fecundity brings about, "pardon."[92]

Thus, it is through the child that Eros evokes in the subject a different way of experiencing oneself and the world. According to Fryer, "in the child the I is drawn back to itself and its possible continuation in the other person who is both other than and yet still myself. Eros challenges traditional notions of subjectivity as the singular subject apart from other existents. Now subjectivity is bound up in an other who is not like myself, but who is myself, without sacrificing his otherness."[93] The relationship with the feminine beloved, the dual egoism of the insular loving couple is ruptured, giving way to self-transcendence in

---

91 Hutchens, *Levinas*, 87.

92 Levinas, *Totality and Infinity*, 283. In *Totality and Infinity* Levinas teases, but does not take up, the relationship between the infinity of time and Jewish messianism. He says in the last line of his book, "The problem exceeds the bounds of this book" (285).

93 Fryer, *The Intervention of the Other*, 82.

and through the child. This is the entrance of the "third party,"[94] the social,[95] and justice and politics.

Most importantly, it is "through the consummation of the erotic life" mainly within the context of the family, that the self of power and subjugation, the "virile being" that is "for oneself," is summoned to responsibility for the Other. The masculine self is called forth to be for the Other before oneself, a call to goodness.[96]

The paternal attitude depicts a mode of responsibility for the Other that needs to be briefly described for it is central to understanding the ethical potential in the erotic and family relations. I should point out, that while Levinas unfortunately usually describes such a mode of being using mainly masculine language, the father and son, in *Totality and Infinity*, he most definitely includes a maternal way of being as the embodiment of such an ethical potential later in his work. Maternity, already discussed in the previous chapter, was analyzed by Levinas in considerable detail in his second great book *Otherwise Than Being*. Maternity was there viewed as the metaphor for the highest ethical relation, personifying responsibility for the Other before oneself, goodness itself.

The paternal attitude, or rather the parental mode of being is evoked by Levinas when he writes:

> Transcendence, the for the Other, the goodness correlative of the face founds a more profound relation; the goodness of goodness. Fecundity engendering fecundity accomplishes goodness: above and beyond the sacrifice that imposes a gift, the gift of the power of giving, the conception of the child.[97]

It is through paternity—"the way of being other while being oneself,"[98] that Levinas puts into sharp focus a mode of being that has applicability beyond one's offspring, to all forms of love. In every authentic love relation, on some level, and to some degree, there is an abiding wish to create the conditions of possibility for the Other to create his or her

94   Levinas, *Totality and Infinity*, 280.

95   Fryer, *The Intervention of the Other*, 81.

96   Wyschogrod, *Emmanuel Levinas*, 136.

97   Levinas, *Totality and Infinity*, 269.

98   Ibid., 282.

own possibilities, especially to enhance the Other.[99] In other words, as with one's own labile teenager, I try to provide him or her with the space and resources to make good decisions in his life—these are the conditions of possibility, but I do not attempt to control his deliberations or make his decisions for him—to realize his own possibilities as he sees it. This is paternity at its best, I am in his world and yet not of his world, I am "inside and outside at once." This is aptly described as the relation of "being towards."[100] Perhaps most importantly, to help bring about the best that is possible in the loved Other requires finding him something like a master teacher and [or] a good mother, as someone who knows with the fullness of her whole being, that her existence, her being, is a secondary matter; what comes first is her responsibility for the Other.

CLINICAL VIGNETTE

By the end of his analysis, John had a deep and wide-ranging capacity to love. Whether it was his wife and children, friends or acquaintances, he related to them in a manner that reflected responsibility and being-for-the-Other, warmth and an open heart. Even the approaching beggars in the subway almost always received some money from him, while the wild birds were daily fed from a makeshift birdfeeder sitting on his window ledge. In other words, he had became a fairly caring and giving fellow to those he felt close to. He worked hard at being compassionate and for the most part his outlook and behavior expressed this sentiment.

However, John's deep and wide-ranging capacity to love was no easy psychic accomplishment. In fact, as he often remarked, his selfishness, his inordinate narcissistic needs and wishes, such as to be taken care of, to be mirrored and affirmed, were the "Devil," with whom he was frequently in hand-to-hand combat. John often quoted Muhammad the Prophet, "We have returned from the Lesser War [with the external enemy], to the Greater War [with the selfish passions]."

---

99   Atterton and Calarco, On Levinas, 47.

100 Stanislas Breton, in Richard Kearney, Debates in Continental Philosophy: Conversations with Contemporary Thinkers (New York: Fordham University Press, 2004) 136, 128.

While John did have what I regarded as excessive narcissistic needs and wishes, most often reflected in his labile self-esteem, he nevertheless made great progress in modulating them and finding more reasonable ways of satisfying them. This movement from inordinate narcissism, from an egoity of the self that was mainly "for himself," towards a greater capacity to love in the Levinasian sense—being for-the-Other—was perhaps best depicted in the evolution of his way of relating intimately to women. In many ways, John's problems with giving and receiving love, both in the erotic and non-erotic context, were manifested in his relationships with three women over many years, culminating in his life-affirming, "for-the-Other" marriage to his second wife, Nicole, the mother of his children. I want to review briefly the development of John's understanding of these important relationships with Betty, Maria and Harriet, and to suggest how he evolved into a man more capable of loving his wife.

Betty was John's first serious girlfriend; he had met her while in high school and described her as very attractive, "with big tits." Betty was regarded as a highly desirable girl by his peers, as she was not only "very hot," but was also the ringleader of the "in" clique. John claimed that he never understood why Betty took a liking to him, though he also said that he was both handsome and a good athlete, both aspects being highly regarded by most high school teenagers. At the time, John felt that Betty was much smarter and more savvy than he was. She received excellent grades, whereas he was a very poor student; she was confident, whereas he felt extremely uneasy about himself "nearly every waking minute." "While I presented a self-assured exterior, inside I was a wreck; I felt stupid, ugly and altogether like a great impostor."

John said that Betty represented a mother figure to him, one who was similar to his own mother, at least the mother he thought he had while growing up (his unfavorable view of his mother was revised, but became more balanced by the end of his analysis). John's mother was seductive and manipulative, but ultimately not very giving or supportive. Betty's appeal to John was that, in his mind, she promised nurturance, symbolized, for example, by her "big tits," which he frequently fantasized about "sucking." Betty also promised pleasure-giving as she was sexually very experienced. Said John, "she fucked like she was a general, she would give me orders—faster, slower, harder, softer. What a controlling bitch. At the time, I did not care, for she was a real piece of ass." John's inordinate expectations for nurturance and pleasure on demand reflected his generally infantile orientation to Betty. His stake in his relationship with her was that she shored up his self-esteem and self-worth, especially because she had high status among his peers and was sexually gratifying. In return, John admired Betty and was a non-threatening boy she could control. The relationship ended in their senior year in high school when Betty "dumped me." He wanted to continue the relationship even though they were going to different colleges that were far away from each other, whereas Betty wanted to cut him loose. "She felt that I was smothering her, that we were too young to be so involved; she wanted to be free. I was devastated and felt like a toddler on the beach who suddenly realizes that he has lost sight of his mother." John said that it took him about a year or two to "get over" Betty. In general, the legacy of Betty was that she engendered an even greater distrust of women, distrust that he claimed was mainly rooted in his early experience of his mother.

It was in his second year of college that John met an Italian woman whom he described "as one of the most beautiful women I ever laid my eyes on and, undoubtedly, the most beautiful woman I ever made love to."

Maria was a gentle and sweet sculptor who had the temperament and outlook of an artist. She was free, flowing and unrestrained, except in making love. Coming from a repressive Catholic parochial school background, she was unable to reach orgasm easily, though she was extremely sensual and deeply devoted to giving John pleasure. Maria was thoroughly in love with him and wanted to marry him. She even said that she was willing to go through an Orthodox conversion if he wanted her to. John however, felt in no way ready for marriage and the subject made him very anxious and wishing to flee.

John was the more powerful one in this relationship in the sense that unlike Betty who was strong and manipulative, Maria was more fragile and accommodating. He indicated to me that he was aware of her more vulnerable nature and that he tried to deal with her sensitively, though he often felt that he was not succeeding. John further said that he derived a fair amount of self-esteem from the fact that Maria was a "head turner" to most men and women. John also found Maria and her extended family very nurturing, as she was a great cook and her family was generous, fun-loving and accepting of him as a Jew.

John said that Maria's appearance in the bedroom was utterly bedazzling. He still remembered the first time he saw her and touched her slender, olive colored body and beautiful long straight black hair: "I use to say to myself, 'love Maria and die.' It was like being in the Garden of Eden." He said that, in general, Maria was an extremely caring and fun-giving woman who "almost worshipped" the ground I walked on. She was easy to please, and to gain her loyalty all I had to do was to be 'nice' to her." Being "nice" said John, was not as easy as it sounds, for he was prone to brooding about one thing or another and feeling not given to.

Despite Maria's being such a lovely woman, John said that he felt that he could not "really handle her." She had a dark intensity that frightened him and made him want "to escape." Maria's open way of being, and sincerity in giving and in desiring closeness, made him feel very uneasy and inadequate. He said he felt unwilling and unable to respond in kind to Maria's openness and deep capacity to give, though he could not offer himself one good reason why. "Maria wanted more from me than I wanted to give to her. Actually, that is not true, she wanted more from me than I had to give." He further indicated that while he adored and idealized her creativity and lovely nature, "I never really 'got' her. She had a temperament, an outlook on life that was so very different than mine, a bit strange, at least to me at the time. I felt inferior to her, she was a free spirit and a much better person than I was. I was bound, tied and gagged by neurosis, and incredibly self-preoccupied."

John said that the differences between Maria's and his outlooks were epitomized in their different fears while in an elevator. "I was deathly afraid that the elevator would suddenly go crashing down, whereas Maria was afraid that it would keep going up and never stop!" In Levinasian terms, Maria's way of being in the world was an abiding mystery to John, perhaps too much so.

In hindsight, John indicated that he felt that Maria represented his longing to free himself from feeling "being twisted up like a pretzel." It was Maria's lightness of being, her openness and generosity of spirit, and her transcendent beauty that he found so compelling. This was strikingly different from his usual heaviness of being, with a proneness to self-absorption, depressive moodiness and cynicism. By having known Maria, John said that he felt that he was less "closed off," more spontaneous and hopeful. "Maria's sweetness and generosity rubbed off on me. Finding her was like accidentally finding a small gem on the street."

Prior to meeting Harriet, his first wife, while in medical school, John had had a number of short-term relationships with women from a wide range of backgrounds. These relationships were largely mutually instrumental in nature. For the most part, "I used them and they used me," especially in the sexual realm. In one six-month relationship with a Latino woman about ten years his senior with whom he worked, he experienced a level of reckless sexual abandon that nearly got him fired, including almost being caught copulating on his desk. He described this woman as "oozing sexuality, as proof of the street wisdom that Latino women give the best sex on the planet."

In looking back on these brief relationships, John noted that all of these women were very nice people, most of whom probably felt that he was a promising candidate for a serious, long-term relationship and marriage. Thus, while initially these women settled for a mutually utilitarian type relationship as, in part, a kind of strategy to win him over, once John sensed that they were about to fall in love with him, "I bolted." John said that he left behind a trail of women who hated him because "he [had] led them on." "Once they fell for me and wanted more of a commitment, I dumped them. I guess I acted like a typical man though I never misled any of the women into thinking that there was a possibility of getting married in the foreseeable future. Still, they thought I was a manipulative bastard and I guess I was."

Harriet, a teacher and child of Holocaust survivors, the woman he cheated on to be with Nicole, whom he ultimately married, has been described in the Chapter 2 vignette. She was a kind, giving and gentle woman whom John had met when he was a resident in medical school. At the time, John said that Harriet represented to him a return to a more infantile mode of relating, one in which he mainly sought nurture, support and stability. In return, he was expected to be loyal and loving, both qualities "I was extremely short on." John further indicated that, in hindsight, Harriet symbolized the mother he wished he had had, totally devoted and caring. The problem was, he said, that "incest got boring." That is, his relationship with Harriet was quickly desexualized, not literally, but it lacked the erotic stirrings and animating power of Eros. "Harriet should have been my best friend, not my wife. She was a fine person, trustworthy, always available and kind, but we were not compatible as husband and wife. Actually, at the time I was probably not able to relate maturely to any woman over an extended period, let alone in a traditional marriage." To John's mind, Maria, like Harriet, was a better person than he was, someone who taught him about fidelity and care. Even more important, he said, was the the guilt he felt after he cheated on Harriet, which ultimately ended his marriage and made him face the painful, unintended consequences of his selfishness and aggressiveness against someone he cared about. John indicated that while he realized that Harriet had also contributed to the demise of the marriage, he felt that his deceitfulness and self-centeredness still deserved a measure of guilt.

Nicole, a pediatrician, represented an amalgamation of John's previous relationships with women, including the first woman in his life, his mother. Like his mother and Betty, Nicole, who came up to him at a party and began to flirt with him even while knowing he was married, could be seductive, a bit manipulative, and was very intelligent and insightful. Similar to Maria, Nicole had a dark intensity and doeish sadness, as well as an artistic bent and outlook, as she had majored in fine arts while in college, and was an accomplished painter. Like Harriet, Nicole was solid, dependable and kind.

That being said, Nicole was more than the sum of these other women, for it was she, more than any woman he knew, who taught him how to say Thou, to be responsible for-the-Other. It was through Nicole's ceaselessly performed acts of love that were aimed at reducing if not eliminating John's pain and defensive need to be selfish, that John began to realize his own potential for giving love without expecting payback. It was within the context of sharing in the being of Nicole, in her otherness, that John was encouraged both outside and inside the bedroom, to love with the fullness of his whole being and more selflessly. This development culminated in the couple's having two children. Nicole, in her gentle but firm constructive criticism, her high expectations, and faith that John could "do better" as a husband and father, acted as a powerful source of motivation for him to be for-the-Other, for Nicole, for his children, and for his friends.

However, as John pointed out, his increased capacity to love was not only brought about by his exemplary and decisive bond with Nicole. In addition, the widening and deepening of his capacity to love emerged through a parallel love relationship he had with an elderly man, his analyst. As Freud said, psychoanalysis "is actually a cure by love."[101] It cures through the analyst's love for the analysand, and the analysand's love for the analyst. John had largely worked through

101 Sigmund Freud, *The Freud/Jung Letters*, 12-13.

his numerous neurotic conflicts, his Oedipal and aggressive wishes, as well as strengthened his self-esteem, all within the context of the transference. It was only then that John's egoity of the self and his inordinate narcissism gave way to a self that was more capable and willing to be responsible for-the-Other as his primary, consciously embraced way of being in the world. As John said at his last session, "My ability to more selflessly love Nicole and my children could have only come about through a process of individuation that traveled through You. For this I am eternally grateful."

6

MAKING SUFFERING SUFFERABLE

To be human is to suffer for the other, and even within one's own suffer-
ing, to suffer for the suffering my suffering imposes upon the other.[1]
Levinas

Psychoanalysis is one of the great master narratives that attempts both to understand the nature of pain and suffering as
well as provide a technology of the self that is meant, at least
at its best, to help the suffering person "manage" his pain in a more
reasonable and life-affirming manner. For Freud, the entire continuum
of pain and suffering, whether a toothache, the stress of everyday life,
the death of a loved one, or a genocidal universe, is to varying degrees
an existential challenge to one's autonomy, integration and humanity.
All suffering, however, whether imposed from without, such as in tor-
ture or an earthquake, or from within, as in neurotic misery, are not
only an assault on one's integrity, dignity and healthy narcissism; in
addition, such pain and suffering, especially of the normative variety
such as being abruptly "thrown over" by one's girlfriend or boyfriend
or the death of an elderly parent, represent an opportunity for growth
and development. Moreover, as some Holocaust survivors have noted,
even in the extreme situation of the concentration and death camps,
inmates derived insights into themselves and others that transformed
their lives for the better in the years following their incarceration. Such
hard-earned moral insights reflect the ancient truth that suffering is
the mother of all wisdom.

As has been mentioned in an earlier chapter, Levinas was no stranger to pain and suffering. As a survivor of imprisonment in a Nazi-
administered forestry commando unit for Jewish prisoners of war he
felt "stripped" of his "human skin." He was treated as if he was "a sub-
human" and "no longer part of the world."[2] Moreover, not only did he

---

1 Levinas, *Nine Talmudic Readings*, 188.

2 *Difficult Freedom*, 152-153. The brutality and dehumanization of the stalag in Germany where Levinas was interned is exemplified in Levinas's

have to endure the horror of Nazi brutality and imprisonment, at the same time he had to bear the anxiety of his wife and daughter being in hiding, and if discovered, being murdered. By the end of the war, Levinas's parents, brothers, in-laws, much of his extended family, and community had been murdered by the Nazis. It is perhaps, for this reason that he described himself as one of the "survivors,"[3] while Derrida noted that "...all of Levinas's thought, from beginning to end, was a meditation on death."[4]

Similar to Job in the whirlwind, Levinas's personal confrontation with the Nazi assault provided the conditions of possibility for an attempt at generating moral insights. His writings on pain and suffering, of the self and of the other, are efforts to reveal the ethical dimension of suffering. Such efforts speak to the heart of psychoanalysis when conceived as a life- and identity-defining narrative that helps those who strive to comprehend, bear, and possibly overcome the problems that assail the human condition: anguish, conflict, despair and loss.

The subject of pain and suffering encompasses a wide range of phenomena. In medicine and psychology, for example, there is a sub-

reminiscence: "When, over the grave of a Jewish comrade whom the Nazis wanted to bury like a dog, a Catholic priest, Father Chesnet, recited prayers which were, in the absolute sense of the term, Semitic" (*Difficult Freedom*, 12).

3 Levinas, *Of God Who Comes to Mind*, x.

4 Levinas, *Adieu*, 120. The important theme of death in Levinas's work is touched upon in this chapter and elsewhere in this book, though it is not a subject that I discuss in a separate chapter. Suffice it to say, for Levinas there is no more extreme encounter with alterity than in facing one's own death. Death is ambiguous, mysterious and menacing. Being a hostage to death is a way of being a hostage to the other. Levinas is here challenging Heidegger's being-toward-death formulation in which death is viewed as the subject's ultimate trial of "mastery," "virility," "heroism" and authenticity (*Time and the Other*, 72). Instead, Levinas views death as unfathomable and radically disruptive, as pointing towards a mindfulness of otherness, of the face-to-face, in other words, of love as responsibility for the Other. Richard A. Cohen writes that "Levinas rejects Heidegger's analysis of being as being-toward-death, arguing that the death that matters most and cuts most deeply into my own psyche is not my own but the other's. Furthermore, it is not the other's death per se, but the other's mortality, meaning the other's aging and suffering, the other's vulnerability, that calls me to myself as responsibility for the other, responsible 'not to let him die alone'" (Personal communication, 9/10/06).

specialty called pain management, which deals with the reduction of physical pain. Pain and suffering has long been a major concern to philosophers and theologians in terms of the problems of evil and theodicy, subjects I will touch upon in more detail in the following chapter on religion. To the average person, the question of why bad things happen to good people still unsettles, while the claim, following Ecclesiastes and Albert Camus, that life is meaningless and absurd,[5] resounds in the modern mind.

In this chapter, I will limit my comments to the aspect of pain and suffering that is most relevant to psychoanalysis, the helping profession: how do individuals make suffering "sufferable?"[6] How do they draw on their "symbolic world,"—their "particular way of looking at life,"[7] and other resources, in the face of extreme pain and suffering, such that they are better able to sustain their autonomy, integration and humanity?

My claim, following Levinas, is that those people who are best able to sustain themselves as persons are those who are steeped in a form of life characterized by steadfast, though flexibly applied, affectively animating, transcendent moral values, beliefs and modes of conduct, that are mainly "for the Other." Such people, says Levinas, live "above all with the sense that belonging to humanity means belonging to an order of responsibility."[8]

I will support my claim by returning to a subject that I discussed in chapter two, the observation that those concentration and death camp inmates who embraced an ethic of responsibility for the Other were, in general, best able to sustain themselves as persons. The latter includes those inmates who were "lone wolves," merely out for themselves, and/

---

5 For Ecclesiastes, our existence, our experience of life's struggles and all that we attempt to achieve, is like a vapor or breath. That is, the entire human enterprise is fundamentally empty and ultimately meaningless "Vanity of vanities, all is vanity," Ecclesiastes famously and bluntly asserts. For Albert Camus, the absurd is the distressing clash between our rational expectations of the world, such as for happiness, justice and gratification, and the fact that we appear to live in an ethically indifferent universe.

6 Clifford Geertz, "Religion as a Cultural System." In *The Interpretation of Cultures* (New York: Basic Books, 1973), 105.

7 Ibid., 110.

8 *In The Time of the Nations.*, 168.

or committed to a "survival at any price" approach to their ordeal.[9] That being said, it is important to be mindful of the fact that Levinas's commitment to the primacy of the Other is not meant to show that this primacy facilitates personal development, including moral development and the ability to cope better. Such personal benefits are an outcome; in Levinas's account, it is the other, not self-development, that is primary.[10]

In this chapter I want to go beyond describing the "what" of responsibility for the Other. I want to elaborate the "how" and "why" a particular mode of being, one that is infused with an ethic of responsibility for the Other, can make extreme pain and suffering and, by extension, its other "lesser" forms such as the variety analysts often see in their clinical work, more endurable, that is, more sufferable. To accomplish this goal, I will compare two modal types of camp inmates: the "intellectuals," as Auschwitz survivors Jean Améry, Primo Levi and Elie Wiesel called them, and the "believers," who were those with unwavering transcendent religious, political, or moral convictions, such as Jehovah's Witnesses, devout Catholics and Jews, militant Marxists, or Zionists.[11] Whether the intellectual was a man of letters, a philosopher of science, a naturalist, a sociologist, a mathematician, or I would add, a psychoanalyst, these intellectuals were more vulnerable to the Nazi assault than the believers.

My hope is that this "thought experiment," this comparison between the religious believer and the psychoanalytic intellectual, will put into sharp focus what is possibly missing in psychoanalytic accounts of how people can best "manage" their pain and suffering. By identifying and describing some of those personal qualities, beliefs, values, and group affiliations that were most helpful to them as they faced the extreme situation, I hope to shed some light on how other painful and distressing experiences in life can be better borne, made more sufferable. More generally, perhaps, the mode of practicing and acting upon the world

9 Paul Marcus, *Autonomy in the Extreme Situation. Bruno Bettelheim, the Nazi Concentration Camps and the Mass Society* (Westport, CT: Praeger, 1999), Chapters 4-6.

10 Edith Wyschogrod. Personal communication, 3/5/06. I am grateful to Professor Wyschogrod for her helpful suggestions to improve this chapter.

11 This chapter is an expanded version of my article "The Religious Believer, the Psychoanalytic Intellectual, and the Challenge of Sustaining the Self in the Concentration Camps."

of the "believers," with their strongly held moral convictions—their ethic of responsibility for the Other—can provide some new insights into the human condition, and human potential at its best.

I will focus my discussion mainly on Freudian psychoanalysis, although much of what I will discuss has some bearing on other psychoanalytic perspectives. I do this because the only existing, systematic discussion of survival in a concentration camp written by a psychoanalytic intellectual is that of Bruno Bettelheim, who was lodged in a broadly-based Freudian outlook, as were most of the survivor psychoanalysts I have spoken to.[12] The "believers" whom I will be describing are mainly devout Jews. This is because they are both the most written-about group in the pertinent Holocaust literature and the group of survivors I have had the most personal and clinical contact with. Finally, as Levinas was an Orthodox Jew, his outlook on life, as mainly deduced from his confessional writings and interviews and, to a lesser degree, his philosophical writings, most resonates with the devout Jews whom we are calling the "believers." For example, as Wyschogrod points out, it is from the Talmud that Levinas develops his stress "upon the unique relation with the Other, not as the most immediately given datum of experience, but as a datum that is ethical in its very upsurge."[13] Moreover, Levinas characterizes Judaism as "an extreme consciousness,"[14] which may reverberate with the "extreme situation" of the concentration camp, as it possibly does with "extreme consciousness,"[15] as he calls the ordeal of physical suffering.

---

12   I have communicated with Dori Laub, Louis J. Michaels, Marion M. Oliner, Anna and Paul Ornstein, and many years ago, with Jack Terry and Fred Wolkenfeld. For a critical review of many of the other well-known psychologically-based narratives of survival in the camps, including the writings of Viktor E. Frankl and Elie A. Cohen among others, see my *Autonomy in the Extreme Situation: Bruno Bettelheim, The Nazi Concentration Camps and the Mass Society.*

13   Wyschogrod, *Levinas,* 176. By extreme consciousness Levinas means, "consciousness more conscious than consciousness," "a consciousness that is no longer subjectivity (that never was subjectivity): *logos*"(italics in original).... The consciousness of there being no way out," *Proper Names,* 80, 81, 162.

14   Levinas, *Difficult Freedom,* 6.

15   Levinas, *Totality and Infinity,* 239.

SOME IMPORTANT DEFINITIONS:
SYMBOLIC WORLD, EXTREME SITUATION, THE
INTELLECTUAL, THE BELIEVER

Before getting to the heart of this chapter, it is necessary to define some of the key terms that are used throughout my discussion.

Symbolic world. A symbolic world is roughly equivalent to a perspective, "a particular manner of construing the world."[16] Religion, politics, and psychoanalysis can operate as symbolic worlds. Psychoanalysis, for example, as a life-narrative, has its own version of the human condition and its own idea of what the "good life" is and how to achieve it. Perhaps most important, it has its own notions about how to effectively assimilate the emotionally dissonant experiences of life, including suffering and death, "into a comprehensive explanation of reality and human destiny."[17] In a certain sense, those who seek out psychoanalysis are attracted to its "vision of reality," to the system of meaning and metaphor that it promulgates.[18]

Extreme Situation. In an extreme situation, especially as it applies to concentration camp inmates, an individual feels deprived of any close, affirming, and need-gratifying personal relationships. Deprived of hope, he feels utterly powerless in relation to those in authority, and fears that the extreme situation is inescapable and interminable.[19] Levinas says about physical suffering that "The whole acuity of suffering lies in the impossibility of fleeing it, of being protected in oneself from oneself; it lies in being cut off from every living spring. And it is the impossibility of retreat."[20] Many analysands frequently feel as if they are in something of an extreme situation, real or imagined.

---

16   Geertz, "Religion as a Cultural System," 110.

17   Peter and Brigitte Berger, *Sociology: A Biographical Approach* (New York: Basic Books, 1972), 352.

18   Roy Schafer, "The Psychoanalytic Visions of Reality," in *A New Language for Psychoanalysis* (New Haven, CT: Yale University Press, 1976), 22.

19   Bruno Bettelheim, "Schizophrenia as a Reaction to Extreme Situations," in *Surviving and Other Essays* (New York: Knopf, 1979) 112-126.

20   Levinas, *Totality and Infinity*, 238. Halpern usefully criticizes Levinas for making a sharp distinction between physical pain and moral and psychological pain, the latter she says, Levinas mistakenly believed one can detach oneself from compared to physical pain which is inescapable in its suffering (Cynthia Halpern, *Suffering, Politics, Power. A Genealogy in Modern Politi-*

The "intellectual" and the "believer." Tentative definitions of an intellectual as it applies to the death camp, Auschwitz in particular, are offered by Jean Améry and Primo Levi. About the person with an "intellectual background and intellectual basic disposition," Améry writes: "An intellectual, as I would like it to be understood here, is a man who lives within what is a spiritual frame of reference in the widest sense. His realm of thought is an essentially humanistic one, that of the liberal arts. He has a well-developed esthetic consciousness."[21] Most psychoanalysts and psychoanalytically-oriented intellectuals can be included in this broadly-conceived skeptic-humanistic category. For those psychoanalytic intellectuals who are religious or political believers, ideological commitments, along with the concomitant potential benefits, tend to be somewhat blunted by their skeptical psychoanalytical intellectualism. Like the author of this book, these analysts may have religious beliefs, but their commitment to their faith lacks the passionate emotional commitment and absolute leap of faith of the "true believer." They tend to be more ambivalent, critical, and questioning of their faith and more angst-ridden, reducing the belief's psychological usefulness and possibility of transcendence in extreme situations and life in general.[22] Likewise, though Levinas was an Orthodox Jew, albeit "a rather heterodox one,"[23] the consolation that Judaism offered him was hardly straightforwardly traditional.

---

cal Theory (Albany: State University of New York Press, 2002, 10).

21 Jean Améry, *At the Mind's Limits: Contemplations by a Survivor on Auschwitz and Its Realities*, transl. Alvin Rosenfeld and Stella P. Rosenfeld (Bloomington, IN: Indiana University Press, 1980), 2.

22 Ernst Federn, a psychoanalyst/survivor who had strong Marxist commitments when he was incarcerated in Buchenwald for many years, as far as I know never stresses in any of his writings on the subject that his Marxist background helped him to remain human or cope more effectively (in a psychological sense) with Nazi barbarism in the day-to-day grind of everyday life. Federn and Bettelheim were incarcerated together in Buchenwald in 1939. (Ernst Federn, *Witnessing Psychoanalysis*, London: Karnac, 1980).

23 Hilary Putnam, "Levinas and Judaism," in *The Cambridge Companion to Levinas*, 51.

THE INTELLECTUAL AND THE BELIEVER IN THE
CONCENTRATION CAMPS

As I have said, this chapter deals with the problem of sustaining the self in the extreme situation from the point of view of those who were less capable of surviving as "human beings"[24] in the camps, the intellectuals, the psychoanalytic intellectual in particular. There is considerable support for this claim, including from three famous Auschwitz survivors, Jean Améry, Elie Wiesel and Primo Levi.[25] Bruno Bettelheim, who was in a concentration camp, made a similar observation.[26] As Améry writes:

> One way or the other, in the decisive moments their political or religious belief was an inestimable help to them, while we skeptical and humanistic intellectuals took recourse, in vain, to our literary, philosophical, and artistic household gods. Their belief or their ideology gave them the firm foothold in the world from which

---

24 Bruno Bettelheim, *The Informed Heart* (Glencoe, IL: The Free Press, 1960), 16. I am aware that what constitutes surviving as "human beings" or "remaining human," as I later call it, in the concentration camps, is a radically philosophical question whose answer depends on one's form of life and frame of reference. It is beyond the scope of this chapter to elucidate these distinctions. Likewise, "remaining human" cannot be reduced to one explanatory factor. For Levinas, to be human is to be the self as responsibility, subjectivity as suffering and obsession for the other, hostage to the other.

25 Primo Levi, *The Drowned and the Saved* (New York: Summit Books, 1988), 145-146.

26 Bruno Bettelheim, "Surviving," in *Surviving and Other Essays* (New York: Knopf, 1979), 296. Says Bettelheim, "It is a well-known fact of the concentration camps that those who had strong religious and moral convictions managed life there much better than the rest. Their beliefs, including belief in an afterlife, gave them a strength to endure which was far above that of most others. Deeply religious persons often helped others, and some voluntarily sacrificed themselves—many more of them than of the average prisoners." It should be noted that Bettelheim was incarcerated in a concentration camp, not a death camp. The former was much more benign situation, relatively speaking, compared to a death camp, which was a methodical, efficient slaughterhouse. While there are major differences between the two types of camps, for the purpose of this chapter, the terms will be used to signify the "extreme situation." The particular kind of camp will be designated when known.

they spiritually unhinged the SS state. Under conditions that defy the imagination they conducted Mass, and as Orthodox Jews they fasted on the Day of Atonement although they actually lived the entire year in a condition of raging hunger. They survived better or died with more dignity than their irreligious or intellectual comrades, who often were infinitely better educated and more practiced in exact thinking.[27]

Wiesel writes:

> Within the system of the concentration camp...the first to give in, the first to collaborate—to save their lives—were the intellectuals, the liberals, the humanists, the professors of sociology, and the like...Very few Communists gave in...They were the resisters... Even fewer to give in were the Catholic priests...yet there were exceptions. But you could not have found one single rabbi—I dare you—among all the *kapos* or among any of the others who held positions of power in the camps.[28]

Bettelheim, who himself was incarcerated in Dachau and Buchenwald in 1938-39, and who at the time of his imprisonment, could reasonably be described as a psychoanalytically-oriented intellectual, made a crucial observation that prompted my interest in comparing the psychoanalytic intellectual and the religious believer:

> Most surprising of all, psychoanalysis, which I had come to view as the best key to all human problems, offered no suggestions or help toward the solution of how to survive and survive halfway decently in the camps. For that I had to fall back on qualities that my psychoanalytic experience and thinking were of little importance, if not of negative valence, while those qualities I had learned to stress were often as much of a hindrance as a help.[29]

---

27 Améry, *At the Mind's Limits*, 13.

28 Elie Wiesel, "Talking, and Writing and Keeping Silent," in *The German Church Struggle and the Holocaust*, eds. Franklin H. Littell and Hubert G. Locke (Bloomington, IN: Wayne State University Press, 1974), 273. The context of Wiesel's remarks are important to appreciate for, as far as I can tell, they have a somewhat rhetorical quality. Wiesel made his comments as part of his improvised reply to a controversial lecture given by Richard Rubenstein to the question of "What can be told, what can be written, where must silence be kept, what can be witnessed only by living?" (the quote is cited by the editors, p. 269).

29 Bettelheim, *The Informed Heart*, 15-16.

What Bettelheim is stressing is that his psychoanalytic perspective did not significantly help him maintain his autonomy, integration and humanity in the concentration camps. Bettelheim's psychoanalytic experience and thinking did not help him achieve his goal: "If I should try to sum up in one sentence what my main problem was during the whole time I spent in the camps, it would be: to protect my inner self in such a way that if, by good fortune, I should regain my liberty, I would be approximately the same person I was when deprived of liberty."[30] Bettelheim writes that his psychoanalytic perspective "strangely enough, and to my sharp disappointment, did not help me in any specific ways to protect myself from that danger [i.e. personality disintegration], nor to understand why those who stood up well under the experience were able to do so."[31]

Why was psychoanalysis, which can be conceptualized as a symbolic world, a master narrative with a particular angle of vision on life, including its own way of assimilating the painful and frightening experiences of life, and even death itself, so unsuited for helping individuals to sustain themselves as "human beings" in the extreme situation?

To help answer this question, and to suggest what moral and other resources a believer could use to "remain human," including making his suffering sufferable, resources that were generally not available to the psychoanalyst, I will further discuss the one existing "classic" concentration camp narrative written by a psychoanalytic intellectual, Bruno Bettelheim's *The Informed Heart*.

BRUNO BETTELHEIM'S AMBIVALENCE TOWARD THE USEFULNESS OF HIS FREUDIAN PSYCHOANALYTIC FRAMEWORK IN THE CONCENTRATION CAMP

It is appropriate to begin with the ambivalent reflections of Bettelheim, the only psychoanalytic thinker/survivor that I am aware of who directly raises the issue under investigation in this chapter. Bettelheim struggles with the limitations of psychoanalysis in helping him and other inmates "survive as human beings" in the camps.[32] Moreover, Bettelheim has been regarded by many as the embodiment of the "European intellectual." He received a classical education at the University

---

30   Ibid., 126.

31   Ibid., 24.

32   Ibid., 16.

of Vienna and was well-versed in literature, history, sociology, mythology, and the humanities of Freud.[33]

In *The Informed Heart*, Bettelheim defines psychoanalysis before he indicates which aspects of his psychoanalytic framework were useful to him while incarcerated at Dachau and Buchenwald. He notes that technically "psychoanalysis is really at least three different things: a method of observation, a therapy, and a body of theories on human behavior and personality structure. They are valid in descending order, the theory of personality being the weakest link of a system quite in need of revision."[34]

Bettelheim further points out that as a personal method of observation psychoanalysis

> more than proved its value and was most helpful to me. It gave me a deeper understanding of what may have gone on in the unconscious of prisoners and guards, an understanding that on one occasion may have saved my life, and on other occasions let me be of help to some of my fellow prisoners, where it counted."[35] "Without the understanding gained from psychoanalysis I would not have been able to comprehend what the concentration camp did to people, nor why.[36]

Such understanding was "psychologically reconstructive" for Bettelheim in the camps in that part of his "old psychoanalytic system of

33 David J. Fisher, *Cultural Theory and Psychoanalytic Tradition* (New Brunswick, NJ: Transaction Publishers, 1991), 163. Bettelheim has been accused by Richard Pollack, his "vengeful biographer," as a *New York Times* book reviewer called him, of having been a brilliant charlatan. Pollack claims, for example, that Bettelheim was a lumber dealer who grandly reinvented himself by means of a forged set of academic credentials after emigrating to the United States in 1939 (*The Creation of Dr. B.*, New York: Simon and Schuster, 1996). Whatever the facts are, in my view Bettelheim's many thoughtful, provocative, and at times brilliant books and essays indicate that he was an impressive and well-rounded intellectual. For a more balanced and sympathetic view of Bettelheim, see Nina Sutton's biography *Bettelheim: A Life and a Legacy* (New York: Basic Books, 1996) and Theron Raines's (Bettelheim's friend and literary agent) *Rising to The Light: A Portrait of Bruno Bettelheim* (New York: Knopf, 2002).

34 Bettelheim, *The Informed Heart*, 19.

35 Ibid., 19-20.

36 Bettelheim, "Owners of Their Faces," in *Surviving and Other Essays*, 107.

mastery" was saved, his "belief in the value of rational examination."[37] For Bettelheim, the strength of psychoanalysis in the concentration camp was as a "instrument of understanding": "The explanatory value of psychoanalysis is beyond question, always."[38]

In contrast, however, Bettelheim also has serious reservations about psychoanalysis as a body of theories explaining human behavior and a personality structure that could adequately comprehend inmate behavior in the camps. He makes the point that psychoanalytic theory, and the views on personality that derive from it, were "inadequate to explain fully what happened to the prisoners."[39] Bettelheim reasons that "outside of its particular frame of reference"—the uniquely-controlled context of the analyst's consultation room—psychoanalysis cannot explain human behavior unless it is modified to take into consideration radically changing social environments. Thus, Bettelheim believes that psychoanalysis "distorted" the meaning of the ways in which individuals survived and maintained their humanity amidst the radically changing social environment of the concentration camps.[40]

A primary example of the inadequacy of psychoanalytic theory for understanding the camps as a radically extreme social environment was, according to Bettelheim, its deficiency in explaining "what constitutes a well-integrated personality" in the camps, "which behavior is preferable, or which personality more adequate."[41] He says that some of the prisoners who maintained their "old personality structure, stuck to their values in the face of extreme hardships, and, as persons, were hardly touched by the camp experience," were people whom psychoanalysis would have viewed "as extremely neurotic or plainly delusional, and therefore apt to fall apart, as persons under stress."[42] This was exemplified by the Jehovah's Witnesses, "who not only showed unusual heights of human dignity and moral behavior, but seemed protected against the same camp experience that soon destroyed persons considered very well integrated by my psychoanalytic friends and myself."[43]

37 Bettelheim, "The Ultimate Limit, in *Surviving and Other Essays*, 13.

38 Fisher, *Cultural Theory and Psychoanalytic Tradition*, 167.

39 Bettelheim, *The Informed Heart*, 18-19.

40 Ibid.

41 Ibid., 20.

42 Ibid.

43 Ibid., 21. The Jehovah's Witnesses who were incarcerated in Buchenwald

Those persons who, according to psychoanalytic theory, should have endured best under the severity of the camp experience were often the first to succumb to the extreme stress. Behavior in the camps could not be explained by an inmate's personal history and his previous personality, by "those aspects of personality" that, at the time, seemed important in then-current "psychoanalytic thinking."[44] Bettelheim points out that this conclusion emanates from his own disappointment with psychoanalysis as a self-sustaining frame of reference in the camps. "Other aspects of psychoanalysis, the introspection, the self-criticism, are not very useful in an extreme situation."[45]

There seems to be a tension in Bettelheim's relationship to his psychoanalytic framework, especially as it relates to the question of its usefulness to him in his struggle to survive and "remain human" in the camps, to make his suffering sufferable. On the one hand, as already quoted, Bettelheim says that psychoanalysis "proved its value and was most helpful" to him, "that on one occasion [it] may have saved" his life. On the other hand, he says that it offered "no suggestion or help toward the solution of how to survive and survive halfway decently in the camps." Perhaps Bettelheim's comments refer to his earlier distinction between psychoanalysis as a method of observation, as he calls it, and a theory of human behavior and personality structure. For example, Bettelheim's psychoanalytic training and mode of understanding may have helped him maneuver effectively against an individual prison guard, but as a general theoretical framework for understanding his overall predicament and how to survive and "remain human" in the camps, it may have been largely unhelpful. Similarly, Bettelheim may have found aspects of his psychoanalytic framework helpful in observing the behavior of his fellow inmates, but the theory, as a master narrative, as the "key to all human problems," as he described it, he found severely lacking.

---

were particularly ideologically steadfast, especially in light of the fact that, according to Eugen Kogon, "On September 6, 1938, the SS offered them the chance to abjure their principles in writing, especially their refusal to swear oaths and render military service, and thus to purchase their liberty. Only a very few failed to withstand this temptation," *The Theory and Practice of Hell* (New York: Berkley Publishing Corporation), 1958, 42.

44 Bettelheim, *The Informed Heart*, 17.

45 Fisher, *Cultural Theory and Psychoanalytic Tradition*, 167.

One important reason Bettelheim felt that classical psychoanalysis was inadequate to explain what had happened to the camp inmates was that it did not give enough theoretical importance to the powerful influence of the social environment in changing the individual. Eventually he did realize that psychoanalysis as a treatment modality is not the most potent influence in fostering personality change. Rather, an extreme environment, such as the camps, could more invasively and swiftly shape the person, for better or worse. Furthermore, this realization dramatically altered his previous view that only personal changes in man, in his subjectivity, can effect changes in society. He explains:

> My experience in the camps taught me, almost within days, that I had gone much too far in believing that only changes in man could create changes in society. I had to accept that the environment could, as it were, turn personality upside down, and not just in the small child, but in the mature adult too. If I wanted to keep it from happening to me, I had to accept this potentiality of the environment to decide where and where not to adjust, and how far. Psychoanalysis, as I understood it, was of no help in this all important decision... We should never again be satisfied to see personality change as proceeding independent from the social context.[46]

For Bettelheim, psychoanalysis could not adequately address the dramatic influence of the environment on the inmate's personality, and psychoanalytic theories were inadequate to explain what constituted a well-integrated personality within the camps. Nor was what would have been considered a well-integrated personality by psychoanalytic criteria be predictive of who could withstand or adapt to the onslaught of the camp environment and remain human.

Bettelheim believes that the main reason that a psychoanalytic frame of reference was not helpful in his struggle to remain human in the camps was because of its emphasis on "what...[goes] wrong in people's lives" and on "what can be done to correct the mishaps." He

---

46 Bettelheim, *The Informed Heart*, 15, 37. Bettelheim, like Erich Fromm and other early psychoanalytic writers, was in a certain sense ahead of his time. Contemporary psychoanalysis, in its relational and intersubjective versions, is more concerned with social context than in earlier theorizing. However, in my view psychoanalysis has yet to develop a sophisticated social psychology that adequately integrates the external world into its theorizing. This especially includes the findings from experimental social psychology.

further says that this has always been the domain of psychoanalysis and notes that this is entirely appropriate. However, psychoanalysis "does not offer a theory of personality giving positive guidance toward the good life."[47]

Psychoanalysis emphasizes the pathological and tends to neglect the positive. In the camps, the issue was not how to rid oneself of one's distorted pathology, but rather how to identify and draw from one's strengths in order to behave in a manner that enhanced physical and spiritual survival. If pathology is one's frame of reference for human action, the camp inmate had little direction in helping him determine what to do. Bettelheim says that

> Psychoanalysis is the best method for uncovering and understanding the hidden in man, but by no means an especially good tool for understanding man in his entirety, least of all for understanding what makes for "goodness" or "greatness" in him. The conclusion then seems warranted that while psychoanalysis can explain the psychological upheaval, the pathology that got something started, it is much less successful in explaining why and how, from such starts, positive developments take place.[48]

What this could have meant for a camp inmate is that if he were lodged in a psychoanalytic perspective, his ability to sustain himself as a person would have been strained, since his frame of reference offered very little helpful direction on how to behave. In the camps, the way a man acted, rather than why he acted a certain way, became of prime importance. It also altered how the inmate saw himself and acted throughout his ordeal. Bettelheim observes:

> Only dimly at first, but with even greater clarity, did I also come to see that soon how a man acts can alter what he is. Those who stood up well in the camps became better men, those who acted badly soon became bad men; and this, or at least so it seemed, independent of their past life history and their former personality make-up,

---

47 Ibid., 25.

48 Ibid., 27. Freud's answer to his question, "Why should analyzed men and women in fact be better than others?" is supportive of Bettelheim's observations, specifically about "goodness." According to Freud, "Analysis makes for integration but does not of itself make for goodness." (Letter to J.J. Putnam, 6/17/15, in Nathan G. Hale, *James Jackson Putnam and Psychoanalysis*,188).

or at least those aspects of personality that seemed significant in psychoanalytic thinking.[49]

Furthermore, in the camps, the psychoanalytic view that the unconscious processes underlying an action were equal in importance to the overt behavior was not tenable. As Bettelheim indicates:

> It just would not do under conditions prevailing in the camps to view courageous, life-endangering actions as an outgrowth of the death instinct, aggression turned against the self, testing the indestructibility of the body, megalomaniac denial of danger, histrionic feeding of one's narcissism or whatever category the action would have to be viewed from in psychoanalysis. These and many other interpretations have validity in terms of depth psychology or the psychology of the unconscious, and they certainly did apply. Only viewing courageous behavior by a prisoner within the spectrum of depth analysis seemed ludicrously beside the point. So while psychoanalysis lost nothing as far as it went, it went unexpectedly, and in terms of my expectations, shockingly short of the mark.[50]

Bettelheim thus highlights what he thinks are the deficiencies of Freudian psychoanalysis in terms of what it does not or can not adequately take into account, chiefly the social world and the individual's strengths and positive attributes. In the next section, by contrasting the believers, mainly devout Jews, and the psychoanalytic intellectual, I hope to illuminate what individual and group resources, in particular, what resources rooted in a transcendent ethic of responsibility for the Other, believers used to remain human, to make their suffering sufferable, resources that were in most instances not accessible to the psychoanalyst.[51]

---

49 Ibid., 16-17.

50 Ibid., 17.

51 It should be categorically stated that this chapter in no way attempts to judge the "truth claims" of psychoanalysis, religion or politics. Rather, my intention is to try to understand how the devout Jewish and the Freudian psychoanalytic frameworks were used by individuals and groups to help or hinder their psychological and spiritual survival, their ability to "remain human" in the extreme situation.

SOME DIFFERENCES BETWEEN THE PSYCHOANALYTIC INTELLECTUAL
AND THE BELIEVER IN RESPONSE TO THE NAZI ASSAULT[52]

SELF-TRANSCENDENCE IN THE FACE OF
SUFFERING AND DEATH

In his masterpiece, *At the Mind's Limits*, subtitled "Contemplations by a Survivor of Auschwitz and its Realities," Améry writes: "Whoever is, in the broadest sense, a believing person, whether his belief be metaphysical or bound to concrete reality, transcends himself. He is not captive of his individuality; rather he is part of a spiritual continuity that is interrupted nowhere, not even in Auschwitz."[53]

Primo Levi elaborated on this point when he described "the saving force" of the believer's faith:

> Their universe was vaster than ours, more extended in space and time, above all more comprehendable, they had a key and point of leverage, a millennial tomorrow so that there might be a sense to sacrificing themselves, a place in heaven or on earth where justice and compassion had won, or would win in a perhaps remote but

---

52   While I stress the "positive" aspects of the believer's mode of being and the limitations of the intellectual perspective in this chapter, I am aware that the matter is extremely complex. For example, in certain instances maintaining a strong religious conviction could diminish an inmate's chances of personal survival as well as threaten the lives of fellow inmates. Langer tells of a group of Hasidim who declined to work in a brush factory on Yom Kippur, deciding rather to pray. Other inmates "pleaded with them, fearing for their own safety if the Germans discovered that the output was less than expected." The Hasidim however, refused. The SS became aware of the situation and shot the Hasidim, "and began beating and randomly executing some of the" other inmates, Lawrence L. Langer, *Holocaust Testimonies: The Ruins of Memory* (New Haven, CT: Yale University Press, 1987, 70-71). It should also be pointed out that in some instances engaging in certain intellectual activity, such as remembering or discussing a poem, helped an inmate remain human by providing him with a "tiny island of freedom" and "a moment of spiritual transcendence," Tzevetan Todorov, *Facing the Extreme: Moral Life in the Concentration Camps* (New York: Henry Holt and Company), 1996, 93). Moreover, some inmates were able to sustain aspects of their humanity and continue to struggle to survive by virtue of moral convictions that were not lodged in religious or political transcending ideologies, such as devotion to a wife or child they hoped to see again, or "bearing witness" for the sake of future generations.

53   Améry, *At the Mind's Limits*, 14.

certain future: Moscow, or the celestial or terrestrial Jerusalem. Their hunger was different from ours. It was a Divine punishment or expiation, or votive offering, or the fruit of capitalist putrefaction. Sorrow, in them or around them, was decipherable and therefore did not overflow into despair.[54]

As I will elaborate shortly, for the devout Jew his self-transcending belief had a very specific form, as it was lodged in a passionately felt, direct relation to the Cosmic Other, to God.[55] His God evoked devotion and worship, and perhaps most importantly, He commanded ethical conduct—responsibility for the Other—as prescribed in sacred texts. Moreover, the devout Jew's suffering was to be understood and responded to in terms of his love and awe of God, who was characterized by inexhaustible mystery and sacredness, radical alterity, compassion and justice. This point was expressed by the Hassidic Rabbi Levi Yitzhak of Berditchev, whose words convey this animating feature of the devout Jew's capacity to make his suffering sufferable via his heartfelt, dialogic relation to the Eternal One: "Master of the universe. I do not know what questions to ask. I do not expect You to reveal Your secrets to me. All I ask is that You show me one thing—what this moment means to me and what You demand of me. I do not ask why I suffer. I ask only this: Do I suffer for Your sake?[56]

For the devout Jew, at the deepest level of the self, God was an intimate presence, an exemplary Other, a partner in the never-to-be finished work of creation and *tikkun olam* (repairing the world). Though at times the Cosmic Other was experienced as enigmatic and ambiguous, "a relation without relation,"[57] the Holy and Blessed One participated in the pain and suffering of His creatures, of Israel and of indi-

---

54 Levi, *The Drowned and the Saved*, 146.

55 Levinas does not like the terms God, "the absolutely Other," "the other par excellence," or other such expressions. Rather, he prefers "to-God." This is because it moves against "thematic rationality and the ontology of power" (Hutchens, *Levinas*, 118). I use the term Cosmic Other simply to evoke the relational and personal aspect of the devout Jew's experience of God (Levinas, *Entre-Nous*, 174-175).

56 *Passover Haggadah: The Feast of Freedom*, ed. Rachel Anne Rabinowicz, 2nd edition (Rabbinical Assembly, 1982), 94.

57 Levinas, *Totality and Infinity*, 80. "Relation without relation" roughly means that there is no parity, no equality of status or position, nor "common ground," conceptual or otherwise, between God and man.

vidual Jews. Levinas writes that "In our suffering God suffers with us. Doesn't the Psalmist say (Psalms 91:15): 'I am with him in distress?' It is God who suffers most in human suffering. The I who suffers prays for the suffering of God, who suffers by the sin of man and the painful expiation for sin."[58] This partnership in suffering in which God is concerned and implicated in the fate of His people, is injured by their pain and suffering, and liberated by their redemption, in part, constituted the divine pathos from which the devout Jew experienced, understood and to some extent, transcended his particular suffering.[59]

Does the psychoanalytic intellectual have a similar ability to transcend the extreme situation by virtue of his psychoanalytic thinking and experience? First, it should be noted that Freudian psychoanalysis is anti-ideological; it sees itself as not having its own distinct *Weltanschauung*. As Alan Bass has indicated, for Freud, to seek out or create a *Weltanschauung* is anti-psychoanalytic,[60] it goes against the basic thrust of psychoanalysis in that for Bass, following Freud, it cannot be systematic. Philosophers, theologians, and psychotics, according to Freud, strive towards systematicity, but psychoanalysis should not, in part because it fundamentally concerns itself with "unconscious energic processes" that by definition are contradictory, paradoxical, and ambiguous, and therefore must challenge our habitual conscious patterns of organizing data. For Bass, like Freud, to seek out or create a *Weltanschauung* is to succumb to an "illusory wish fulfillment."[61] Levinas's belief that thematization and conceptualization suppress and possess the other, and his extensive use of ellipsis, paradox, contradic-

---

58   Levinas, *Alterity and Transcendence*, 182.

59   Arnold Jacob Wolf, "Heschel's 'Torah from Heaven.'" *Judaism*, 53, 3-4 (Summer/Fall 2004): 303-304.

60   This is of course a debatable claim, as many psychologists view psychoanalysis as lodged in a so-called "scientific" worldview, one with strong positivistic and materialistic elements. The current wave of interest in neuroscience and psychoanalysis, "neuropsychoanalysis," as Mark Solms calls it, also suggests that psychoanalysis sees itself, or strives to be, a scientific account of human experience.

61   Alan Bass, "Sigmund Freud: The Question of a Weltanschaung," in Marcus and Rosenberg, *Psychoanalytic Versions of the Human Condition*, 415-446. My summary of Bass is taken from my introduction to his essay, p. 412.

tion and circular reasoning in his writings, are in harmony with the anti-systematicity of psychoanalysis.

The implications of such a psychoanalytic viewpoint could be catastrophic for the camp inmate, for it rejects the very notion of the desirability of an "all-embracing," coherent "fabric of meaning[s]" "that comprehends him and all of his experiences" and by its very nature, involves "a transcendence of individuality."[62] Without an ideologically informed overarching universe of meaning, including a consistent, though flexibly applied set of emotionally infused transcending beliefs that are meant to guide a person, and that are believed by the individual to be absolute, psychoanalytic inmates were seriously limited in their ability to make sense of and endure their nightmarish situation. Améry remarks that for the believer, "the grip of the horror reality was weaker where from the start reality had been placed in the framework of an unalterable idea. Hunger was not hunger as such, but the necessary consequence of atheism or capitalist decay. A beating or death in the gas chamber was the renewed sufferings of the Lord or a natural political martyrdom."[63]

In contrast, psychoanalysts have no transcending concepts that can transport them to a different dimension of the spirit, or that can protect them from the extreme situation by radically altering the meaning of their suffering. To the psychoanalyst, religion and politics, at least the type that we are referring to as they relate to the camp inmates, are an "admirable and redeeming illusion, but an illusion nonetheless." As Charles Hanly points out, "Psychoanalysis finds itself at odds with ideologies because they are governed by visionary ideas and values that are exempted from critical investigation."[64]

While psychoanalysis has certain ideological aspects, such as its orthodoxies and dogmatic creeds, Hanly's view more closely approaches the core of psychoanalysis. Thus, psychoanalysts could not generate their own enduring and enabling "illusions" by drawing from the psychoanalytic framework. Not even the immortal unconscious could redeem them, for they were too tied to "reality" as they construed it. This particular way of constructing reality is one that is, according to

---

62 Peter Berger, *The Sacred Canopy* (Garden City, NJ: Doubleday, 1967), 54.

63 Améry, *At the Mind's Limits*, 13.

64 Ibid.

Améry, decidedly different from that of the believer. In the camps, he implies, this may have made the difference between sustaining oneself as a person and surrendering to Nazi barbarism. Says Améry,

> He [the believer] is both estranged from reality and closer to it than the unbelieving comrade. Further from reality because in his Finalistic attitude he ignores the given contents of material phenomenon and fixes his sight on a nearer or more distant future; but he is also closer to reality because for just this reason he does not allow himself to be overwhelmed by the conditions around him and thus can strongly influence them. For the unbelieving person, reality, under adverse circumstances, is a force to which he submits; under favorable ones it is material for analysis. For the believer, reality is clay that molds, a problem that he solves.[65]

As Geertz points out in another context,[66] in contrast to the believer the psychoanalytic intellectual "questions the realities of everyday life out of an institutionalized skepticism which dissolves the world's givenness into a swirl of probabilistic hypotheses." However, says Geertz, the religious perspective questions everyday reality in terms of a "wider, non-hypothetical" truth. "Detachment" and "analysis," the watchwords of the psychoanalytic intellectual, are replaced by "commitment" and "encounter," if you will, subjectivity. It is "the imbuing of a certain specific complex of symbols—of the metaphysic they formulate and the style of life they recommend—with a persuasive authority which, from an analytic point of view, is the essence of religious action." In the camps, this meant that religious inmates had the symbolic capacity to transform their reality, at least to some extent, and episodically, into something other than the dehumanizing reality. Through their faith, including the rituals that they participated in, frequently in a communal context, they had the ability to move beyond the realties of everyday life to more transcendent realities that, says Geertz, corrected and completed the painful realities of the camp.

In contrast, psychoanalytic intellectuals were lodged in a more common sense mode of experiencing the world. This, says Geertz, involves "a simple acceptance of the world, its objects, and its processes as being just what they seem to be," even after they are coated with a psycho-

---

65 Améry, *At the Mind's Limits*, 14.

66 All of the Geertz quotes in this paragraph are from "Religion as a Cultural System," 112.

analytic gloss. Such a view, with its "pragmatic motive," i.e., "the wish to act upon the world so as to bend it to one's practical purposes, to master it, or when that proves impossible, to adjust to it," does not allow psychoanalytic intellectuals to fuse together "the world as lived and the world as imagined" into one world under "a single set of symbolic forms"[67] (as a religious person does by means of religious ritual), thus transforming their consciousness into another mode of existence. Unlike religious inmates, the psychoanalytic intellectuals did not have the symbolic capacity to place the proximate acts in ultimate meaning-giving, life-affirming contexts and, in so doing, decisively alter the Nazi landscape. Devout Jews viewed Nazi brutality against the background of The Fall and other Jewish calamities which, though it does not adequately explain the brutality, at least places it in a moral, cognitive and affective context. The devout Jew's beliefs tended to render their experience intelligible and within cognitive understanding.

For example, Améry notes that in the camps the believers and non-believers had very little or nothing to do with one other. Religious and political comrades, says Améry, "paid no attention to us, be it in tolerance, in the willingness to help, or in anger. You must realize one thing, a practicing Jew once told me, that here your intelligence and your education are worthless. But I have the certainty that our God will avenge us." The point is that such inmates, mainly through their meaning-giving relationship with the Cosmic Other, "transcended themselves and projected themselves into the future. They were no windowless monads; they stood open, wide open onto a world that was not the world of Auschwitz."[68] Psychoanalytic intellectuals could not derive a similar conceptual capacity from their psychoanalytic thinking and experience.

For the Freudian, and most other psychoanalysts lodged in different versions of psychoanalysis, life has a tragic dimension. Hostility, aggression, and self-destructiveness are inevitable, as is death. In fact, Freud indicates in his formulation of the death instinct that the purpose of life is death. For Freud, death is absolute. Since the individual knows for sure that he or she is going to die one day, the crucial question becomes how one relates to the inevitability of one's death. Does one face up to it or does one seek cover inside a form from this exis-

---

67 Ibid., 111.
68 Améry, *At the Mind's Limits*, 14.

tential fact? How that is to be accomplished is difficult to imagine, but I think that for the skeptical psychoanalytic intellectual, accepting the inevitability of one's death entails recognizing that this world is all we have and that our only reasonable option is to make the best use of the time we do have. This results from viewing the world as a wall rather than a gate, which is the view of the devout Jew.

The approach has its obvious limitations within the context of the concentration camp in that it does not allow psychoanalytic intellectual inmates to "lose themselves" in a meaning-giving, transcending symbolic world. Thus, their terror can be overwhelming. The situation was quite different for the devout Jew. For example, a religious Jew could draw comfort from the doctrine of *Kiddush Hashem*, the sanctification of the Divine Name, often through martyrdom. This notion and behavioral instruction acted as a guide for Jewish responses to crisis and catastrophe.[69] In the camps, the belief that one's death in some way sanctified God served to diminish the inmate's death panic by giving an other-worldly meaning and focus to his or her death. The belief that he would be rewarded in the world-to-come for his sacrifice, and that there would be some kind of Divine retribution against their enemies, reassured and comforted the devout Jew in the face of his death. Such religious Jews did not feel that they were merely passive victims in the face of Nazi assault. They did not wish to die, but their capacity to interpret their death as a holy act of *Kiddush Hashem*, as the ultimate expression of their responsibility to their beloved God, indicates choice and action. They were able to will meaning into their suffering and death. By anchoring their identity in a cosmic reality, religious inmates were, to some extent, protected from the terror associated with anticipating and facing death. In contrast to psychoanalytic intellectuals, devout Jews and other religious inmates were better fortified against many of the dehumanizing Nazi realities.

MAINTAINING A MODICUM OF DIGNITY AND SELF-RESPECT AMIDST THE NAZI ASSAULT

As Primo Levi points out, for a number of reasons the intellectual was more likely to feel tortured by a sharp sense of "humiliation" and

---

69   Shimon Huberband, Jeffrey S. Gurock and Robert S. Hirt, *Kiddush Hashem: Jewish Religious and Cultural Life in Poland During the Holocaust* (Hoboken, NJ: KTAV Publishing House, 1987).

"destitution" in both death and concentration camps.[70] Bettelheim indicates that without "a consistent philosophy, either moral, political, or social," non-believing inmates had no way to protect their integrity or to derive strength to stand up, even if only within themselves, against Nazism. Such inmates had few or "no resources to fall back on" when they faced the shock of incarceration. Their self-esteem and self-concept was mainly based on the "status and respect" that emanated from their professional position, their place as "head of a family," or similar outside factors.[71] Fromm also noted that without the "props" on which their self-esteem and self-identity rested, these non-religious, non-political middle-class inmates collapsed "morally like a deflatable balloon."[72]

The radical loss of self-respect played havoc with prisoners in relation both to their former social status and to their sense of personal worth. It should be noted that social status and a sense of personal worth that is confirmed by the social world are not unimportant to most people, including believers. However, to a deeply religious person such as the Orthodox Jew, the social world as described above was frequently less significant. As Berkovitz says with regard to devout Eastern European Jews, "Ultimately, what really matters is what kind of Jew one is, that alone is the source of one's self-respect."[73] To the extent that the devout Jew lived a life of heartfelt and exacting responsibility—to God and tradition, the Jewish people, and to his fellow human beings—he viewed himself as worthwhile, dignified and deserving of God's blessings in this world or the world to come.

However, without their social status, psychoanalytic intellectuals were unable to restore a connection with their past, and were thereby unable to rescue it "from oblivion."[74] In contrast, deeply religious or avidly political inmates' reliance on the outside world was less pronounced. They were more rooted inside themselves, in a realm of the spirit that was less susceptible to the influence of their unsure destiny

---

70   Levi, *The Drowned and the Saved*, 132.

71   Bettelheim, *The Informed Heart*,120-121

72   Erich Fromm, *The Anatomy of Human Destructiveness* (Greenwich, CT: Fawcett Crest Books, 1973), 86.

73   Eliezer Berkovitz, *With God in Hell* (New York: Sanhedrin Press, 1979), 55.

74   Levi, *The Drowned and the Saved*, 139.

in an outside reality.[75] They were better able to sustain themselves as persons because, in their view, they did not fashion their identity primarily from the values and standards of the Christian, capitalist Western society that was consuming them.[76] However, the world to which psychoanalytic intellectuals belonged plunged into moral and spiritual bankruptcy, and because their identity was so enmeshed in that world, they were left bereft of self-esteem and self-respect.

THE ROLE OF GROUP MEMBERSHIP

Those inmates who were part of a community or group in the camp were also more likely to survive physically, sustain themselves psychologically, and "remain human." The community was a crucial source of emotional sustenance, morale building, and practical help to its members. Such social support also allowed the inmate to sustain his counter-narrative to the dehumanizing Nazi reality. Devout Jews, Jehovah's Witnesses and Marxists were all able to recreate, usually in a highly modified form, their former communities. In the camps, these inmates stayed together and assisted each other. In the case of devout Jews, they participated in communal religious rituals such as secretly meeting to pray together, observing the Sabbath and the holidays, lighting Hanukah candles, keeping kosher, studying Torah, baking matzahs, and "conducting" Passover Seders.[77] Some Hasidim in Bergen-Belsen

---

75   Berkovitz, *With God in Hell*, 54.

76   Ibid.

77   Daniel Landes, "Spiritual Responses in the Camps," in *Genocide: Critical Issues of the Holocaust*, eds. Alex Grobman and Daniel Landes (Chappaqua, NY: Russell Books, 1983), 261-278. As Todorov points out, group membership, while almost always a helpful resource, was a morally ambiguous issue. For example, it could mean that a group member automatically helps all of the members of his group and does not concern himself with the needs of those who do not belong. The Communists, for example, fashioned insular groups "from which all those who did not share their convictions were excluded." Moreover, unlike religious believers, an enemy of the Communists, say a kapo or Nazi informer, would in some instances be killed by a group member. The Jehovah's Witnesses were the most tightly knit, their love for Jehovah being so passionate that they refused all accommodation and compromise with the Nazis. However, according to Todorov, none of their fellow prisoners benefited from that love. He quotes Ravensbruck survivor Margarete Buber-Neumann, "If they took any risks at all, it was only in the service of Jehovah—and never of their fellow pris-

even made a sukkah (a hut in which observant Jews reside during the seven-day festival of Sukkot, commemorating God's providence over the Israelites in the desert). Straw from a torn and dirty mattress acted as a make-shift roof.[78]

For the devout Jew, the community was considered to have intrinsic spiritual value and meaning, it was a kind of holy Other. The preservation of "mitzvah-based communities"[79] was a way of maintaining and expressing the Jew's deeply internalized values, which gave individual Jews the feeling that their pre-Holocaust sense of self was not completely destroyed. This aided the inmates' survival as it tended to help them reconstitute their ontological security, thereby defending themselves against the Nazi attempts at dehumanization and depersonalization. As Auschwitz survivor/analyst Anna Ornstein points out,[80] sustaining deeply internalized values within the camps indicated that the nuclear self more-or-less maintained its continuity in space and time regardless of the radical changes in one's body and disruptions in one's physical environment. Furthermore, she says that in the camps, "the creation of small groups provided an opportunity to experience and express aspects of the nuclear self, specifically related to the pole of ideals, and it provided the all-important empathic selfobject[81] matrix that reinforced a modicum of self-esteem."

For psychoanalytic intellectuals, however, the likelihood of their establishing a strong group membership was diminished not only because of practical considerations, such as a paucity of psychoanalytically-oriented members, but also in part because their way of understanding their relationship to the community was influenced by their grim individualistic assumptions. For example, as Greenberg and Mitchell point out,

---

oners" (Todorov, *Facing the Extreme*, 57-58, 83).

78   Yaffa Eliach, "Jewish Tradition in the Life of the Concentration Camp Inmate," in *The Nazi Concentration Camps: Proceedings of the Fourth Yad Vashem International Historical Conference* (Jerusalem: Yad Vashem, 1980), 201.

79   Landes, "Spiritual Responses in the Camps," 265.

80   Anna Ornstein, "Survival and Recovery." *Psychoanalytic Inquiry*, 5, 1, (1985): 115.

81   A selfobject refers to the person's experience of someone else as part of the self or as essential to satisfy a need of the self such as for affirmation and idealization.

The unit of study of (Freudian) psychoanalysis is the individual, viewed as a discrete entity. Man is not, in Aristotle's terms, a "political animal"; he does not require social organization to allow him to realize his true human potential. Society is imposed on an already complete individual for his protection, but at the cost of renunciation of many of his of his most important goals. It is thus possible and even necessary to speak of a person divorced from his interpersonal context.[82]

The pre-incarceration "mind-set" of the psychoanalytic inmate was not geared to seeing other people, in the communal context, as a resource. Rather the Freudian version of the person hypothesizes an atomistic, autonomous, self-regarding individual more or less devoid of an intrinsic social or communal existence. Moreover, Freud portrays human society as fundamentally unstable, trying to control and fend off forces antagonistic, if not subverting to its very existence. For Freud, the battle between primordial human instinct and civilization is inevitable. Aggressiveness is a deep and abiding feature of human nature. Such a view neither facilitates reaching out to others nor fosters community. While relational theories of psychoanalysis have to some extent revised the above-described cynical and gloomy Freudian version of the human condition, they still mainly understand subjectivity, as Freud did, as initially for itself, not as Levinas believes, for the Other.

Finally, while psychoanalysis provides an intellectual orientation and a camaraderie with other analysts, it does not generate the same kind of communal loyalty and devotion that religion or a fundamentalist political ideology does. A psychoanalytic worldview does not confer upon the individual a spiritual membership in a community that, theoretically at least, has existed for thousands of years and is

---

82   Jay R. Greenberg and Stephen A. Mitchell, *Object Relations in Psychoanalytic Theory* (Cambridge: Harvard University Press, 1983), 44. While relational versions of psychoanalysis have tried to correct this Freudian-based deficit, they nonetheless focus mostly on the intersubjective context. They do not adequately consider the role of external reality, including external interpersonal reality, such as obedience to authority and group pressure, in human behavior. As in Freudian and other versions of psychoanalysis, relational psychoanalysis lacks a comprehensive and dynamic psychology of "everyday" situational behavior (Paul Marcus, "Psychoanalysis and Social Psychology." *Journal of The American Academy of Psychoanalysis*, 14, 1 (1986): 115-123).

inspired by thought of contact with the Eternal. Such membership, for the devout Jew and all such religious believers, is mainly brought about through living a life of selflessness, compassion and justice, that is, a life of responsibility for and to the Other, a holy life.

SUMMARY: WHY DID RELIGIOUS BELIEVERS FARE BETTER THAN THE PSYCHOANALYTIC INTELLECTUALS IN SUSTAINING THEMSELVES AS PERSONS IN THE CAMPS?

Unlike the psychoanalytic intellectuals, the believers, in particular the devout Jews, had a symbolically mediated relation between themselves and the extreme situation that gave a specific meaning to their environment in the camps, one that was "symbolic of a transcendent" truth,[83] that gave them a more helpful general orientation through which to view the horror they were experiencing. This self-sustaining transcendent truth was rooted in a deep-seated sense of responsibility for the Other, a truth that that to some extent, made the devout Jew steadfast and immovable, maybe even serene, relatively speaking. As Geertz points out in a different context, for the devout Jew the extreme situation of the camps had a greater degree of "interpretability."[84]

In contrast, psychoanalytic intellectuals felt utterly overwhelmed by a situation that was "at the limits of their analytic capacities, at the limits of their powers endurance, and at the limits of their moral insight."[85] Geertz further says, if situations of "bafflement, suffering, and a sense of intractable ethical paradox" become intense enough or are endured long enough, they radically challenge people's ability to orient themselves effectively within them. Such situations threaten "to unhinge" one's mind.[86]

Thus, the psychoanalytic intellectual did not have the symbolic resources to make the extreme situation "sufferable." However, devout Jews had religious symbols which provided "a cosmic guarantee not only for their ability to comprehend the world, but also, comprehending it, to give a precision to their feeling, a definition to their emotions" that enabled them to better endure the extreme situation. Intense, relentless brute pain could be endured "by placing it in a meaningful

---

83   Geertz, "Religion as a Cultural System," 98.

84   Ibid., 100

85   Ibid.

86   Ibid.

context, providing a mode of action through which it can be expressed, being expressed understood, and being understood, endured."[87] Psychoanalytic intellectuals did not have such symbolic resources by virtue of their psychoanalytic thinking and experience.

It should be emphasized that the Nazi concentration camp was not only a situation to be suffered; as in intense neurotic conflict, it also threatened the inmates' ability to make moral judgments. The camps challenged the inmate's "resources to provide a workable set of ethical criteria, normative guides to govern" their actions in the face of radical evil.[88] For Levinas, evil is both "inside" suffering and a notion we use to evoke it: "the evil of pain, the deleterious per se, is the outburst and deepest expression, so too speak, of absurdity." That is, "the least one can say about suffering is that, in its own phenomenality, intrinsically, it is useless: 'for nothing.'"[89]

Unlike devout Jews, who could draw on what they viewed as a God-given sacred moral code to give direction to their actions, psychoanalytic intellectuals were faced "with intractable ethical paradox, the disquieting sense that one's moral insight is inadequate to one's moral experience."[90] Such ethical paradox is of course characteristic, to some degree, of how all analysands experience their problems in living, especially in the moral realms of love and other such interhuman contexts. Psychoanalytic intellectuals were faced with the shattering sense that their intense pain lacked not only any manageable "emotional form," but that their life in the camps lacked any "moral coherence."[91] Consequently, they were prone to experience a high degree of "analytic, emotional, and moral impotence" in the face of evil and suffering.[92]

Though devout Jews had their doubts, uncertainties, questions, and made protests to their God for their suffering and the evil they were facing, they did have the faith that, while elusive, there was a moral, intellectual, and emotional explanation for their encounter with evil. The certainty that there was a principle or explanation that could, and maybe would, in this world or the next, eventually make their

---

87   Ibid., 104, 105.

88   Ibid., 106.

89   Levinas, *Entre Nous*, 93.

90   Geertz, "Religion as a Cultural System," 106.

91   Ibid., 108.

92   Ibid.

suffering intelligible and meaningful, meant that they could sustain the moral structures of their world. The believing inmates thus maintained a sense of agency, efficacy, and control over their situation. As Erving Goffman writes, "Strong religious and political convictions have served to insulate the true believer against the assaults of a total institution."[93]

It should be noted, however, that the above findings are not entirely in harmony with Levinas's thinking about suffering. For Levinas, we reside in an era "of gratuitous human suffering, in which evil appears in its diabolical horror," in an era that reflects the "end of theodicy" in both its theological and secular expressions, such as in atheistic progressivism. That is, theodicy is a seductive "temptation," an effort "in making God innocent, or in saving morality in the name of faith, or in making suffering bearable."[94] For Levinas, intellectual integrity demands that any attempts to justify or reconcile ourselves to useless, meaningless, unendurable suffering, as in the Holocaust, Hiroshima or the Gulag, is futile and disingenuous. Theodicy is over, Levinas boldly declares.[95] He is of course right in a certain sense. There are no grand theodicies that account for the Holocaust and similar horrors that are generally regarded as adequate and satisfying, that settle the problem of evil and undeserved suffering. However, Levinas is not right when it comes to the real-life, hellish world of the Kingdom of Night. As I have reported, eye witness accounts and compelling testimonials of concentration camp inmates and survivors, like Améry, Levi and Wiesel, at least on the level of the individual trying to sustain himself as a person, to preserve his autonomy, integration and humanity, challenge Levinas's sweeping conclusion that theodicy and other such self-sustaining, transcendent notions, are over.

MAKING SUFFERING SUFFERABLE:
THE CHALLENGE TO PSYCHOANALYSIS

Helping people to endure and possibly overcome their pain, sorrow and suffering is the heart of all versions of clinical psychoanalysis. By comparing the psychoanalytic intellectual and the believers, mainly

---

93 Erving Goffman, *Asylums* (New York: Anchor Books, 1961), 66.

94 Levinas, *Entre Nous*, 96-97.

95 Richard J. Bernstein, "Evil and the Temptation of Theodicy," in *The Cambridge Companion to Levinas*, 255.

devout Jews, in the extreme situation of concentration camp, I have
tried to demonstrate some of the limitations of psychoanalysis as a
symbolic world, in helping individuals to sustain themselves as persons, maintain their autonomy, integration and humanity, the same
goals all analysands have when they suffer, whether facing suffering
caused by the outside world, such as "when rocks fall from the sky," or
suffering caused by others, or when faced by suffering in their internal
world, such as neurotic misery. The testimonials of camp inmates and
survivors of the concentration camps, of believers and non-believers,
strongly suggest that something crucial is missing in the psychoanalytic
"way of looking at life." Its "particular manner of construing the world,"
its "vision of reality," and the technology of self that it advocates, as
it engages the problems of pain, sorrow and suffering, needs expan-
sion and deepening. As I have insinuated throughout this chapter, a
Levinasian-animated perspective on the challenge of making suffering
sufferable, one that understands suffering as "an ethical relationship"
prior to "anything else,"[96] as demanding an ethical response that is for
the Other, may supply the needed augmentation.

According to Isaiah Berlin, there are two types of intellectuals,
"hedgehogs," who know "one big thing," and "foxes," who know "many
small things."[97] Levinas is more a hedgehog than a fox. The "one big
thing" that he knows about individual suffering is that while the suffering person tries with all of his mind and heart to rid himself of
his suffering, his suffering can best become "sufferable" when it is conceived as for the Other. As we have seen, this Other can be a self-
transcending God/sacred tradition, or an equivalent secular notion,
and of course, a person(s):

> There is a radical difference between *the suffering in the other*, where
> it is unforgivable to *me*, solicits me and calls me, and suffering *in me*,
> my own experience of suffering, whose constitutional or congenital
> uselessness can take on a meaning, the only one of which suffering is
> capable, in becoming a suffering for suffering...of someone else.[98]

Such suffering for the Other, and here Levinas is pushing his point
to the ethical extreme, includes suffering that my suffering causes the

---

96   Robert Kugelmann, "Pain, Exposure, and Responsibility," in Gantt and
     Williams, *Psychology-for-the-Other*, 99.

97   Quoted from Putnam, "Levinas and Judaism," 58.

98   Levinas, *Entre Nous*, 94.

Other. In other words, my suffering is "useless," meaningless, insurmountable and ambiguously evil, a derivative of the "there is," anonymous being, to the extent that it stays for itself to the extent that it remains "a question of perceiving oneself locked within a self-preoccupation, a self-enclosed ego or state of narcissism."[99] Rather, when one construes one's suffering as a problem of responsibility for the Other, it assumes a transcendent meaning, one that goes beyond the "savage malignancy" of, for example, physical pain or "the immanent and savage concreteness of evil."[100] A bad toothache is "useless" suffering. But the suffering one feels for one's dying spouse, and the devoted love and concrete care of her that it evokes, is not.

Put somewhat differently, all pain and suffering undermines the self-encapsulation, self-sufficiency, narcissism and autonomy of the self, especially the conquering, mastery-oriented, "virility of being" we described in the previous chapter. Such undermining of the virile self puts the sufferer in touch with a fundamental feature of pain and suffering, namely that, to some extent, all pain is inherently interhuman, whether it is the drill of the dentist or the loss of a loved one, the sufferer begs for relief from his pain, and this almost always involves wishing for the helping hand of a caring and compassionate other. Levinas aptly makes this point concerning physical pain, though his observation has more general relevance, especially for the psychoanalyst and psychotherapist whose job it is to care for the suffering analysand:

> The caress of a consoler [i.e., the kind and insightful words of the analyst], which softly comes in our pain does not promise the end of suffering, does not announce any compensation, and in its very contact, is not concerned with what is to come with afterwards in *economic* time; it concerns the very instant of physical [and psychological] pain, which is then no longer condemned to itself, is transported "elsewhere" by the movement of the caress, and is freed

---

99 Noreen O'Connor, "Who Suffers?" in *Re-Reading Levinas*, 230. Nietzsche makes a related observation when he writes, "What really arouses indignation against suffering is not suffering as such but the senselessness of suffering" (*On the Genealogy of Morals*. Translated by Walter Kaufmann. New York: Random House, 1957, 7). Viktor E. Frankl, the psychiatrist/survivor has famously created a form of psychotherapy, Logotherapy, around this assumption.

100 Levinas, *Entre Nous*, 93, 100.

from the vice-grip of "oneself," finds "fresh air," a dimension and a future.[101]

By compassionately embracing the other's pain, a form of consolation we gratuitously give, we release the sufferer from his agonizing isolation and solitude,[102] his feeling of being trapped in a maze of grotesque happenings, at least to some extent. Through our caring words and deeds we give the sufferer the beginning of a way out, a measure of relief and hope that, mercifully, there is a light at the end of the tunnel. One way or the other, if not for just a moment, the sufferer feels the liberatory effect of our unconditional giving, serving and solidarity with his pain.

The limitations of the psychoanalytic understanding and "management" of suffering is rooted in its being too influenced by a particular vision of the human condition, one that is lodged in the Western intellectual tradition that Levinas profoundly calls into question. I am mainly thinking of none other than the founder of modern philosophy, René Descartes. It is Descartes' understanding of the human condition, with his narcissistic and self-referential version of subjectivity, personified by his fundamental principle, the "*cogito ergo sum*" ("I think therefore I am"), that psychoanalysis has in general, too uncritically appropriated as its guiding assumption of what constitutes the core of the human condition. *Cogito ergo sum* was Descartes's attempt to demonstrate the existence of the self in any act of thinking or doubting as the singular "certainty," a path-breaking view that made Descartes the extraordinarily significant philosopher he became. Rather, as Levinas believes, after Auschwitz, a radically new self-world relation needs to augment, if not override Descartes influential view. It can be aptly suggested in one sentence uttered by Elie Wiesel: "I suffer, therefore you are." That is, "Levinas's I does not 'think'; it suffers; it is obsessed; it is nothing but 'for the other.'"[103] This is the view of subjectivity as responsibility for the Other, especially the willingness to suffer for the other. Such subjectivity was the subjectivity that mainly governed the actions of the believers in the camps. In ordinary life, such subjectiv-

---

101 Levinas, *Existence Without Existents*, 93.

102 Robert Kugelman, "Pain, Exposure, and Responsibility," in Gantt and Williams, *The Psychology-for-the-Other*, 99.

103 Paul Davies, "Sincerity and the end of theodicy: three remarks on Levinas and Kant," in *The Cambridge Companion to Levinas*, 171.

ity is most clearly perceived in those whose lives are characterized by a deep and wide altruism and loving kindness. Saints and *tzadikkim* (righteous people) personify such subjectivity at its very best. From the Holocaust, the names of Father Kolbe, Dr. Janusz Korczak and Miep Giese come to mind,[104] as do those of Rabbis Leo Baeck, Kalonymus Kalman Shapira and Ephraim Oshry.[105] Such people, says Levinas in another context, give us consolation, they exemplify "the invincible but unarmed goodness of the just and the saints."[106] It behooves psychoanalysis to study further the nature of this extraordinary, largely non-narcissistic subjectivity. More generally, psychoanalysis can be enhanced as a theory and clinical practice by appropriating insights into the human condition, including how to make suffering

---

104 Bettelheim mentions these "righteous ones" who represent the "hope for humanity: Father Kolbe, a Polish priest, who, while in Auschwitz, volunteered to die in place of a Polish political prisoner, allowing him to survive and return to his wife and children (the priest had no such family). He was starved to death by the Nazis; Janusz Korczak steadfastly refused many offers to be saved from extermination in the death camps in order to stay with the orphaned children under his care, until they were all murdered by the Nazis; Miep Giese, at great personal risk, provided Anne Frank and her family, and others who hid out with them, with the essential food and supplies that kept them alive, and with the human companionship they required to endure their terrible isolation. See my discussion and references in *Autonomy in the Extreme Situation: Bruno Bettelheim, the Nazi Concentration Camps and the Mass Society*, 192-195.

105 Rabbi Baeck's moral courage and saintliness while serving his community in Berlin and in the Theresienstadt concentration camp, including his refusal to abandon the Jewish community and save himself, are legendary. See Albert H. Friedlander, *Leo Baeck: Teacher of Theresienstadt* (New York: Holt, Rinehart, & Winston, 1968); Rabbi Shapira, the Rebbe of the Warsaw Ghetto, succored his flock during the Destruction through unwavering faith and deeds of kindness and personal sacrifice. See Nehemia Polen, *The Holy Fire, The Teachings of Rabbi Kalonymus Kalman Shapira, the Rebbe of the Warsaw Ghetto*, Northvale, NJ: Jason Aronson, 1994); Rabbi Ephraim Oshry, a survivor of the Kovno ghetto, through his relentless dedication to the Torah and to observing Jewish law as recorded in his extraordinary *Halachic Responsa* (Jewish legal decisions), written mainly within the ghetto, and his unyielding service to his fellow Jews, has been lauded by both religious and secular writers, *Responsa from the Holocaust*, trans. Y. Leiman (New York: Judaica Press, 1983).

106 *In the Time of the Nations*, 90.

sufferable, through its respectful study of the instructive, illuminating and uplifting forms of life of the believers.

Thus, following Levinas, my claim is that the "one big thing" that psychoanalysis has not adequately appropriated into its thinking about pain, sorrow and suffering is the "usefulness" of helping the analysand give meaning to his suffering by developing an ethical response to it, one that is for the Other. Whether it is my, or the other's suffering, or the suffering that my suffering causes the other, the way to make such suffering "sufferable," at least in general terms, is to perceive it as an ethical problem requiring an other-directed, other-regarding response. Such an ethical response is an asymmetrical and non-reciprocal responsibility to and for the other, whether another person, or one's God or its secular equivalent, or both. For Levinas, this is the surest way of becoming most fully human and, in doing so, being able to come out of the whirlwind of pain and suffering, as did Job, with self-transforming moral insight. This moral insight is quite simply an infinite compassion for the other person, and for all life, but also, I would add, for oneself.[107]

CLINICAL VIGNETTE

John's internal world was often like an emotional rollercoaster. In one session he would come in incredibly energized, full of interesting associations and stories and looking to the future with hope and optimism. A day or two later, he would come in down in the dumps, saying little, reverting to his familiar pessimistic soliloquy about how futile life was. In these sessions, the zestfulness and playfulness of the previous day were overwhelmed by his bleak cynicism and sarcasm. John would snap at me if I said what he took to be the wrong thing, or if he perceived that I was not listening attentively enough. Most of the time, however, John's depressive outlook soon changed to a more upbeat one, at least until the next disappointment, frustration or stress in his everyday life. John and I worked hard to help him "manage" his work and love life more reasonably, though by his own admission, he was something of a "drama queen,"—the last of the great male hysterics I sometimes thought to myself.

---

107 As O'Connor points out, it is only through the suffering that I feel for the suffering of the analysand, that I can be an effective psychotherapist ("Who Suffers?" 232-233).

However, there was a three-year period in John's analysis where his ups and downs became much more extreme and worrying. Soon, it became obvious to John and me that he had become clinically depressed. His agitated depression became so unmanageable that he needed medication, something that he was not that willing to take. This horrible experience of clinical depression was a form of suffering that challenged John's internal resources, including a near-suicide attempt. Eventually, through his analysis and the crucial help of medication, but also much exercise and meditation and a supportive wife and extended family, John began to return to the "world of the living," as he called it.

In a sense John's depression came out of nowhere, that is, it seemed to have had a strong biological component to its emergence. There were, however, a number of psychosocial stressors that were also precipitating factors.

John's brother-in-law, also a doctor, with whom he worked in the same office, developed cancer, which he ultimately survived after going through surgery, chemotherapy and radiation. However, his brother-in-law's and his brother-in-law's family's suffering, together with his own fear of losing him, caused him great distress. That a perfectly healthy young man could get so sick reminded him of his own physical vulnerability, as well as that of his wife and children and other dear ones. John's traumatic medical history made him especially reactive to illness and partly accounted for his pervasive anxiety that the world could suddenly turn very nasty and come crashing down on him.

The second likely precipitating factor of John's depression occurred a month or two after his brother-in-law's cancer diagnosis. John had a peanut allergy and inadvertently ate a food with a trace of peanut, triggering an allergic emergency, requiring him to use his "Epi Pen," and call "911." John spent about six hours in the emergency room until the allergic reaction subsided. The experience especially frightened him because he was alone at home when it occurred, and even though he was a doctor, he felt completely out of control, fearful, including being afraid of dying as he came close to losing consciousness before the EMT arrived and took care of him.

The third factor contributing to John's depression was the fact that he had possibly missed a key symptom in a young woman patient eight months earlier. She subsequently discovered on a routine visit to her "OB-GYN" that she had an extremely serious illness requiring radical surgery. John felt that he should have caught the earlier symptom, though his colleagues and I thought he was being unrealistic and unreasonably severe on himself. Nevertheless, John, who always had an over-active super-ego, felt very guilty for what he took to be his mistake. He was also worried about a lawsuit, something that he had been overly stressed out about throughout his career.

It was in this context that John's depression emerged. His normal eating, sleeping, and energy level were seriously disrupted, as were his concentration and motivation to work. His interest in his wife and children, together with his ability to experience pleasure, were greatly reduced. Though John never missed a day of work throughout his depression, nor ever mistreated a patient, two points I kept reminding him of when he hit near rock bottom, he nevertheless felt he was sliding further and further into the abyss. John told me that he felt helpless in his struggle with his own mind and feared that he was going "crazy." He also made it clear that I, too, seemed unable to stop his free fall into the void.

After many months of John's trying to manage his agitation and depression without medication, he finally agreed to see a psychiatrist. As is often the case, John had to mix and match medications before he found the right combination, though there were, as is often the case, unpleasant side effects. All of this mixing and matching of medications took time, while John was in what could be described as an "extreme consciousness," one that alternated between severe agitation and intense despair. When not feeling one of these extremes, he said he felt numb, probably an effect of the anesthetizing medications he was taking.

My conversations with John focused on the reasons for his depression, how he managed it, and his sense of helplessness and pessimism that he would never feel "normal" again.

John's understanding of possible causes for his illness, as he called it, ran the gamut of possibilities. At one end of the continuum, he irrationally thought that his depression was a consequence of his misdeeds and basic badness, a punishment from God. After discussing this absurd hypothesis, he admitted that he was not such a bad person that God would do this to him and that he was looking for someone to blame for his suffering. At other times, John believed that his depression was due to a basic bio-psychological design fault, and there was nothing he could do about it. Though John's depression did seem to have a chemical component to it, he gradually agreed that he would never know for sure, and the crucial issue was how he would respond to his illness, that is, would he give up hope or keep fighting.

Finally, John and I discussed his depression in terms of conventional psychoanalytic themes, such as repressed anger turned in on the self, incomplete mourning of an "internal object," not an actual person in whom he had ambivalently invested and was dependent on, and who, through his hostile wishes he had destroyed, early narcissistic deficits and self-esteem problems, his masochistic need for punishment and other such psychodynamic understanding. All of this, as he informed me, was helpful. John's basically positive transference to me as his "good enough" parental caretaker also helped him to endure his extreme psychic pain. Moreover, John knew I cared deeply about him and that I would do everything that I could to help him get through his ordeal.

The turning point for John in overcoming his depression occurred one night when he was alone in his house and felt extremely anxious. He reached for some Klonopin, an anti-anxiety medication, only to find out that he had run out of pills. John went into a panic, so much so that he actually licked the inside of the pill bottle in a frantic effort to at least get some of the pill residue into his body. At that moment, John said, he became aware of his desperation and the futility of his struggle against his depression. "Fuck it," he told himself. "I've had it." He went upstairs into his closet and reached for the loaded pistol that he kept for home protection. He had decided that it was a hopeless struggle against his intensely painful anxiety and depression. He had been reduced to a pathetic creature, a burden to his family and an altogether useless person. He'd rather "check out" than stay alive. Taking the gun in his hand, he later said that he felt as though he was in a fugue state, as if what was happening during these few moments was not really happening. All that he cared about was to feel no pain, to feel nothing. Deciding to pull the gun's trigger, he heard the front door to his house open; it was his teen-age daughter returning home from an after-school program. She yelled "mommy, daddy, where is everyone." John shouted, "Here I am, upstairs in my room." He put the gun away.

John came in the next day and told me the details of what had happened the night before. I was, needless to say, extremely troubled by the incident. In a certain sense, I had not been aware at that particular time that John felt as bad as he did and was capable of killing himself.

Still, his suicidal gesture and its aftermath were something of a break-through, at least in terms of his rededicating himself to not giving in to his depression and to bear his pain no matter what. Through our discussions John came to view his suicidal gesture as an act of narcis-sistic manipulation and deep hostility, mainly directed toward his wife and children, and symbolically towards his childhood parents, for no good reason that he or I could think of.

Most importantly, it was John's deeply felt conviction that his re-sponsibility for his children and wife was sufficient reason to conquer his terrible illness, rather than to abandon them by killing himself. It was only when he fully embraced the notion that his life was not chiefly about his self-satisfaction, including his peace of mind, but, rather, that his responsibility to his wife and children took priority, that John was able to find the motivation to bear his pain and suffer-ing with greater strength, tolerance, patience and dignity. Eventually, John's depression began to give way and eventually passed.

As John told me, though grateful for his reprieve, he was trauma-tized by his encounter with his illness. That he could be so helpless against his own mind, to the point of wanting to kill himself, was a chilling awareness that he could never lose. John's traumatization was especially manifested by the pervasive background sense of worry and sadness that he lived with. He feared that his depression would return. John reported being deeply frightened when he felt the transient rum-blings of panic and despair that crept into his consciousness from time to time, sometimes when he least expected it. It made him cringe. "The fear never really goes completely away. Oh God, I hope I can remem-ber how much my wife and kids need me so I can find the strength and motivation to fight it, and beat it, the next time."

RELIGION WITHOUT PROMISES

*"You know, they often speak of ethics to describe what I do,
but what interests me when all is said and done is not ethics,
it's the holy, the holiness of the holy."*
Levinas[1]

Levinas, an Orthodox Jew, who spent much of his adult life as the director of a Jewish teachers college, has written many important books and essays about Judaism, the Bible and Talmud, Jewish education, and to a lesser extent, religion in general. Indeed, Derrida has noted that Levinas's "ethics" is so saturated with religious values and concepts that it is impossible to tell them apart.[2] For example, in *Otherwise Than Being*, Levinas describes responding "to and for the other," of being the other's hostage, to the extent of insisting on "justice" and responding to the third party's insistence for "justice"[3] as "religiosity of the self." "Beyond egoism and altruism it is the religiosity of the self."[4] Elsewhere, Levinas actually declares, "I am a religious thinker," that "the Bible is essential to thinking" because "it renders the Greeks [philosophy] necessary."[5] "Philosophy, for me, derives from religion."[6] Many other examples can be given of a religious infusion

---

1 Levinas, in conversation with Derrida, as reported in Derrida's funeral oration for Levinas, *Adieu to Emmanuel Levinas*, 4.

2 Jacques Derrida, *The Gift of Death*, trans. David Will (Chicago, IL; University of Chicago Press, 1995), 84. An earlier version of this chapter has been published in the *Psychoanalytic Review*, 93 (6), 923-952 ("Religion Without Promises: The Philosophy of Emmanuel Levinas and Psychoanalysis").

3 Hutchens, *Levinas*. 116.

4 Levinas, *Otherwise Than Being*, 117.

5 Levinas, *Is It Righteous to Be?* 63-64.

6 Levinas, *Nine Talmudic Readings*, 182. By religion Levinas means: "This bond with the other which is not reducible to the representation of the

in Levinas's philosophical writings. While to some, Derrida's claim is debatable, it seems clear to me that Levinas has put forth a most original philosophy that is powerfully animated by what can be called a religious sensibility, one that is rooted in Jewish monotheism[7] and the prophetic tradition.[8] As Simon Critchley has pointed out, "Levinas's thinking is quite inconceivable without Jewish inspiration."[9]

In other words, Levinas aims to universalize Judaism, to bring "biblical wisdom" to the attention of Gentiles (and Jews) lodged in a "Greek lexicon of intelligibility," as he calls it.[10] Levinas attempts to translate the ethos of the Bible into Greek philosophy, explicating the ethical message of Judaism, with its commitment to the Good, into the language of philosophy, with its commitment to the True. Like philosophy, psychoanalysis, which is rooted in, and steeped in the Greek outlook in many ways,[11] can only be enhanced by its encounter with the ethical and spiritual insights of biblical wisdom. Though Levinas tends to privilege Judaism in certain contexts, his outlook is usually inclusive and universalistic. For example, he believes that there is a unity to the great religions of the world, at least in terms of their enduring spiritual insights. "There is not a single thing in a great spirituality that would be absent from another great spirituality."[12]

---

other, but to his invocation, and in which invocation is not preceded by an understanding, I call religion," *Entre Nous*, 7.

7 Levinas, *Difficult Freedom. Essays on Judaism*, 21-22.

8 Peperzak, *To the Other*, 55.

9 Simon Critchley, "Introduction," in *The Cambridge Companion to Levinas*, 22. Jacob Meskin has also noted that "Levinas's philosophical texts…[can be read] as a profound, modern articulation of Judaism" (Meskin, "The Role of Lucrianic Kabbalah in the Early Philosophy of Emmanuel Levinas." Jeffrye Bloechl, editor, *Levinas Studies. An Annual Review. Volume 2*, Pittsburgh: Duquesne University Press, 2007, 75). As Critchley points out, Levinas did not want to be described as simply a Jewish philosopher. He once said, "I am not a Jewish thinker. I am a thinker" (22).

10 Levinas, *Face to Face with Levinas*, 19.

11 Jonathan Lear, "Philosophy," in *Textbook of Psychoanalysis*, Ethel S. Person, Arnold M. Cooper and Glen O. Gabbard, eds. (Washington, D.C.: American Psychiatric Publisihing, 2005), 513-523.

12 Levinas, *Of God Who Comes to Mind*, 93. As for Levinas privileging Judaism: "To be Jewish is not particularity, it is a modality. Everybody is a little bit Jewish, and if there were men on Mars, one will find Jews among

In this chapter I want to give the reader a sense of how Levinas's insights into biblical wisdom and its associated notions of God, transcendence and holiness can deepen and expand the ethical dimension of psychoanalysis.

GREEK AND BIBLICAL WISDOM

Levinas frequently contrasts the Greek way of thinking and speaking philosophy with a very different approach to meaning and truth, that of biblical or ethical wisdom. This is a very complex subject, but I want to give the reader some sense of what Levinas is getting at in order to show how his ideas about religion and spirituality can be illuminating for psychoanalysis, especially as it strives to be a transformative moral discourse. I believe that Levinas has something to teach both the so-called religious/spiritual and or secular analyst/analysand. He writes that[13]

> the most essential distinguishing feature of the language of Greek philosophy was its equation of the truth with an intelligibility of presence. By this I mean an intelligibility that considers truth to be that which is present or copresent, that which can be gathered or synchronized into a totality that we would call the world or *cosmos*. According to the Greek model, intelligibility is what can be rendered present, what can be represented in some external here and now, exposed and disclosed in pure light. To equate truth thus with presence is to presume that however different the two terms of a relation might appear (e.g., the Divine and the human) or however separated over time (e.g., into past and future), they can ultimately be rendered commensurate and simultaneous, the same, contained in history that totalizes time into a beginning or an end, or both which is presence. The Greek notion of being is essentially this presence.

In contrast to this ontology of presence is "the ethical or biblical" outlook that, says Levinas, "transcends the Greek language of intelligibility," as a subject of justice, care and compassion "for the other

---

them." *Is It Righteous to Be?* 164; [Israel] "is a particularism that conditions universality, a moral category rather than a historical fact to do with Israel..." *Difficult Freedom*, 22; Regarding the uniqueness of Judaism: "The harmony achieved between so much goodness and so much legalism constitutes the original note of Judaism." *Ibid.*, 19.

13 Levinas, *Face To Face with Levinas*, 19.

as other;" as a subject "of love and desire," that takes "us beyond the infinite being of the world as presence." It is the difference between ontological intelligibility and ethical responsibility. Levinas continues,

> It is this ethical perspective that God must be thought, and not in the ontological perspective of our being-there or of some supreme being and creator correlative to the world, as traditional metaphysics often held. God as the God of alterity and transcendence can only be understood in terms of that interhuman dimension which, to be sure, emerges in the phenomenological-ontological perspective of the intelligible world, but which cuts through and perforates the totality of presence and points to the absolutely other.[14]

Levinas is not dismissing Greek thought, rather he is claiming that philosophy can be both ethical and ontological, can be at once biblical and Greek, at least in its inspiration and sensibility.[15] "I think that Europe is the Bible and the Greeks."[16] "Judaism is the brother of the Socratic Message."[17] His task was "to try and identify this dual origin of meaning...in the interhuman relationship."[18] That is, continues Levinas, while "biblical thought" has clearly animated his "ethical reading of the interhuman, Greek thought" has mainly influenced "its philosophi-

---

14 Ibid., 20-21.

15 Levinas notes that the Greeks were, to some extent, capable of being "biblical." Says Levinas, "The idea of Plato," to place "the Good above being," is one such example (*It Is Righteous to Be?* 183).

16 Levinas, *Is It Righteous to Be?* 64. Levinas elsewhere says, "I'm in favor of the Greek heritage. It is not at the beginning, but everything must be able to be 'translated' into Greek" (*Alterity and Transcendence*, 177). As Wyschogrod points out (*Levinas*, 219), Levinas maintained that in a sense, all ideas worth thinking have already been generated in the major classical texts immediately prior to and after the Common Era. In my view greatly exaggerating and leaving out Eastern thought, for example, Levinas says, "Has everything been thought? The answer must be made with some caution. Everything has been thought, at least around the Mediterranean during the few centuries preceding or following our era" (*Nine Talmudic Writings*, 5-6). Interestingly, Levinas wisely makes room for one Englishman; he writes that "It sometimes seems to me that the whole philosophy is only a meditation of Shakespeare" (*Time and the Other*, in *The Levinas Reader*, 41).

17 Levinas, *Difficult Freedom*, 233.

18 Levinas, *Face To Face with Levinas*, 21.

cal expression in language."[19] "Greek is a language of impartial thought, of the universality of pure knowledge."[20] In response to a query about the relationship between his philosophical and his biblical-Talmudic writings, Levinas responded: "The difference is the manner. What is communicated in the Jewish writings by warmth must be communicated in philosophy in light."[21]

The upshot of all this as it pertains to the subject of spirituality/religion is that for Levinas there is a significant difference between Greek spirituality and biblical spirituality:

> Greek spirituality is first of all in knowledge. It is a matter of grasping—in both senses of the term—a being: to comprehend and to apprehend him, to unveil and to dominate him. The Bible 'breathes' differently, bringing the idea of social proximity as an original mode of spirituality, meaning and intelligibility. Certainly the Greeks knew about proximity, but for them the truth of being is in contemplation, knowledge, and theory. To this I oppose the dialogical proximity, fraternal or social, of the Bible, different from coincidence within the truth of representation. Proximity without coincidence, which, for that, is experienced as a truth that has been missed.[22]

To simplify, Levinas is contrasting the Greek and biblical traditions, psychoanalysis being in many ways more Greek than biblical. Psychoanalysis, like the Greek conception of life, tends to be animated by a search for "clarity, conceptualization and explanation" in its quest for knowledge and Truth. The biblical outlook, as embodied in its sacred texts, is more "elliptic, elusive" and enigmatic, as it passionately strives to hear the other and searches for the Good.[23] As Bauman aptly describes the Levinasian moral subject, "the moral self is a self always

---

19 Ibid.

20 Levinas, *Alterity and Transcendence*, 178.

21 Quoted from Smith, *Toward the Outside*, 244.

22 Levinas, *Is It Righteous to Be?* 116-117.

23 Davis, *Levinas*, 118. It is worth nothing that in the Hebrew Bible, while Truth is considered to be one of the fundamental elements of God's Universe (it is His "seal"), Goodness, often called "lovingkindness" (*chesed*), precedes truth (*emet*). Moreover, truth telling must always be spoken "in love," it must be moral. J.H. Hertz, ed. and, trans., commentator, *The Pentateuch and the Haftorahs* (London: Soncino Press, 5720-1960), 365, 497.

haunted by the suspicion that it is not moral enough."[24] Thus, the Greco-Latin tradition and the Judeo-Christian tradition differ in how they conceptualize the I and the other. In the Greco-Latin view, "it is the I who is in the center, and the other who only exists in relation to the I." In the Judeo-Christian view, it is "the other who is at the center" and, while the I may have to embrace "absolute responsibility, it is he," who always "exists in relation with the other, who is central."[25] As Levinas says, "The idea of an effective transcendence in sociality itself, in proximity, rather than ecstasy, will remain foreign to Greek thought."[26]

My claim is that psychoanalysis has had to become considerably more biblical and less Greek in its theory and practice in order to become a more compelling, ethically suffused narrative of the human condition. In a word, it is the difference between the spirituality of Athens and Jerusalem, of Ulysses and Abraham.

ULYSSES VERSUS ABRAHAM

One of Levinas's favorite comparisons is between the figures if Ulysses and Abraham as a way to dramatically contrast Western Greek philosophy, which is essentially a comprehension of Being, with a biblical, ethical, outlook as it strives to engage "the Other as Other,"[27] According to Levinas, the history of philosophy and, I would add, to a large extent, the history of psychoanalysis, has been similar to the narrative of Ulysses than to the biblical narrative of Abraham.

Throughout Ulysses' epic adventures he longs to return home to Ithaca where his heroic odyssey originated. He fantasizes returning to Penelope and celebrating his reunion with her and his fellow citizens and forgetting the time of his long separation from his family, friends and country.

---

24 Zygmunt Bauman, *Postmodern Ethics* (Oxford: Blackwell Publishing, Inc., 1993), 80.

25 M. Fresco, in Levinas, *Of God Who Comes to Mind*, 84.

26 Levinas, *Alterity and Transcendence*, 8-9. Levinas further notes, that "sociality, for me, is the best of the human" (103).

27 *En découvrant l'existence avec Husserl et Heidegger* (Paris: Librairie Philosophique J. Vrin, 1974, first edition 1949, with editions in1967), 188, 191, as quoted in Davis, *Levinas*, 33; "On the Trail of the Other," *Philosophy Today* (Spring 1996): 34-48; Levinas, *Otherwise Than Being*, 79-81.

In contrast, there is Abraham. He is uprooted from his country and never looks back, having no hope of returning home. He also knows that leaving involves his descendents, as he does not allow his servants to bring his son back to Ur, even to search for a wife. Abraham is irrevocably uprooted from his homeland.

For Levinas, the history of philosophy is more like the story of Ulysses than of Abraham because, like Ulysses, who only searches for what he has left behind, philosophy has always striven to return to the recognizable, familiar ground of "Being, Truth" and "the Same."[28] In other words, there is a "circular odyssey" to Ulysses' story, just as there is to most Greek and modern philosophies,[29] including most versions of psychoanalysis. In contrast, Abraham bravely and resolutely goes into the unknown, toward a largely unidentified somewhere-else. "Not all those who wander are lost," said J.R Tolkien. Levinas wants to take philosophy in a radically different direction, to make it vulnerable and receptive to an encounter with what has always been ignored, marginalized, suppressed and concealed, "the problem of the Other," that is, thinking "the Other as Other."[30] For Levinas, "the other is what I myself am not."[31] Alterity and heteronomy are thus his preferred terms, rather than sameness and autonomy. The former must never be reduced to the latter as philosophy and psychoanalysis have tended to do. Like other postmodern critics of Western philosophy, Levinas is trying to undermine philosophy's totalizing project, its thematic rationality, that wipes out differences.

The metaphors of Ulysses' and especially Abraham's journeys, have direct bearing on notions that are central to psychoanalytic theory and technique, such as the problems of selfhood, integrity, and ethical subjectivity. It is the Abrahamite self, as it is uprooted and moves into the strange and foreign, that serves as a basis for the development of what Levinas calls in another context, "the authentic spiritual life,"[32] referring to a spirituality that does not, as in the Greek outlook, begin in pure knowledge, but rather in the order of being-for-the-Other.

---

28 Davis, *Levinas*, 33.

29 Peperzak, *To the Other*, 44.

30 Davis, *Levinas*, 33.

31 Levinas, *Time and the Other*, 83.

32 Emmanuel Levinas, *En découvrant l'existence avec Husserl et Heidegger*, from Davis, *Levinas*, 12.

"Spirituality," says Levinas, "is an overwhelming of…being…into proximity, which does not turn into knowing."[33] Elsewhere, he explains, "The spiritual is no longer reduced to an event of pure 'knowledge' but would be the transcendence of the relation with someone, with an other: love, friendship, sympathy."[34] "Transcendence," in this context, says Levinas, "is not a vision of the Other, but a primordial donation… the first ethical gesture."[35]

The story of the odyssey of a hero, Ulysses, is quite different from the story of Abraham, the just and righteous, as he is referred to in Jewish tradition. Says Peperzak, "the attitude of the good person is not the nostalgia of a return to an existence one has always lived"[36] as with the Greek hero Ulysses. Rather, he says, it is the estrangement of the uprooted, the engagement with the unfamiliar and foreign, both externally and internally, that brings about one's individuation, integrity and humanity. For Levinas, the self or, I would say, one's attitude towards one's self, should not be like Ulysses'. Hutchens states that this self mistakenly

> travels where it will in order to return to itself, constructing delusions as it goes, ignoring alternative routes hitherto unexplored. The quotidian farce of always reflecting upon oneself according to the same criteria, or achieving a sort of selfhood always understood before the achievement of itself, in effect, forbids openness to the spontaneous, elusive, or radically foreign elements in one's own being.[37]

The point is that one is most profoundly transformed, especially ethically, through encountering absolute otherness in oneself, while never returning to the precise "point of departure,"[38] to the realm of the same. To think otherwise, to live otherwise, is to be trapped in an endless thicket that obstructs the possibility of any type of authentic selfhood or ethical subjectivity. Remember, unlike other thinkers who speak about authenticity, like Heidegger who urges us to a genuine hu-

---

33 Levinas, *Totality and Infinity*, 97.

34 Levinas, *Is It Righteous to Be?* 201.

35 Levinas, *Totality and Infinity*, 174.

36 Peperzak, *To the Other*, 67.

37 Hutchens, *Levinas*, 43.

38 Peperzak, *To the Other*, 44.

man existence, "to take hold of ourselves," or Sartre, with his emphasis on responsibility for what we do and what we are, authenticity for Levinas consists in the "moral self becoming increasingly aware of its burden of guilt,"[39] of its not working hard enough to fulfill its infinite obligations to compassionately give and serve the Other.[40] The Other, the moral life, says Levinas, is itself "persecution."[41]

In the psychoanalytic context, encountering the absolute otherness in oneself means that, like Abraham, who was forbidden to believe that he could "find himself by cultivating a nostalgia for his past," the analysand must avoid staying lodged in the retrospective consciousness of the familiar and taken for granted past, the perspective on his life often dominated by his child-based self-understandings. Rather, as Chalier further points out, we must be like Abraham, who realizes his integrity and humanity, "as a man called to be a blessing to all families on earth, only on condition that he loses himself."[42] Only on condition that Abraham relinquishes all, or almost all, that keeps him trapped in "his past of words, images, possessions," is it possible for him to move forward and, perhaps enter the Promised Land.[43] Peperzak comments that "The exodus of the just is different from the odyssey of a hero; it

---

39 Wyschogrod, *Emmanuel Levinas*, 232.

40 Unfortunately, mainstream psychoanalysis does not usually use the terms authenticity and inauthenticity, terms that are associated with existentialism. Recently published, *The American Psychiatric Publishing Textbook of Psychoanalysis*, Ethel S. Person, Arnold M. Cooper and Glen O. Gabbard, eds. (Washington, D.C.: American Psychiatric Publishing, 2005), for example, does not even have these turns as entries in its index of glossary. However, as Charles Rycroft points out, while psychoanalysis frequently makes distinctions between actions and behavior "which are done in good and bad faith, which are true and false to the self," it has no rigorous way "of making the distinction, nor the similar one between 'sincere' and 'insincere,'" although clinical work often relies on the analyst being able to make such fine distinctions (*A Critical Dictionary of Psychoanalysis*, Middlesex: Penguin Books, 1972, 9).

41 Levinas, *Basic Philosophical Writings*, 81; Wyschogrod, *Emmanuel Levinas*, 166.

42 Catherine Chalier, "Levinas and the Talmud," in *The Cambridge Companion to Levinas*, 106.

43 Ibid.

leads toward a land promised rather than possessed."[44] It is especially noteworthy, says Chalier, that the Promised Land is the place that Abraham moves towards, struggles towards day in and day out, for his integrity and humanity lie in his existential response to the summoning call form God, the Other, that he heard. However, and this is crucial, the Promised Land is a place into which Abraham has no guarantee of actually "entering and settling."[45] As in psychoanalysis at its most disruptive and deconstructive best, by removing the self from its familiar anchors and self-understandings, from an identity generated under the regime of the same, the analysand is oriented towards an unpredictable, impossible to pin down, future. Says Chalier, "This is a future which forever postpones the possibility of a return to self, for it obliges one to take the path, with no end in sight, of answering to the otherness of God and human beings."[46]

Levinas's conviction that the return to the self lacks the meaningfulness and humanizing, goodness-generating impact of the absolute orientation towards the other,[47] and by extension, engaging the strange, foreign and other in us, probably has its basis in biblical ethics, in the obligation to love the stranger, an obligation that is emphasized thirty-six times in the Bible, and is regarded as equally important as the obligation of "protection of" and "kindness to the widow and orphan."[48] These obligations are frequently referred to in Levinas's confessional writings, as personifications of the ethical life. As Jewish philosopher Hermann Cohen noted, "The alien was to be protected, although he was not a member of one's family, clan, religious community, or people; simply because he was a human being. In the alien, therefore, man discovered the idea of humanity."[49] Whether it is the otherness of the alien or stranger, or that which is alien or strange to oneself, it is, for Levinas, the otherness, engaging the otherness with the fullness of one's being that is the basis for the development of a responsible subjectivity and ethical life.

---

44   Peperzak, *To the Other*, 68.

45   Chalier, "Levinas and the Talmud," 106.

46   Ibid., 112.

47   Ibid., 111.

48   Herz, *The Pentateuch and Haftorahs*, 504.

49   Ibid. Hertz is quoting Cohen (no citation given).

GOD AND TRANSCENDENCE

Levinas's discussion of God has the same problem that any discussion of otherness has, namely, that by thematizing and conceptualizing God in conventional language we diminish his transcendence[50] and otherness, and thus reduce him to the realm of the same, to knowledge, to ontology, something especially made evident in Derrida's critique of his work;[51] Levinas is acutely aware of the difficulties of saying anything without reducing it to consciousness and thematization, and thus he always tries to avoid speaking of God in the language of Being and presence. For example, as Davis points out, to speak of religious or spiritual experience, as analysts, psychologists of religion and philosopher/theologians frequently do, implicitly asserts the ontological way of thinking, in that "God is an object of knowledge revealed to the subject, experienced as a presence." God's assumed transcendence is thus reduced to a form of immanence: God is ultimately comprehend "as part of our own world, a Being that we may experience or refuse to experience, of which we may have knowledge or be ignorant."[52]

In contrast to speaking of God in the familiar terms and questions of the philosophy of religion and theology, for example, can humans know whether the claim "God exists" is true or not? Or, what does it mean to believe, or not to believe in God, to have faith in him or to be an atheist? Levinas offers a very different approach, one that is not lodged in the ontological outlook. Rather, as Levinas says, his focus is on a different question, "What is it to have become conscious of God?" He aims to investigate "the possibility—or even the fact—of understanding the word as a significant word." His concern, he says,

---

50 In general, transcendence has at least two meanings for Levinas. First, it is roughly equivalent to radical alterity, the impossibility of fully comprehending the other; second, transcendence, emanating from the interhuman relation, an "intimate structure of subjectivity," and "a going out from the self." "The face of the other is the" site "of transcendence" (*Alterity and Transcendence*, "Preface" by Pierre Hayat, xii, xi, xiv). "Transcendence," in other words, says Smith, is "the movement of the self (or "same") toward the outside (the "other" or alterity)" *Toward the Outside*, 1.

51 Derrida, "Violence and Metaphysics..." in *Writing and Difference*, 79-153.

52 Davis, *Levinas*, 96.

is to describe "the phenomenological 'circumstances,'" the 'staging' surrounding what gets described in the abstract."[53]

In order to rescue God from the misguided, potentially violence-prone thematic rationality and the ontology of power of conventional philosophical, theological and psychological ways of speaking about God, Levinas speaks of "to-God."[54] By "to-God" he means that God is "surrendered" to, "opened up" to, "approached," or "addressed," but never actually directly encountered or arrived at.[55] This is because God is not a substance or essence and has no independent existence.[56] "I think that God has no meaning outside the search for God."[57] God is thus best understood as a direction rather than an end point, a process rather than a result, a mysterious irruption to be pursued, but never possessed.

Unlike Martin Buber,[58] and the countless "believers" from many of the world religions who claims it possible to address God, to have a direct, personal and reverentially close encounter with the Almighty, Levinas's God is too otherwise to be approached in such unduly common and familiar cognitive and emotional terms. Rejecting any description or evocation of God in rational, negative, mystical or theological terms,[59] Levinas claims that "the idea of God is something other than being, beyond being."[60] "The transcendence of God can neither be said nor thought in terms of being."[61] Levinas further elaborates:

> God is not simply the 'first other,' or the 'other par excellence,' or the 'absolutely other,' but other than the other, other otherwise, and other with an alterity prior to the alterity of the other, prior to the

53 Levinas, *Of God Who Comes to Mind*, xii, xi.

54 Levinas, *Entre Nous*, 174-175.

55 Hutchens, *Levinas*, 118, Davis, *Levinas*, 98.

56 Davis, *Levinas*, 98.

57 Levinas, *Of God Who Comes to Mind*, 95.

58 For a comprehensive treatment of the similarities and differences between arguably the two greatest Jewish philosophers since Maimonides, Buber and Levinas (as the editors claim), see Atterton et al., *Levinas and Buber: Dialogue and Difference*.

59 Hutchens, *Levinas*, 118.

60 Levinas, *Entre Nous*, 119.

61 Levinas, *Of God Who Comes to Mind*, 77.

ethical obligation to the other and different from every neighbor, transcendent to the point of absence, to the point of his possible confusion with the agitation of the *there is [il y a]*" [impersonal being, italics in original].[62]

In a word, God is otherwise than being and beyond essence, beyond intellectual- emotional grasp or apprehension.[63] Levinas calls this radically other aspect of God, *illeity*, an unwieldy French word designating "something present but at a distance."[64] Contra Buber, illeity lies outside the "thou" and "it indicates a way of concerning me without entering into *conjunction* with me."[65] Thus, while a man moves "to-God," it is God who initially approaches man through the face of the other, and commands and "ordains" him to a wide range of deeds of serving and giving, of being for the Other.[66] This is a form of "grace" that is "concretely expressed in the demand" of the other[67] for absolute responsibility, for justice and love. As Levinas notes, such a demand from the other instills a sense of gratitude in the actor. This is not gratitude as conventionally understood, as being grateful for having received something. Rather, continues Levinas, "it signifies that one owes gratitude precisely for having gratitude, gratitude for being in this apparently inferior situation of the one who renders thanks—when the superior one is God…a situation…which is supreme grace."[68]

---

62 Ibid., 69.

63 Levinas's notion of God as beyond intellectual/emotional comprehension is possibly rooted in the biblical passage in which Moses asks God his name and He answers, "I am that I am" (Exodus 111, 14). While this mysterious passage is understood in traditional circles as a philosophical assertion that God is "self-existent and eternal…a unity and spirituality of the Divine Nature," it is also suggested by Rashi that the puzzling phrase implies that there are "no words that can" adequately "sum up all the He is," and most importantly perhaps, "will be to His People" (Hertz, *The Pentateuch and Haftorahs*, 215).

64 Smith, *Toward the Outside*, 89.

65 Levinas, *Basic Philosophical Writings*, 119.

66 Ephraim Meir, "Buber's and Levinas's Attitudes Towards Judaism," in *Levinas and Buber: Dialogue and Difference*, 141.

67 Ibid.

68 Levinas, *Is It Righteous to Be?* 66-67. Grace, viewed as "supreme" "moments" of devotion, when "something wholly other" disrupts self-interest, is the basis of ethics as first philosophy, Jeffrey Bloechl, "Ethics as First

If God cannot be cognitively or emotionally grasped or experienced, at least in the conventional sense of these terms, the how do we gain access to-God? Levinas answers this question in his complicated concept of the "trace," a term usually associated with Derrida, but which Derrida specifically credits to Levinas.[69]

The "strange, illogical notion of a 'command before understanding,' where the other is capable of obligating prior to consciousness and deliberation," is what Levinas calls the trace.[70] "'The neighbor strikes me before striking me, as though I had heard before he spoke'"[71] Atterton and Calarco aptly define the trace:

> the trace is not a sign in the conventional sense in that it does not refer to either a concept or an extra-linguistic entity (e.g., a tree). Rather, it refers to what never presents itself as such to consciousness making it impossible to say who or what it is a trace of. As the trace of a certain 'nonpresence' or 'nonphenomenon,' it signals the relation of *différance* within the test of philosophy, thwarting its pretensions of full intelligibility or 'logocentrism'...For Levinas, the trace is the way in which the Other appears, not as the appearing of a phenomenon, but as a face.[72]

Philosophy," in *The Face of the Other and the Trace of God: Essays on the Philosophy of Emmanuel Levinas*, ed. Jeffrey Bloechl. New York: Fordham University Press, 2000, 146, 149.

69 Jacques Derrida, *Of Grammatology*, trans. Gayatri Chakravorty Spivak (Baltimore, MD: The John Hopkins University Press, 1976), 70. "The Trace of the Other," trans. Alphonso Lingis, in *Deconstruction in Context*, ed. Mark C. Taylor, (Chicago, IL: University of Chicago Press, 1986), 345-59.

70 Atterton, Calarco and Friedman, "Introduction," in *Levinas and Buber*, 14. This idea of a "command before understanding" may have its roots in a famous Biblical passage in which Moses read the Book of the Covenant to Israel, a passage that Levinas was surely aware of. In Exodus 24, verse 7, it says, "and he took the Book of the Covenant, and read in the hearing of people; and they said; 'All that the Lord hath spoken will we do, and obey.'" As Hertz notes, for the Rabbis this "instant and instinctive response to carrying out the will of God," before understanding and reflection, indicates the ultimate "submission to God and self-consecration to His Covenant" (Hertz, *The Pentateuch and Haftorahs*, 321).

71 Levinas, *Otherwise Than Being*, 88.

72 Atterton and Calarco, *On Levinas*, 56-57.

For Levinas the face "is a trace of itself, a trace in the trace of an abandon where the equivocation is never dissipated."[73] This rather inaccessible, contradictory sentence is important in that it seems to suggest that the other comes into view in the form of a trace in which the Other is neither present nor absent per se, but present in its absence![74] "To go toward Him is not to follow the trace, which is not a sign; it is to go toward the Others who stand in the trace of illeity [radical alterity]. It is through this illeity situated beyond the calculations and reciprocities of economy and of the world, that being has a sense. A sense which is not a finality."[75] Hutchens writes that "the face is merely a trace of its own presence and a trace of the passing of the god that abandoned the other person... The trace of god's passing indicates the that the god approaches from, and can only be approached within, the anonymous domain of illeity."[76] God, then is sighted, so to speak, only in the unfamiliar third person, "neither a presence nor an absence" in itself or by itself, "but a trace," "infinitely" near and "absolutely" remote.[77]

In light of Levinas's notion of the trace, it is reasonable to infer that God, the Divine, is co-present in some sense of the term, or at least comes to mind as one approaches the other in responsibility, in justice and love. As Levinas says, "The dimension of the divine opens forth from the human face. A relation with the Transcendent free from all captivation by the Transcendent is a social relation. It is here that the Transcendent, infinitely other, solicits us and appeals to us."[78]

Elsewhere, Levinas notes, "Through my relation to the Other, I am in touch with God."[79] "It is in the encounter with the other man that God 'comes to mind' or 'comes into sense'"[80] "The Other, in his signification prior to my initiative, resembles God."[81] "The Infinite [i.e., God]

---

73 Levinas, *Otherwise Than Being*, 94.

74 Atterton and Calarco, *On Levinas*, 57.

75 Levinas, *Basic Philosophical Writings*, 64.

76 Hutchens, *Levinas*, 120.

77 Davis, *On Levinas*, 99.

78 Levinas, *Totality and Infinity*, 78.

79 Levinas, *Difficult Freedom*, 17.

80 Levinas, *Is It Righteous to Be?* 222.

81 Levinas, *Totality and Infinity*, 293.

comes into the signifyingness of the face. The face *signifies* the Infinite"
[in the sense of "meaning" and "giving orders"][82] "The subject who says
'Here I am!' testifies to the Infinite." [83] "The 'otherwise than being' is
the glory of God." [84] "It is in the human face that...*the trace of God is
manifested, and the light of revelation inundates the universe*" (italics in
original).[85] Many more quotations from Levinas could be given that
indicate that God appears to me in the manner of a trace which is
the face of the Other, that is, the "saintliness of God"[86] is accessed and
affirmed in responsibility for the other, through deeds of justice, love
and goodness.

The above is a partial rendering of Levinas's account of his version of
Judaism, or for that matter, any form of ethical monotheism, at its best,
"a religious for adults."[87] In this view, God is not a "strange magician,"
or "lesser demon," "a fairly primary sort of God" that "dishes out prizes,
inflicted punishment or pardoned sins—a god who, in His goodness,
treated men like children." Rather, an "adult's God," Levinas claims, reveals Himself "precisely through the void of the child's heaven. This is
the moment when God retires from the world and hides His face."[88]
God, always departing, is encountered in the infinity of the Other's
demand for absolute responsibility.

HOLINESS

God, the idea of God, "a thought that thinks more than it thinks,"[89]
the longing for the Infinite, the longing for the other that leaves itself
as a trace in the domain of the same, explodes normal consciousness.
It breaks up consciousness characterized by presence, immanence, being, the "I think" of Descartes. But what follows from the idea of God
as Levinas conceptualizes the irruption of the transcendent that hurls

---

82   Levinas, *Ethics and Infinity*, 105.

83   Ibid., 106.

84   Ibid., 109.

85   Levinas, *Proper Names*, 95.

86   Levinas, *Difficult Freedom*, 14.

87   Ibid., 11.

88   Ibid., 143.

89   Levinas, *Of God Who Comes to Mind*, xv.

the self out of normal "consciousness into insomnia?"[90] "The idea of the Infinite commands the spirit," says Levinas, "God-coming-to-the-idea, as the life of God." A life of "responsibility without concern for reciprocity," "a love without eros," "the order of being-for-the-Other," in a word, a life of holiness.[91]

Levinas claimed that his most passionate interest had always been holiness, rather than ethics per se, so it is worth exploring this mode of being. A few comments by Levinas on the theme of holiness, often equated with sacrifice, will be helpful in giving this notion some real-life, everyday meaning:

> I think about holiness, about the holiness of the face of the other or the holiness of my obligation as such. So be it! There is a holiness in the face but above all there is a holiness or the ethical relation in oneself in a comportment which encounters the face as face, where the obligation with respect to the other is imposed before all obligations; to respect the other, to take the other into account, to let him pass before oneself. And courtesy! Yes, that is very good, to let the other pass before I do; this little effort of courtesy is also an access to the face. Why should you pass before me? This is very difficult, because you, too, encounter my face. But courtesy or ethics consists in not thinking that reciprocity.[92]

> One has to take it as the perspective of holiness, without which means the human is inconceivable. This means that man is responsible for the other man and that he is responsible for him even when the other does not concern him, because the other always concerns him. The other's face always regards me. And this is *de jure* limitless. At no moment can you leave the other to his own destiny.[93]

> Holiness is nevertheless the supreme perfection, and I am not saying that all humans are saints! But it is enough that, at times, there have been saints, and especially that holiness always be admired, even by those who seem most distant from it. This holiness which cedes one's place to the other becomes possible in humanity...[94]

---

90 Fryer, *The Intervention of the Other*, 166, 163.

91 Levinas, *Of God Who Comes to Mind*, xv, ix.

92 Levinas, *Is It Righteous to Be?* 49.

93 Ibid., 99.

94 Ibid., 183.

The priority of the other person begins in this self-effacing gesture in our ceding our place. This is the road that can lead to holiness…[95]

The concern for the other breaches concern for the self. This is what I call holiness. Our humanity consists in being able to recognize the priority of the other.[96]

I could go on and on with quotations from Levinas on the theme of holiness, especially when he tries to show how such a mode of being manifests itself in the concrete historical and social life of real people. It is mainly through his study of the Bible, that paradigm of his ethical transcendental philosophy, rigorously and inspirationally interpreted through the Talmud, that Levinas exemplifies the possibility of a thoroughly God-infused outlook. This outlook is one that emphasizes "the commandment towards the Good" or "a prophecy of the Good," and which also is entirely lodged in the "experience of modernity"[97] The Bible for Levinas is a root text, one that is steeped in responsibility for the other, especially before oneself, a paradigm of religious adulthood and ethical humanism with universal significance. Indeed, as Levinas indicates, the Bible is not only a testament to the presence, to the spirit of God through language, but the "Torah…[is] a force warding off idolatry by its essence as Book, that is, by its very writing, signifying precisely prescription…"[98] Notwithstanding his rejection of comparisons of his work to any versions of normative theory that, he claims, are simply manifestations of the ontology of power, there does seem to be a normative,[99] or at least a "crypo-normative" aspect to his discussions of Biblical and Talmudic ethics, what he elsewhere calls "biblical humanity."[100] Indeed, Levinas's emphasis on responsibility for, and obligation to the other, on selfless love, on giving and serving, all have a privileged place in his philosophy. This may, in part, constitute what

---

95   Ibid., 191.

96   Ibid., 235.

97   Michael Fagenblat and Nathan Wolski, "Revelation Here and Beyond: Buber and Levinas on the Bible," in *Levinas and Buber: Dialogue and Difference*, 162, 157.

98   Levinas, *In The Time Of The Nations*, 58.

99   Fagenblat and Wolski, "Revelation Here and Beyond," in *Levinas and Buber: Dialogue and Differnce*, 169.

100 Levinas, *Is It Righteous to Be?* 120.

Hutchens calls Levinas's "glimmering of prescriptivism buried deep beneath the metaphysical and Ethical descriptions."[101]

GODS, TRANSCENDENCE, HOLINESS AND THE PSYCHOANALYTIC PROJECT

What does all this "God and holiness talk" have to do with the typical cosmopolitan psychoanalyst who, together with his knowing analysand, struggles each analytic hour in the latter's goal of developing greater self-understanding and deeper self-transformation, of living a more satisfying and creative life of love and work and, of course, a life of greater peace of mind, of greater happiness?

Levinas is suggesting that the above-described goals of psychoanalysis are good and necessary, but not nearly sufficient or complete if one wants to fashion what Levinas takes to be a responsible subjectivity striving to live an ethical life. This is a life that is lived through an intelligibility of goodness—of being for the other, of God who comes to mind, and holiness.

While there is no way of proving that a life lived through an intelligibility of goodness is more "True," or ultimately better than any other form of life, it is possible to argue as I do, that such a form of life has its advantages for the analysand. Though commitment to living a life of goodness in order to get something out of it flies in the face of the very for the other, altruistic spirit of such a life, it is still important that analysts and analysands have a basis, perhaps a compelling basis, for choosing to live such a form of life, and to have such an outlook animate, if not suffuse, psychoanalytic work. Put somewhat differently, as a question, in what way is a form of life that is lived by an intelligibility of goodness, giving, serving, sacrificing, responsibility for the other— being for the Other, often before oneself, more commanding and appealing than a wide range of psychoanalytic versions of the human condition and the forms of life that these metanarratives put forth? While I will take up this key question in greater details and rigor in the concluding chapter, I want now to make a few comments, admit-

---

101 Hutchens, Levinas, 156. For example, Levinas sounds prescriptive when he writes, "Man's supreme work –a broad, open welcoming life—is accomplished in transcendence" (Proper Names, 112). Holding up "a broad, open, welcoming life" as "man's supreme work" surely reflects Levinas's valuative attachment. Many other examples of Levinas's "soft" prescriptivism can be given.

tedly polemical ones, to indicate where I am going with all of this in terms of psychoanalysis.

Levinas clearly advocates living an ethical life that is characterized by passionately, unconditionally, giving and serving others, especially before oneself as the most impressive mode of existence: "The only absolute value is the human possibility of giving the other priority over oneself. I don't think there is a humanity that can take exception to that ideal."[102] Indeed, saintly behavior and hagiology are central to his ideal of what being human at its best is all about. Though most of us are not saints, and probably do not have what it takes to be saintly in our inner experience and outward behavior, nevertheless, for Levinas, there are at least three ways one can serve others that are open to the average person.[103]

One can serve others in the realm of knowledge, for example, by teaching. In teaching we open minds and hearts, and thereby give knowledge and insight to others so that they can make better choices in their lives; in the realm of action, by helping someone accomplish a desired task, such as getting a job; in the realm of feeling, by providing for those in need. By such as acts of kindness, we serve others on the emotional level, giving the needed goods, including literal and psychological gifts, and other forms of affective support to help them grow, develop, flourish and enjoy their lives. These modes of serving others are similar to the Jewish belief that we serve God, that is, we make the world a better and more beautiful place through justice (e.g., engaging in ethical behavior by being a lawyer or social activist); through love (e.g., being a caring and competent doctor or social worker, giving charity, performing acts of kindness); and as the Greeks have especially taught us, through beauty (e.g., participating in the fine or performing arts, writing, and demonstrating ecological sensitivity and activism).

Needless to say, serving others as one's primary orientation to the world has its benefits to the helper. Personal gratification and enhancement in the form of increased self-esteem, and an augmentation in our knowledge, skills and sense of empowerment, are just a few of the well-known ways that serving others helps the helper. Indeed, as brain research using MRI technology has shown, doing good for others lights up the reward center of the brain. But there are other, more

102 Levinas, *Is It Righteous to Be?* 170.

103 I am liberally drawing from Kunz, *The Paradox of Power and Weakness,* 168-169.

gripping self-serving reasons to embrace Levinasian-inspired "for-the-Other" lexicon of intelligibility and action, especially as it pertains to those everyday aspects of human experience that are often most important to many analysands. I will mention a few of these crucial aspects of human experience in question form, by referring back to the psychoanalytic "intellectual" and the religious "believer" section of the previous chapter, "Making Suffering Sufferable." Of course, as in any polemic, I am generalizing, stereotyping and oversimplifying to bring my point home.

1) If you were suddenly made poor and homeless, would you be more likely to be helped by someone, especially by someone you don't know, if he was lodged in a "for oneself" psychoanalytic outlook or a "for-the-Other," service-oriented, ethical way of being, an outlook that commands kindness, mercy and charity to the lowly, needy and miserable among us?

2) If you were suffering from a debilitating or life-threatening illness that required long-term care, would you want to be comforted and cared for by a psychoanalytic intellectual or a person rooted in a responsibility for the other, compassion-driven, "biblical humanity," as Levinas describes such an ethical outlook?

3) If you were in a situation where "doing the right thing" was required, where standing up to the "tyranny of the majority," as John Stuart Mill called it, was required, would a psychoanalytic intellectual or a person rooted in a biblical ethic of justice and truth be more likely to rise to the occasion?

4) In making love, would you prefer to be with a psychoanalytic intellection who views his own needs for pleasure as foremost in importance, or a person who regards satisfying the other as his first responsibility and concern?

5) If you were walking in a national park and came upon a beautiful vista, do you think that a psychoanalytic intellectual would be more likely to embrace the moment, or would someone whose perspective on life was steeped in gratitude to God for the grandeur of His universe be more likely to experience the moment with the fullness of his whole being?

6) In raising children, would a psychoanalytic intellectual or a religious believer who views his child as the highest of human treasures given by God be more likely to give himself

selflessly and sacrifice for the sake of raising a healthy and happy child?

7) If you were out with some friends or in a social gathering among strangers, would a psychoanalytic intellectual or a religious believer, lodged in an outlook that emphasizes humility and modesty (i.e., reduced narcissism) be more likely to defer to the other and respectfully and empathically listen?

Given my rhetorical exaggeration, I think that my main point is clear. Fashioning a self that is rooted in an ethic of responsibility for the other, compared to a psychoanalytic perspective on life, one that is built on a self-centric outlook in which behaving in accordance with my desire takes precedence over behaving in accordance "with 'the good'"[104] is not a sufficient or "good enough," technology of the self for the analysand to embrace without reserve. Rather, as Levinas says, and as I will argue with greater rigor and less rhetorical flourish and polemic in the final chapter, psychoanalysis could greatly benefit by embracing a lexicon of goodness, holiness and biblical humanity, as Levinas understood these terms, as core values animating its theory and technique. Freud, as I will suggest, believed that this was a laudable goal, though difficult to achieve, and not one that he ever adequately integrated into his psychoanalytic project. It is to this subject that I now turn.

CLINICAL VIGNETTE

By the time I first saw John he had become a modern Orthodox Jew "of some description," as he said. That is, though he practiced Judaism as if he were Orthodox, his views were often not in harmony with the traditional outlook of his religious community. His belief in God, for example, sometimes ran "hot," while on other days he claimed, "God leaves me cold." John said he frequently felt out of step with fellow Jews at his centrist synagogue, except for a few other "odd ball" intellectual types who were also marginal for one reason or another. Most of his fellow "shul"-goers, John indicated, were the usual suspects for an affluent Jewish community: doctors, lawyers, accountants and business people, "all very successful and all very boring for the most part." Still, in spite of all his complaints, John reliably went to synagogue on the Sabbath and sometimes on weekdays for morning prayers. For the most part, he lived an Orthodox lifestyle, including sending his children to a yeshiva through high school years, which he felt steeped

104 Fryer, *The Intervention of the Other*, 227.

them in the best of Judaism while protecting them from the dangerous elements of the secular world.

Perhaps the most interesting fact about John's religious life was the he grew up in a basically non-religious home, as a Reform Jew in an affluent suburb. His father and mother were strong Zionists, at least ideologically over the breakfast table, but for the most part, John viewed them as ignorant and self-hating Jews, typical of the second generation of immigrant parents, who wanted to "make it" in America. This often meant giving up or denying their Jewishness, that is, engaging in rapid, mindless, assimilation. Their's was the generation of the "Gentleman's Agreement."

As with most people, John's religious and Jewish identity was an evolving process that was thoroughly enmeshed, at least initially, with his family dynamics and personal history. It is worth briefly reviewing some of this history as it unfolded in his analysis, for it is a way of illuminating how John' s Judaism became such a crucial resource in his efforts be the kind of "morally better" person he wanted to be. John's wish to be a better human being—kinder, gentler and more generous—were goals that he had from the beginning of his analysis in one form or another. He felt that Judaism and his analysis were the two best forms to help him to accomplish this self-transformation and self-mastery. In addition, John said that he felt that religion, that is, in some form of Judaism, could help him find his way in this "mad" world and live a life that "I could look back on my death bed and feel worthy of living." A justified life, Levinas might say.

John's interest in Judaism surfaced in earnest while a teenager. While his Bar Mitzvah was mostly a spiritually meaningless and uncomfortable event (e.g., John was shy and had performance anxiety), about a year later or so later, he felt himself drawn to "things Jewish," as he called them. He began to read books with Jewish themes, such as *Exodus* and *The Chosen*, and sought out teachers who could educate him and nurture his unfolding intellectual interests. These activities were developmental attempts to separate and individuate, that is, they were identify-defining and empowering endeavors, especially in relationship to his ambivalently-loved father, whom John viewed as having cheated him out of a solid and meaningful Jewish background. In John's eyes, his father was weak, ignorant and pathetic, not the strong, educated, noble Jewish patriarch he wished he had come from.

In contrast, John identified with his mother's paramour, Reul, who was a refugee from Nazi Europe, a former French resistance fighter and gunrunner during the Israeli War of Independence. This cosmopolitan and polyglot (including Hebrew) man had come to the United States after World War II, having lost most of his family during the Holocaust. He came to this country with only the shirt on his back and became a very successful businessman and charity giver to Jewish and other causes. For John, Reul, a Holocaust survivor, provided a properly masculine and positive basis upon which to build his Jewish identity. However, Reul was not an easy man to relate to, let alone get close to. He could be hard-assed and hostile, bitter and angry, as he felt that he had been cheated out of what he always wanted to do with his life, to be a doctor and rabbi. Reul had given up his career plans after the war because he had had to earn a living. He had also, like many survivors, lost his faith in God because of the Holocaust. That he was having an affair with John's mother also made him a competitor, though John said that he felt, at least in hindsight, that he and Reul were secretly conspiring against his father toward whom John had had extremely ambivalent feelings throughout his childhood. There were other instances, said John, where Reul and he went at it; as if they were in competition for his mother, Reul would "put me down," resent my education and success. Still, John said that, for the most part, he admired Reul because "of what he had been through during the war and how he transformed himself into such an effective person." Compared to his rigid, habit driven, emotionally remote and critical, anti-intellectual scientist/businessman father, Reul was "easy to manage."

John's Jewish identity turned seriously religious when he went to college. There, while pre-med, he had studied Hebrew and Jewish philosophy, established strong ties with various rabbi's and gradually took on a religious life, which he maintained inconsistently until his first marriage. John spent one year in Israel studying at a university. There he became considerably more inspired and motivated to educate himself as a Jew, though he said that he never felt like the "real thing." Running throughout John's Jewish story was the feeling that his religious identity was inauthentic, that he did not fit in, and would never quite fit in: "I am like a man with a high fever trying to find a comfortable position to sleep in. I keep twisting and turning, and am only comfortable for a few minutes at a time. What I would give to be a 'real believer.'"

Throughout his analysis, John and I tried to understand his unusual turn to Judaism, considering his non-religious upbringing. We explored the developmental and psychological meanings to his involvement with Judaism form its onset. We analyzed why he chose to be a doctor, the Jewish profession as he called it; why he chose two Jewish wives, both daughters of Holocaust survivors; why he chose to live as an Orthodox Jew, though an ambivalent one. We explored his shifting beliefs and concept of God, and, most importantly, his deep-abiding quest for spiritual self-transformation and self-transcendence, especially on the ethical front (to be a kinder, gentler, more generous person), a recurrent, strong wish on his part. As we analyzed all of these ideas, almost always holding John's religious thinking and convictions in considerable suspicion, as possibly reflecting neurotic, self-deceptive and illusive aspects of his psychic functioning, it gradually became clear that John was trying to refashion himself by means of his spiritual and religious resources, that is, through Judaism, to a "higher" level of autonomy, integration and ethical living. Once John had sufficiently analyzed his involvement in Judaism as being, to some extent, an obsessional neurosis, a childhood neurosis, with a strong Oedipal aspect, a form of masochism, a reaction formation against unacceptable impulses, a delusion and the like, it became clear to us both that Judaism had become a largely life-affirming aspect of his existence and a psychosocial asset. John was working at creating a new form of subjectivity. In his own way, by living a more moral life along Jewish ethical lines, John was expressing and fortifying his long-standing wish for self-transformation and self-transcendence, what Levinas would call ethical transcendence, a trace of "Goodness" and the "holy."

8

TOWARDS A LEVINASIAN-INSPIRED, ETHICALLY-INFUSED PSYCHOANALYSIS

That psychoanalysis has not made the analysts themselves better, nobler,
or of stronger character remains a disappointment for me.
Perhaps, I was wrong to expect it.
Sigmund Freud[1]

The unworthiness of human beings, including the analyst,
always impressed me deeply,
but why should analyzed men and women in fact be better.
Analysis makes for integration but does not itself make for goodness.
Sigmund Freud[2]

When I ask myself why I have always striven honestly to be considerate
of others and if possible kind to them and why I did not give this up when
I noticed that one is harmed by such behavior and is victimized because
others are brutal and unreliable, I really have no answer.
It surely was not the sensible thing to do.
Sigmund Freud[3]

As the first two passages above taken from letters to his good friend James Jackson Putnam strongly suggest, Freud wanted psychoanalysis to be an ethical enterprise, wanted analysts and analysands to be exemplary people in their moral life. Freud, perhaps secretly, longed for psychoanalysis at its best to be a technology for helping analysands makes themselves into people characterized by moral excellence—"better, nobler, stronger" and devoted to "goodness"

---

1 Nathan G. Hale, editor, *James Jackson Putnam and Psychoanalysis*. Translated by J.B. Heller, (Cambridge: Harvard University Press, 1971). Letter from Freud to Putnam, 11/13/13, 163-164.

2 Ibid., Letter to Putnam, 6/17/15, 188.

3 Ibid., Letter to Putnam, 8/7/15, 189-190.

as a core principle in their moral lives. As the third quotation suggests, this commitment to an ethical way of being, similar in certain ways to Levinas, was rooted in his devotion to moral excellence in his personal life. This moral excellence was expressed above all in terms of "kindness" towards others, often ahead of utilitarian motive and self-interest. Levinas, according to Kunz, actually indicated in a conversation before his death that the lived essence of his philosophy boils down to a "*la politesse*"—politeness or kindness.[4] Says Levinas, "The only morality is therefore one of kindness."[5]

Taking my lead and inspiration from Freud, and using Levinas as my main intellectual resource, I have tried to suggest how psychoanalysis, conceived as a theoretico-practical matrix, an intellectual technology for rendering existence "thinkable and practicable," can become a more ethical life—and identity-defining narrative of the human condition and technology of the self. I have tried to propose how psychoanalysis as a theory of human behavior and clinical technique can be enhanced, deepened and expanded, to become the radical ethical enterprise that Freud always wanted it to be. Freud's followers have recognized the ethical and moral component to psychoanalysis, including the concept of the superego, the role of moral values in treatment,[6] the moral values inherent in psychoanalysis,[7] psychoanalysis as a movement of social reform (as in law[8]), psychoanalytic contributions to the good or well-lived life.[9] But to the best of my knowledge, no one has attempted

---

4 Kunz, *The Paradox of Power and Weakness*, 199. A shorter version of this chapter has been published in a special issue I edited on "Levinas and Psychoanalysis," in the *Psychoanalytic Review*, 94(4), August, 2007, 515-527 (Editor's introduction. "'You are, Therefore I am': Levinas and Psychoanalysis").

5 Levinas, *Difficult Freedom*, 154. This claim is perfectly compatible with Levinas's Talmudic-animated outlook: "The Torah begins in acts of loving kindness and ends in acts of lovingkindness" (*Sotah*, 14a).

6 Heinz Hartman, *Psychoanalysis and Moral Values* (New Haven, CT: International Universities Press, 1960).

7 Ernest Wallwork, *Psychoanalysis and Ethics* (New Haven, CT: Yale University Press, 1991).

8 Anna Freud, Joseph Goldstein and Albert Solnit, *Beyond the Best Interests of the Child* (New York: The Free Press, 1973).

9 Jeffrey B. Rubin, *The Good Life: Psychoanalytic Reflections on Love, Ethics, Creativity and Spirituality* (Albany, NY: SUNNY, 2004).

to make ethics, conceived as responsibility for the other, especially before oneself, central to psychoanalytic theory and practice. There have been a few books on the "common ground between ethics and psychoanalysis,"[10] but there has been little, if any attempt to develop a version of a humanized psychoanalysis that has a Levinasian devotion to Goodness as its fundamental premise and orientation, including its praxis.

In the remainder of this final chapter, I want to elaborate and summarize what Levinas, one of the major ethical thinkers of the twentieth century, has to offer psychoanalysis as it tries to transform itself into a radically ethical theory and technique. While working out the exacting details of such an ethically-infused, humanized psychoanalysis will have to await a future publications, I now want to offer some preliminary, orienting comments that will, I hope, put the reader on the right track, at least right as I conceive it.

By way of organizing my comments I will address three questions that are central to any psychoanalytic theory,[11] including the development of a Levinasian-inspired ethically-infused psychoanalysis, namely:

1. What is Levinas's conception of the human condition?

2. In light of Levinas's conception of the human condition, how are individual "problems in living" and psychopathology understood?

3. How does this conception of the human condition inform a Levinasian-inspired clinical psychoanalysis as it attempts to alleviate individuals' "problems of living" and psychopathology?

I. RECONCEPTUALIZING THE HUMAN CONDITION

As I pointed out in Chapter One, and following Roy Schafer, psychoanalysis has a number of "master narratives" and storylines about the human condition that guide its practice, its way of conceptualizing psychopathology and doing treatment. For example, analysts have very different narratives about the self: the self fashioned by its defenses against instincts (Freud), the self formed by its inner objects (Klein),

---

10 Meissner. *The Ethical Dimension of Psychoanalysis.*

11 Paul Marcus and Alan Rosenberg, eds., *Psychoanalytic Reflections of the Human Condition. Philosophies of Life and Their Impact on Practice,* 6.

the self shaped by its internalized relationships (Kohut),[12] and "the self as a narcissistic misrecognition, represented through the symbolic order of language" (Lacan).[13] Moreover, depending on which master narrative one is lodged in, the goals of psychoanalytic treatment tend to be conceptualized differently. We have for instance, "the taming of the beast within" through reason and love (Freud), the "mad person within raging about" who becomes transformed through compensatory reparative activities (Klein), the "discovery of the self within" and the development of compensatory self-structures (Kohut), "to speak what heretofore been unspeakable," to reclaim the voice of one's desires (Lacan), and the enhancement of responsibility from "self-as-victim of unknown psychic forces to master in one's own house" (Schaefer).[14]

Most recently, we have had many newer, broadly conceived relational,[15] intersubjectivist[16] and interactional theories[17] that stress the need to create and sustain relationships, the ability and predisposition to partake in the experience of others[18] as the main motivation of behavior, and tracking and understanding the dynamic interaction between the analysand and analyst's subjectivity, especially the co-produced transference/countertransference ebb and flow, in the clinical

---

12   James W. Jones, *Contemporary Psychoanalysis. Religion, Transference and Transcendence* (New Haven: Yale University Press), 135.

13   Anthony Elliot, *Psychoanalytic Theory: An Introduction* (Oxford: Blackwell Publishing, Inc., 1994), 113.

14   Paul A. Roth, "The Cure of Stores, Self-Deception, Danger Situations, and the Clinical Role of Narratives in Roy Schaefer's Psychoanalytic Theory," in Marcus and Rosenberg, *Psychoanalytic Versions of the Human Condition*, 327.

15   Stephen Mitchell, *Relationality: From Attachment to Intersubjectivity* (New York: Analytic Press, 2000).

16   George Atwood and Robert Stolorow, *Structures of Subjectivity: Explorations of Psychoanalytic Phenomenology* (Hillsdale, NJ: Analytic Press, 1984). 1990.

17   Dale Boesky, "The Psychoanalytic Process and its Components." *Psychoanalytic Quarterly*, 49 (1990): 527-531.

18   Kohut has famously developed this notion through his concept of "empathic immersion." As Simon Critchley points out, for Levinas "there is a certain affective disposition towards alterity within the subject, as the structure or pattern of subjectivity" (*Ethics, Politics Subjectivity*, London: Verso Books, 1999, 183).

context. Attachment theory, one of the most popular expressions of this trend,[19] claims that there is "an innate need for attachment to a caregiver" that is central motivation in development. Diverse "patterns or failures in early attachment" supposedly incline a person to future "development pathologies," and these patterns or failures are also correlated with certain kinds of adult modes of relating to oneself and to others.[20] These modes are often pathological, including narcissistic, borderline, schizoid and other characterological disorders.

All of the above described master narratives and storylines have been extremely important to the development of psychoanalysis, including providing some useful insights into the development of morality. However, none of these master narratives has put ethics, at least in the Levinasian sense, at the center of its theorizing and practice. This is where Levinas fits in, as none of these versions of psychoanalysis make the ethical demand of the Other as the ultimate affect-integrating, meaning-making, and action-guiding hermeneutic horizon. In a Levinasian-inspired psychoanalysis we have a very different version of the human condition, one that makes ethics, that is, being for the other, goodness, holiness, "otherwise than being" its main focus and ideal mode of being. The self, in this context, is said to be a "hostage"[21] to the other, to the other's needs for love and justice. "Strictly speaking, the other is the end; I am a hostage, a responsibility and a substitution supporting the whole world in the passivity of assignation, even in an accusing persecution, which is undeclinable."[22]

Thus, the self is not fundamentally and firstly "for oneself," "for itself," and "by oneself." Rather, prior to freedom of choice and assertion of identity, it is the "for the other" of responsibility that ultimately defines the self. "Perhaps the possibility of a point in the universe where such an overflow of responsibility is produced ultimately defines the

---

19   Morris Eagle, "Attachment and Psychoanalysis." *British Medical Journal* (1997), 70: 217-229; Peter Fonagy, *Attachment Theory and Psychoanalysis* (New York: Other, 2001).

20   "Glossary." In Ethel S. Person, Arnold M. Cooper and Glen O. Gabbard, eds., *Textbook of Psychoanalysis* (Washington, D.C.: American Psychiatric Publishing, 2005), 548.

21   Levinas, *Otherwise Than Being*, 112, 118.

22   Ibid., 128.

I."[23] Levinas cogently describes his demanding version of the self or subjectivity by contrasting his view of the interhuman encounter with that of Martin Buber who, Levinas claimed, believed that the relationship between the I and Thou is directly lived as reciprocity:

> My point of departure is in Dostoyevsky and in the phrase 'Each of us is guilty before everyone and for everything, and I more than the others.' The feeling that the I owes everything to the Thou, that its responsibility for the other is gratitude, that the other has always —and rightfully, a right over me: all that I said to you earlier about this 'I' submitted to obligation, about this 'I' commanded in the face of the other—with the double structure of human misery and the word of God—all this perhaps represents a theme basically different from the one that Buber approached.[24]

Hostage, responsibility, substitution, persecution, the self in the accusative, these are some of the evocative Levinasian tropes that Derrida probably had in mind when he noted that when we read Levinas we "tremble." Levinas offers an awesome and humbling version of the human condition that feels utterly insurmountable. Such a narrative goes against, it radically disrupts, undermines and challenges our usual way of thinking about ourselves and others, including about what ultimately matters in life and what is possible in terms of self-constitution, self-transformation and intersubjectivity. The question for psychoanalysis is whether such a narrative of the human condition could be illuminating and useful in our theorizing and clinical work. I believe it is for reasons that I will discuss in greater detail at the end of this chapter. I want now to suggest how such a Levinasian conception of the human condition—the responsible self as hostage to the other—expands, deepens and, most importantly, ethicizes four key notions in psychoanalysis: "personality," or its interchangeable term, "character,"[25] affect, or what Levinas calls affectivity, the unconscious, and the private faculty that Freud thought could guide us to be more healthy, authentic and sensible, namely, reason.

---

23 Levinas, *Totality and Infinity*, 244.

24 Levinas, *Is It Righteous to Be?* 72.

25 Burness E. Moore and Bernard D. Fine, editors, *Psychoanalytic Terms and Concepts* (New Haven, CT: The American Psychoanalytic Association and Yale University Press, 1990) 141.

PERSONALITY AND CHARACTER

In mainstream psychoanalysis personality has been defined as "the observable, ego-syntonic and, under ordinary circumstances, relatively predictable behavior pattern that characterizes an individual's day-to-day life."[26] Character is defined as "the enduring, patterned functioning of an individual...it is the person's habitual way of thinking, feeling and acting,...the person's habitual mode of reconciling intrapsychic conflicts."[27]

These standard definitions are useful to the clinician, but they leave out what I think is most important, namely, the ethical nature of the person. In this Levinasian view, personality becomes "a point where responsibility is concentrated." That is, personality is best understood as "moral personality," as a subjectivity that comprehends itself as responsibility for the other.[28] This place where responsibility is concentrated is a kind of "resource for moral recognition," "ethically sound practical reasoning" and, ultimately, moral "recovery" or repossession of ourselves.[29] In other words, personality or character can be viewed as the action-guiding nexus for enacting our moral values, of responsibility for the other. In this view, a personality or character disorder, at least most generally, can be defined as the habitual conscious and unconscious way that a person is inadequately responsive, misguided and or deaf to ethical considerations, that is, to the summoning call of the Other as one's normative horizon of feeling, thought and action.

For example, in the narcissistic personality disorder the person's habitual way of perceiving, relating to and thinking about the other is marked by grandiosity, envy and an inordinate need for admiration. Such an outlook cuts him off from properly empathizing with and responding to the reasonable needs and desires of the other. Instead, the other is exploited to advance his own ends, that is, to have his excessive need for self-aggrandizement self-importance and specialness affirmed again and again. The borderline personality, who has marked lability in his sense of self, emotions and impulse control, has volatile, unstable and explosive interpersonal relationships that make it near im-

---

26 Ibid.

27 Ibid., 37.

28 Wyschogrod, *Emmanuel Levinas*, 125.

29 Jonathan Jacobs, *Choosing Character. Responsibility for Virtue and Vice* (Ithaca, NY: Cornell University Press, 2001), 43.

possible to consider the other's need needs and wishes in any sustained and reasonable manner. His fear of abandonment, his inordinate need for idealization and quick sense of devaluation, his boundless rage all diminish, if not arrest, his ability to give and receive love. The paranoid person whose inner life is typified by all-encompassing distrust and suspiciousness of others such that their intentions are viewed as malicious, makes him largely incapable of giving to, and serving the other. Frequently questioning the devotion, honesty and reliability of friends and acquaintances, giving humiliating or menacing interpretations to inoffensive comments or benign events, prone to holding grudges and disinclined to forgive insults and hurts, and imagining infidelity in his partner, make him unable to care properly for the other in any genuinely other-regarding manner. The dependent personality, characterized by an inordinate, infantile need to be nurtured and taken care of, often leading to submissiveness, demanding and clinging relatedness, and fears of separation and abandonment, is severely limited in his ability to love, let alone experience "mature" love that respects the separateness and autonomy of the other.

Likewise, the mode of being in the world of schizoid, avoidant, antisocial and obsessive-compulsive personalities can also be fruitfully analyzed in terms of their ethical meaning and significance, as evidenced in their diminished capacity to respond empathetically to the other's needs for love and justice: the schizoid's aloofness and indifference to social relationships and his emotional restrictedness, coldness and prickliness; the avoidant's detachment from the social world, social anxiety and low self-esteem; the antisocial's harmful, disruptive, inconsiderate interpersonal approach, always at the expense of the other's rights and needs; the obsessive-compulsive's tendency to control others, his perfectionism, cheapness, fussy orderliness and lack of positive emotional expressiveness. In all of these and other personality disorders, the individual is ethically corrupted, unable to respond with the fullness of his whole being to the reasonable needs and desires of the other in an ethically healthy, genuinely other-regarding manner. As a result of their truncated ties to empathy, those analysands with personality or character disorders, whether they acknowledge it or not, are suffering greatly, for they reside in a loveless hell.

AFFECT

Affect, a "clinical manifestation," a "neurobiological concomitant," and a "metapsychological concept" in psychoanalysis, has been conventionally defined in classical psychoanalysis as "emotions, and particularly their physiological manifestations, that are derivative (i.e., transformed) expressions of libidinal and/or aggressive drives."[30] This definition is a serviceable one but it leaves out "the lived mode of morality...an immediate and instinctive attachment to the Good"[31] that is beyond being (i.e., "to think him or her straightaway before affirming oneself").[32] In other words, affect is our "experience" of obligation to the other.[33] This reflects a fundamental aspect of the person, *disponibilite*, as Levinas's friend and colleague Gabriel Marcel called it, our "readiness to respond, availability, openness, welcoming and abandonment to"[34] the Other. As Stern[35] and others have noted, in psychoanalysis this theme is often described in terms of a "core intersubjectivity," including those nonverbal empathetic, participatory, and resonating elements of intersubjectivity.

For Levinas, such an experience of the social as he calls it, does not originate in oneself but, first and foremost, in the other. Moreover, such an experience is not intentional or conscious as we usually use these terms. Such an experience of the other is, pre-reflective, something that immediately happens to and disrupts me. Critchley says that "The Levinasian ethical subject is a sentient self...before being a thinking

---

30   Moore and Fine, *Psychoanalytic Terms and Concepts*, 9; Ethel S. Person, Arnold M. Cooper and Glen O. Gabbard (eds.), *Textbook of Psychoanalysis*, 547.

31   Wyschogrod, *Emmanuel Levinas*, 231.

32   Levinas, *Is It Righteous to Be?* 106.

33   James E. Falconer, "Levinas. The Unconscious and the Reason of Obligation," in Gantt and Williams, *Psychology For The Other*, 113-115.

34   Daniel Guerriere, "Continental Theistic Philosophers," in Richard Popkin, editor, *The Columbia History of Western Philosophy* (New York: Columbia University Press, 1999), 718.

35   Daniel Stern, "Intersubjectivity," in Person et al, *The Textbook of Psychoanalysis*, 80. See also Michael Eigen's interesting psychoanalytic discussion of Levinas's notion of "face," "The Significance of the Face," in *The Electrified Tightrope* (Northvale, NJ: Jason Aronson, 1993), 49-60.

ego."[36] This relation with the other, using Levinas's language, who "is absolutely weak...exposed, naked, and destitute," moves, solicits and summons me. "Affectivity itself," "feeling itself," "human emotion and its spirituality" have their "initial place," and "source" in the relation with the other, in the for-the-Other, in being affected by the other. Levinas continues, "The great event and the very source of affectivity is in the other."[37] Affectivity in this sense, as receptivity, sensibility, susceptibility, as the lived mode of Goodness, is what lies beneath and guarantees ethicality.[38] It is one of "the ultimate structures of the human" that psychoanalysis needs to be more mindful of, if not centrally integrate into its theoretical and clinical understanding.

THE UNCONSCIOUS

Having been trained in the phenomenological tradition, Levinas did not have much interest in the dynamic unconscious as Freud and contemporary psychoanalysts describe and use the concept (e.g., that unconscious mental processes are motivated). Indeed, like phenomenological psychiatrists Ludwig Binswanger and Medard Boss, Levinas denied that something lay behind or beneath phenomena, including psychological phenomena, that accounts for, motivates, or drives their emergence. Clarification and elucidation of human experience in terms of unconscious psychological or physical energies, instincts, drives, brain waves or neurochemistry were unacceptable. In this view, phenomena, their manifestation, are what they are in terms of how they "show up" in all of their perceived immediacy; they are not a façade, copy or offshoot of something else. Phenomenological description, clarification, and illumination of human experience, not cause and effect explanation or formal proof, constitutes the main thrust of Levinas's methodology.

Thus, says Wyschogrod, for Levinas "the unconscious is a contradiction in terms, for if it is unconscious it must remain so in order for the unconscious to be applicable. We could not possibly discover the

---

36   Simon Critchley, "The Original Traumatism: Levinas and Psychoanalysis," in *Questioning Ethics: Contemporary Debates in Philosophy*, ed. Mark Dooley and Richard Kearney (New York: Routledge Books, 1999), 239.

37   Levinas, *Is It Righteous to Be?* 63, 53.

38   Jacobs, Choosing *Character. Responsibility for Virtue and Vice*, 103,107, 102.

unconscious, for then it would cease to be what it is."[39] As Levinas indicated, the only definition of the unconscious that he could accept would be "If the concept of the unconscious were to signify a lived mental experience which is not reducible to re-presentation and to the present, thus giving it all the significations of temporality, then it suits me fine."[40] For Levinas, says Wyschogrod, there is not a dark domain of the unconscious that acts as the storehouse for secret sexual and aggressive desires, the so-called "cellar" view of the unconscious. Nor did Levinas believe as Freud did, that these desires cannot come into consciousness because the impact of gratifying these desires would obliterate social structure and societal stability.[41] What Levinas wanted to do was to eliminate any notion of a second consciousness that somehow motivates behavior and from which any deterministic theory can be developed. He wants to eradicate "from consideration the possibility of that which is *eo ipso* closed to the illumination of consciousness as being in any sense part of what can be termed the world."[42] Levinas's reflections on the unconscious are interesting, though says Wyschogrod, they clearly do not signify a fully worked out set of criticisms of classical Freudian, let alone post-Freudian notions of the unconscious.[43] While Levinas's understanding and appreciation of the dynamic unconscious as psychoanalysts conceive the notion was extremely limited, it should not obscure what I think he does have to offer to the ways in which psychoanalysts conceive of and work with the unconscious in their everyday work with analysands.

It is Levinas's conception of the human condition, the responsible self as hostage to the other, and his implied ethics, that suggests a view

---

39 Wyschogrod, *Emmanuel Levinas*, 19.

40 Levinas, *Is It Righteous to Be?* 118.

41 Wyschogrod, *Emmanuel Levinas*, 74.

42 Ibid., 19.

43 One wonders for example, what Levinas would make of Atwood and Stolorows' psychoanalytic phenomenological definition of the dynamic unconscious: "that set of configurations that consciousness is not permitted to assume, because of their association with emotional conflict and subjective danger. Particular memories, fantasies, feelings and other experiential contents are repressed because they threaten to actualize these configurations" (George E. Atwood and Robert D. Stolorow, *Structures of Subjectivity. Explorations in Psychoanalytic Phenomenology.* Hillsdale: The Analytic Press, 1984), 35.

of the unconscious that could be useful to the analyst, especially when the concept of the unconscious is placed in a historical context. As May noted, Freud's monumental contribution to the historical meaning of the unconscious "was to enlarge the sphere of the human personality beyond the immediate voluntarism and rationalism of the Victorian man, to include in this enlarged sphere the "depths," that is the irrational, the so-called repressed, hostile, and unacceptable urges, the forgotten aspects of experience, *ad infinitum*. The symbol for this vast enlarging of the domain of the personality was 'the unconscious.'"[44]

What Levinas adds to our understanding of the unconscious is to give it an ethical significance. While there is a human tendency to repress unacceptable sexual and aggressive wishes and painful affects, human beings also repress their ethical wishes, especially to be a more moral self, one that is the for-the-Other. Individuals repress, deny, ignore and disavow their prosocial wishes, to help, share, cooperate, comfort, donate and serve others, just as they repress threatening wishes associated with affectively discrepant and painful experiences from their past. A simple example: a man can not be regularly kind and generous to his wife, friends and employees because to do so makes him feel vulnerable to their imagined insatiability and criticism, just what he felt in the presence of his needy and judgmental mother.

Mainstream psychoanalysis has largely conceived of the unconscious as "containing" threatening sexual and aggressive wishes and drives derivatives (classical theory), affect states that have been evoked and improperly responded to within the child-parent dyad and defended against to avoid retraumatization, (intersubjective perspective), and wishes for self-sustaining, self-enhancing and self-verifying relationships (self-psychology). What I am suggesting is that in addition to these important formulations of what constitutes the content of the unconscious, we add Levinas's conception of the human condition: that the mind, fundamentally, has an ethical cast and, therefore, that within the unconscious there exists somewhere a "repressed angel" that reflects the fact that human beings seem to strive for ethical self-transformation and self-transcendence. Humans have deep within their nature, perhaps their biology, the wish to live a life animated by altruistic motivation and characterized by prosocial behavior, an attachment to Goodness, as Levinas would say. In this view, it is the

44   Rollo May, "The Origins and Significance of the Existential Movement in Psychology," in *Existence*, 91.

analyst's job, in collaboration with the willing analysand, to access this repressed Goodness, and make it conscious. By doing so, this de-repressed Goodness, these now accessible non-neurotic, life-affirming, for-the-Other moral strivings, can become a positive resource for living one's life with greater ethical vigor, if not grandeur, as Levinas and others have described it. For the biblically-inspired Levinas, as in most of the ancient religious wisdom traditions, it is the ethical life that always references the needs, rights and dignity of the Other, that is the surest way to a modicum of so-called happiness.[45] This is to be contrasted with Freud, who was steeped in the Greek outlook, specifically an Aristotelian one, says Wallwork, where happiness is "a matter of functioning well"[46] in such sublimated activities as love and work.

REASON

Reason, or rather the proper use of reason, says Freud, is the key to mental health and sensible, decent living:

> Intellect —or let us call it by the name that is familiar to us, reason—is among the powers which we may most expect to exercise a unifying influence on men—on men who are held together with such difficulty and whom it is scarcely possible to rule...Our best hope for the future is that intellect—the scientific spirit, reason— may in process of time establish a dictatorship in the life of man... The common compulsion exercised by such a dominance of reason will prove to be the strongest uniting bond among men and lead the way to future unions. Whatever, like religion's prohibition against thought, opposes such a development, is a danger for the future of mankind.[47]

The above passage clearly defines reason as the voice of "intellect" and also emphasizes Freud's alliance with the deep faith in the value-laden system he calls the "scientific spirit." Though Levinas would probably agree that reason understood in this way has its value in prac-

---

45 Levinas discusses the notions of happiness in *Totality and Infinity*. "Life is *love of life*" (112) and this love of life is best expressed in responsible social relations.

46 Ernest Wallwork, "Ethics in Psychoanalysis," in Ethel S. Person, Arnold M. Cooper and Gary O. Gabbard, eds. *Textbook of Psychoanalysis* (Washington D.C.: American Psychiatric Publishing, 2005), 287.

47 Freud, Introductory Lectures on Psycho-analysis, S.E., vol. 22, 171-172.

tical living, he also thought that reason has its dark side. In Levinas's language, "reason is the faculty for maintaining identity through all the variations of becoming; it therefore finds nothing alien to itself."[48] In other words, reason can be understood as totalizations's tool; it applies "logical argumentation" to discern "neutral and universal themes" that is, "to reduce the other to the same," to "the ontology of power".[49] Totalization, the perspective of the whole that wipes out the otherness and difference of the Other is a primordial act of violence.[50]

For Levinas, however, reason can be conceptualized differently, in terms of its ethical functioning and significance. That is, reason emanates from the engagement "with the face of the other." This engagement brings about the "first signification" and founds "language from which intelligibilty" emerges. Reason, in this scene, "is something we share with the other."[51] According to Levinas,

> If the face to face founds language, if the face brings the first signification, establishes signification itself in being, then language does not only serve reason, but is reason. [Elsewhere he says that] Proximity [i.e., the for-the-Other of responsibility to the point of substitution, the source of all compassion] thus signifies a reason before the thematization of signification by a thinking subject... It is a reason before the beginning, before any present, for my responsibility for the other commands me before any decision, any deliberation.[52]

The point is that one can be said to be reasonable in a positive Levinasian sense to the extent that one has the rational and critical capacity, and emotional intelligence and empathy, to be sensitive, mindful and responsive to the integrity, autonomy, alterity, and transcendence of the other. Put somewhat differently, reason is what allows the person to recognize both the fact that, and the manner in which, "moral requirements," the needs of the Other, "have gone unmet."[53] Such a

---

48   Wyschodgrod, *Levinas*, 14.

49   Hutchens, *Levinas*, 56-57.

50   Wyschogrod, *Levinas*, 245.

51   Neve Gordon, "Ethics and the Place of the Other," in Atterton et al, *Levinas and Buber*, 111.

52   Levinas, *Totality and Infinity*, 207; *Otherwise Than Being*, 166.

53   Neve Gordon, "Ethics and the Place of the Other," in Atterton et al, *Levinas and Buber*, 111.

view of reason points beyond Freud's notion of reason as equivalent to intellect, the faculty of knowing, the capacity to draw logical conclusions, and/or in terms of the ego, as the center of rational awareness and effective action. While these formulations are of course useful, Levinas is drawing attention to reason's ethicality as emanating from "the original," primordial "ethical relation," that is, as moral obligation and responsibility. For Levinas, obligation and responsibility is what the other evokes in me by putting my self into question, by making me feel the insufficiency of my intention, "reason is that with which I respond, that with which I" may not, "cannot," cease "responding."[54]

2. RECONCEPTUALIZING INDIVIDUAL PROBLEMS IN LIVING AND PSYCHOPATHOLOGY

For Levinas, the analysand's problems in living and psychopathology are best understood in terms of their being "ethically disabled." As Jacobs observes, their mode of being in the world, "their characters, are such that sound ethical considerations," that is, the for-the-Other of responsibility, are largely "inaccessible to them." Moreover, such analysands have a seriously limited and restricted capacity for moral self-transformation, "for ethical self-correction." In Levinasian language, an ethically disabled analysand is more-or-less consistently and significantly estranged from the Good.[55] Such an analysand can be said to lack ethical integrity and "good" character, the irreproachable character that Freud believed was a pre-requisite to being a competent treating analyst.[56]

Put differently, in general, to the extent that the natural inclinations of the selfishness of the self, the ego, dominate one's life conduct, especially in one's interhuman relations, one is more likely to suffer in terms of guilt, anxiety, depression and alienation. This is a basic, widely accepted spiritual/moral insight of all major ancient religious wisdom traditions.[57] It is important to recognize, however, that the Levinasian subject, at least in some basic sense, acts according to spon-

54 Faulconer, "The unconscious and the Reason of Obligation," in Gantt and Williams, *Psychology For the Other*, 114-115.

55 Jacobs, *Choosing Character*, 1, 74.

56 Freud, "On Psychotherapy," S.E., vol. 7, 267.

57 Paul Marcus, *Ancient Religious Wisdom, Spirituality and Psychoanalysis*, 177-200.

taneous selfishness, that the subject is fundamentally egotistical. In fact, egotism is not a despicable flaw on the part of the subject, but the subject's very nature.[58] "Egotism is not an ugly vice on the part of the subject, but its ontology..."[59] This view is very much in harmony with Freud, who wrote, "Narcissism is the universal and original state of things, from which object-love is only later developed, without the narcissism necessarily disappearing on that account."[60] Levinas, the Holocaust survivor, is no innocent; he understands that the self can probably never be completely modified in that it is inherently "for itself," that is, selfish and self-referential. Levinas evocatively makes this point when he writes, "No one is good voluntarily. No one is enslaved to the Good." And elsewhere he notes that "responsibility for the other is the good. It's not pleasant, it is good."[61] Levinas, like Freud and his followers, recognizes that overcoming, even significantly modulating, our inherent selfishness, infantile narcissism and tendency toward egocentricity is no easy task.

What Levinas is suggesting is that a human being in his ethical expression is an exception to selfishness, infantile narcissism and egocentricity, to this central striving in existence, "to preserve oneself in being" (*conatus essendi*) as Spinoza called it.[62] There is an alternative mode of being worth moving towards, the search for "the Good," that is beyond being (i.e., following Plato, everything, including Being, is to be apprehended in terms of the Good). This "otherwise than being" is depicted, for example, in the biblical/prophetic tradition in Judaism, in which ethics is its very center,[63] and in all of the ancient religious wisdom traditions.[64] Saints, *tzadikkim* (righteous people) and all those who live lives of holiness, of radical selflessness and kindness, characterize the otherwise than being that Levinas has in mind.

Thus, many problems in living, and in their extreme, psychopathology, emanate in part, from the selfish self-undermining, if not taking over, of the ethical self. The needs and aspirations of the selfish self,

58   Smith, *Towards the Outside*, 147, 256, 150.

59   Levinas, *Proper Names*, 70-71.

60   Freud, Introductory Lectures on Psychoanalysis, S.E., vol. 16, 416.

61   Levinas, *Otherwise than Being*, 11; *Is It Righteous to Be?* 47.

62   Smith, *Toward the Outside*, 65.

63   Levinas, *Difficult Freedom*, 16, 17.

64   Levinas, *Is It Righteous to Be?* 62.

the ego, have priority over the life-affirming needs of the other. When the ego is tied to the self in this manner, the fundamental isolation and loneliness of the subject remains continuous and steady. Psychoanalysis, with its interest in narcissistic pathologies, has provided much insight into the development and tragic course of such a way of being. For Levinas, to the extent that one avoids and ignores, or is ignorant of, one's infinite responsibility for the other, including what we do in carelessness, inadvertently, and unconsciously, one can be said to be ethically disabled, lacking in what Levinas calls "humaneness." In one of his Talmudic discussions, he asks: "To shelter the other in one's own land or home, to tolerate the presence of the landless and homeless on the ancestral soil, so jealously, so meanly loved—is that the criterion of humanness? Unquestionable so."[65]

Elsewhere, Levinas elaborates, that "The others's hunger—be it of the flesh, or of the bread—is sacred; only the hunger of the third party [every one else] limits its rights; there is no bad materialism other than our own."[66]

Both of these quotations speak to Levinas's criterion for the ethical life, infinite responsibility and compassion, in the form of responding with the fullness of one's being to the life-affirming material, psychological or spiritual needs of the other. Says Levinas, "Sociality, for me [the for-the-Other that commands the I], is the best of the human."[67] Pathology, so to speak, can be conceptualized as those habits of mind, heart and behavior that impede the movement of transcendence toward otherwise than being, towards living a life characterized by love and justice for the other before oneself. Indeed, from a Levinasian point of view, a person's capacity for critical, ethical self-reflection, acknowledging when moral requirements and obligations to the Other have not been properly met and responded to, is a good prognostic indicator for a successful analysis.

In mainstream psychoanalytic terms, the above refers to the transmutation of narcissism from infantile to more mature forms and the development of deep and wide-ranging emotional capacities for empathy, compassion and love. Psychoanalysis has been masterful in its ability to describe, understand and ameliorate the many developmen-

---

65 Levinas, *In the Time of the Nations*, 98.

66 Levinas, *Difficult Freedom*, xiv.

67 Levinas, *Alterity and Transcendence*, 103.

tal, conflictual and other impediments that blunt, impair and block individuals' capacity to live a life guided by love and justice, as Levinas defines these terms.

As I have tried to show throughout this book, including the clinical vignettes taken from my analysis of John, there are conceptual and practical advantages to the psychoanalyst's embracing a Levinasian perspective on the subject matter that is at the heart of psychoanalysis, namely, reducing the suffering of analysands. In particular, I have suggested that pain, sorrow, conflict and other forms of suffering are fruitfully viewed in terms of helping the analysand give meaning to his suffering by developing an ethical response to it, one that is for-the-Other. Whether it is my, or the other's suffering, the way to make such suffering "sufferable," at least in general terms, is to perceive it as an ethical problem acquiring a self-transcending, other-directed, other-regarding response. Such a Levinasian-inspired angle of vision, "ethics as optics," provides fresh, thought-provoking ways of understanding previously inadequately illuminated aspects of responsibility, guilt, anxiety (roughly the "there is"), forms of love, extreme anguish and affliction, death, spirituality and religiosity, and other important themes that are pertinent to psychoanalytic theory and practice.

3. RECONCEPTUALIZING PSYCHOANALYTIC THERAPY

Overall, following Levinas, I have tried to suggest that human existence, including problems in living and psychopathology, are best illuminated in terms of the self's responsibility for the other as being more basic, more summoning, than its freedom and choice. While to actualize my infinite responsibility for the other, I myself must be free, autonomous and self-governing, the fundamental "sense of my selfhood is my being-for-the-Other."[68] That is, "exposure to the Other is the bedrock of my selfhood; it is the condition of subjectivity, not an aspect of it."[69] Moreover, an ethics of responsibility, not the ontology of freedom, should be the guiding premise of psychoanalytic theorizing, understanding and practice. In such a view, the individual is, at least in some sense, consciously or unconsciously, always moving towards the transcendent, towards the "more," conceived in ethical terms as the Good, Goodness or "to-God." This Good or Goodness

---

68 Peperzak, *To The Other*, 25.

69 Davis, *Levinas*, 80.

"to which responsibility for the other is directed," commanded and obligated, is more important than the Truth that the self freely decides to search for.[70] The self-analysis that Freud calls for mainly leads the analysand to discover his ignorance of his unconscious sexual and aggressive wishes and anxieties. The self-reflection demanded by Levinas mainly leads a person to the discovery of his moral limitations and guilt. Psychoanalysis in this context, becomes a way of helping people move from ethical disablement or impairment towards a fuller, deeper, wider and freer expression of responsibility for the Other, toward a mode of being in which love, justice, compassion and selflessness are continuously animating influences and regulative principles in one's daily life. As Levinas said in his famous essay "A Religion For Adults,"[71] which is about Jewish ethical monotheism at its best, this Levinasian-animated version of psychoanalysis, and the form of life it implies, is a "psychoanalysis for adults," it requires considerable self-discipline, self-mastery and moral armature.

What I am arguing for, following Levinas, is a radical reorientation of psychoanalysis, in which the goal of analysis is helping the analysand awaken "to a moral life" that is coterminous "with the discovery that the other is the first to be" valued, appreciated, "served," that is, tended to before oneself. It is the development of a moral consciousness, defined as the mindfulness of "the privilege the other has relative to me" that mainly characterizes a so-called "successful analysis."[72] Only when there has been a self-transfiguration "of a being-for-itself into a being-for-the-Other through moral responsibility and obligation"[73]—in a sense, an unchosen, undeclinable, obligation emanating from "my condition as a subject," in which "I am given over to the Other"[74]—has the analysand reached the end of analysis. Paraphrasing and playing off Freud, a Levinasian-inspired psychoanalysis, with its demand for infinite responsibility and obligation to the other—there is always more giving and serving to do—makes analysis, in a certain sense, interminable.

70 Hutchens, *Levinas*, 8.

71 Levinas, *Difficult Freedom*, 11-23.

72 Peperzak, *To The Other*, 111-112.

73 Richard A. Cohen, "Maternal Psyche," In Gantt and Williams, *Psychology For The Other*, 60.

74 Davis, *Levinas*, 81.

In this context, the role of the analyst is to expand the analysand's awareness and understanding of what conscious and unconscious personal factors (e.g., thoughts, feelings, wishes and fantasies) and especially valuative commitments, impede, diminish or take the place of, an ethic of responsibility for the other, as well as for oneself.[75] This includes, for example, (1) deconstructing the many ways that analysands defend, insulate, and deceive themselves from feeling appropriate guilt, shame, remorse and self-reproach for their misdeeds towards others; (2) understanding why the analysand is unmoved to reflect on, and critically re-evaluate his selfish and immoral acts, or even perceive that he has acted selfishly or hurtfully towards others. This involves analyzing the analysand's valuative attachments, especially within the context of his personal background and moral history, including the vulnerability, anxiety, pain, confusion, and conflict that almost always sustains such misguided valuative attachments and self-serving behavior; (3) understanding why the analysand is often unmoved by conscious reasons and unconscious motivations for willingly causing suffering to others, for being unjust in his relationships. This means encouraging the analysand to see how his various moral lapses, often rooted in interference by his selfishness and inordinate desire for self-affirmation and gratification, make his own, and his loved one's lives miserable.

Thus, we can say, that in such a Levinasian-inspired form of psychoanalysis, we are always doing "character analysis." The aim is to help the analysand recognize and deeply appreciate in the widest sense, ethical considerations, being-for-the-Other. Most importantly, this means being motivated by such a valuative action-guiding commitment, towards living what in theological circles is called a virtuous life.[76] In a Levinasian-glossed psychoanalytic language, this means helping the analysand become a morally autonomous and integrated individual, one who has the effective cognitive, emotional and motivational capacity to be stably devoted and attached to the Good.

What kind of inner attitude does the analysand need to engage, receive and embrace the Other in this "for the other," before oneself,

---

75 I have liberally drawn on Jacobs, *Choosing Character*, for the following comments.

76 In the "positive psychology" literature, one good book that takes up this theme is Blaine J. Fowers, *Virtue and Psychology: Pursuing Excellence in Ordinary Practices* (Washington D.C.: American Psychological Association, 2005).

manner? First, it requires that the analysand ask different and tough questions of himself. While the typical analysand asks: "why do I exist rather than not?"[77] the Levinasian-inspired analysand also asks, "Have I the right to be, am I worthy of being?"[78] The typical analysand asks, "What do I hope for, what do I desire to be happy?" The Levinasian-inspired analysand also asks "What must I do?" In other words, the psychoanalyst prompts the analysand to ask additional existential questions, ethical questions that cut deeper and are altogether more disruptive. For the Levinasian-inspired anaylsand, his first words do not follow Descartes', I think, or I want, or even, I feel, but rather, like Abraham's response to the summoning call of God to serve Him, "Here I am." In this context, the meaning, truth and value of the anaylsand's life is approached in terms of his response to the other's call; the analysand lives less in terms of his self-serving desire, say for power or acquisitiveness, and more in terms of the Good. He pursues a life devoted less to questing after fame and fortune and more to service to others. Responsibility for others thus becomes the fundamental meaning of his self-identity.

The analysand also needs help from the analyst in being open to embracing a second set of related tropes that orient values and sensibility in his analysis, storylines that speak to the heart of psychoanalysis, namely, living a life of love and justice. I have written two chapters on Levinas's views on love and its possible meaning for psychoanalysis. In this view, the grounding of love is responsibility, and kindness its very perfection. Justice, rooted in love, has not been commented on, especially as it plays out in one's personal and everyday life. A word about this is in order, though Levinas's views on justice, law and politics are an important and complex dimension of his overall philosophy, with interesting applicability to real-life social problems.[79] I, however, only

---

77   Levinas says in *Otherwise Than Being*, "To be or not to be is not the question when it comes to transcendence," (3). Rather as Cohen notes, "The question is to be or not to be *good*" ("Maternal Psyche," in *Psychology For The Other*, 42).

78   Levinas, *Alterity and Transcendence*, 165.

79   Two very good books that deal with the theme of justice in Levinas's writings are Catherine Chalier, *What I Ought to Do? Morality in Kant and Levinas*, trans. Jane Marie Todd (Ithaca, NY: Cornell University Press, 2002) and Howard Caygill, *Levinas and the Political* (New York: Routledge Books: 2002).

want to comment on justice as it pertains to the individual analysand who strives to live a life that is "for-the-Other."

Justice, for Levinas, is essential for implementing "the intention of love" in the social world.[80] As Atterton and Calarco point out,[81] in Levinas's early work the term was used to characterize the ethically asymmetrical face-to-face relation with the Other. Levinas remarks that "Justice consists in recognizing in the Other my master." "We call justice this face to face approach, in discourse."[82] In this later work, Atterton and Calarco further claim, justice takes on an additional meaning, one that is the basis for his social philosophy, what he calls sociality, in that it relates to the third party, everyone else, who stands outside the face-to-face relation. "It is the proximity of the third party that introduces, with the necessities of justice, meaning, measure, thematization, appearing and justice."[83]

Levinas's concept of justice is, to some extent, rooted in the biblical/Talmudic conception of the notion. By briefly contrasting it to the Greek conception of justice, it puts into sharp focus the ethical meaning of justice and its implications for living the moral life as Levinas conceives it. As Hertz points out,[84] in Plato's *Republic*, for instance, justice implies a harmonious configuration of society, "by which every human peg is put into its appropriate hole, so that those who perform humble functions shall be content to perform them in due subservience to their superiors." This formulation emphasizes the inequalities and disparities of human existence, whereas in the biblical notion of justice, absolute equality and parity is most important. To comprehend the biblical notion of justice, says Hertz, one must be mindful of the "Biblical teaching that man is created in the image of God," that in every person there exists a Godly aspect, "a Divine spark," and that each person is holy and of infinite, indisputable value. Thus, a human being cannot be related to as an object, a thing, but must be related to as a dignified personality. Moreover, as a worthy of respect personality, every person is "the possessor of the right to life, honor, and the fruits of his" efforts. Justice, in this view, "is the awe-inspired respect for the

80   Smith, *To the Outside*, 12.

81   Atterton and Calarco, *On Levinas*, 73.

82   Levinas, *Totality and Infinity*, 72, 50.

83   Levinas, *Otherwise Than Being*, 196.

84   J.H. Hertz, editor, *The Pentateuch and Haftorahs*, 821.

personality of others, and their inalienable rights; even as injustice is the most flagrant manifestation of disrespect for the personality of others." While the Greek notion of justice was equated with harmony, in the biblical view, it is equated with holiness, a key term for Levinas. As the prophet Isaiah says, "The Holy God is sanctified by justice." In other words, concludes Hertz, where there is no justice, no appropriate and pragmatic appreciation of, and respect for, the human rights of all people as the creations of the God of righteousness, we have a radical subversion of ethical monotheism and, for that matter, all religions with similar ethical and moral commitments.

Finally, in the biblical view, the work, the purpose of justice, is peace. It must be spoken, it must be guided by mercy and infused with love in some form. Levinas says:

> I call love *peace*. It is extraordinarily important, particularly in Judaism. The last word in the Talmud is the word peace. The first word of the meeting is also peace, *shalom*. Peace is sociality; it is to attend to the other...man always cedes his place to the other.[85]

On a personal level, from a Levinasian perspective, living a life guided by justice means that in my treatment of others I am guided by a high degree of fairness and reasonableness. This is based on a conviction that it is crucial to give each and every person the respect that they deserve. Justice is, in part, the continual and permanent commitment to give everyone his or her rightful share, a love that does not desire to keep for itself the good things of life but knows how to share them equally with others.

However, for Levinas, at least in my reading of him, justice is more than fairness, reasonableness, and giving each person his equal share. Justice, on the personal level, requires working for the "peaceful," kindhearted "resolution of infinite responsibilities" for the other, and secondarily, the satisfaction of my interests and rights.[86] In other words, living a just personal life means living according to an ethic that makes responsibility for the other, especially in terms of demanding justice for others who are suffering, before being concerned with oneself. This may be what Levinas was insinuating when he wrote that "The

---

85 Levinas, *Is It Righteous to Be?* 113. Elsewhere Levinas says that "the highest duty, 'when all is permitted,' consists in feeling oneself responsible with regard to these values of peace" (*Proper Names*, 121).

86 Hutchens, *Levinas*, 99.

foundation of the consciousness of being is justice itself."[87] Needless to say, psychoanalytically speaking, to live a just life as described above, especially in one's everyday personal life, requires a high degree of autonomy and conscience fused with empathy and compassion. Perhaps most importantly, it requires the transformation of inordinate and infantile narcissism into its more mature forms, as Kohut would say, from exaggerated egoism, grandiosity and self-centeredness, towards a more selfless for the Other way of being in the world.

This last point, the reduction of inordinate and infantile narcissism, on the way to "otherwise than being," is an observation that Levinas was well aware of. In fact, as Smith points out,[88] Levinas viewed the undoing or emptying out of the selfish self, the naturally egotistical I, as it is ethically solicited, summoned by the other in responsibility, as the prerequisite for "otherwise than being." The imprisonment of self within itself, and its tendency to assimilate otherness to itself, to the same, by knowledge, possession, mastery, needs to be gradually challenged, disrupted and ultimately emptied out and transformed by the other, by being hostage to the other. It is, says Smith, through an "unselving or transelving," by being roused, stirred and troubled by the other that one moves towards the Good, Goodness, "to-God," that is to the transcendent state of being for the Other. Such an approach is entirely in keeping with those all too few psychoanalytic theorists who wisely argue that it is the development of a "dereified, decommodified, non-selfcentric subjectivity" that should be the main goal of any psychoanalysis.[89] To some extent, mainstream psychoanalysis recognizes this point when it distinguishes so-called "normal narcissism" as manifested in ample self-care, level-headed self-confidence and reasonable self-regard from "heightened narcissism" as expressed in conceit and smugness, a demand to be treated specially, a haughty sense of superiority over others, or utter grandiosity.[90] To help an analysand achieve

87   Levinas, *Otherwise Than Being*, 160.

88   Smith, *Toward the Outside*, 12, 42, 104.

89   Rubin, *Psychotherapy and Buddhism. Towards an Integration*, 8, 190; Mark Epstein, *Thoughts without a Thinker* (New York: Basic Books, 1995), 69-70; Marcus, *Ancient Religious Wisdom, Spirituality and Psychoanalysis*, 52, 185-188.

90   Ethel S. Person, Arnold M. Cooper and Glen O. Gabbard, eds., *Textbook of Psychoanalysis* (Washington D.C.: American Psychiatric Publishing, 2005), 555.

a modicum of happiness, probably the best we can do is to help him transform his selfish cravings and infantile narcissism into "Goodness."

It should be noted that Levinas is not suggesting that individuals embraces a limitless altruism at the expense of appropriate self-development,[91] including the kind of saccharine, soppy altruism sometimes associated with certain "do good" religious and other traditions. "Certainly, my responsibility for everyone can also manifest itself by limiting itself: the ego may be called in the name of this unlimited responsibility to concern itself about itself as well."[92] For example, the development of a separate identity, self-knowledge, and a range of skills and talents, expressions of the inherent dynamism of being in the world, are necessary attributes for learning to be "for the Other." Altruism, continues Kunz, becomes mindless and even wrong when it involves being taken advantage of, or would violate another other, the third party, or when one's good works are used to do harm to others.[93]

My reading of Levinas indicates that, like Freud, he understood that a modicum of self-love, self-regard and self-affirmation were basic human strivings and are psychic prerequisites for reasonable and generous serving and giving to others. Moreover, Levinas believed that fundamentally, the self's pleasure-seeking, enjoyment[94] and happiness are worthwhile and good, though there are of course ethical constraints operative when others are involved. The infinitization of responsibility, suggests Levinas, begins in the obedience, both literally and metaphorically, to the biblical commandment, "Thou Shall Not Kill."

What I believe Levinas was hinting at was the need for a radical reconfiguration of self-identity, similar to what Michael Foucault advocated when he noted the need "to promote new forms of subjectivity through the refusal of the kind of [normalized, for Levinas, self-centric] individuality which has been imposed on us for centuries." Else-

---

91 Kuntz, *The Paradox of Power and Weakness*, 171-176.

92 Levinas, *Nine Talmudic Readings*, 50.

93 Kunz, *The Paradox of Power and Weakness*, 174.

94 Levinas has a thoughtful and original analysis of enjoyment and *Totality and Infinity*.

where, Foucault says, "we have to create ourselves as a work of art,"[95] which for Levinas means the ethicization of one's life. In other words, Levinas is suggesting radical changes in character structure and values and beliefs that make being for the Other, before oneself, seem "natural," or almost "natural." In psychological language, this requires in part, the capacity to imagine a moral order beyond oneself, one that is rooted in a transcendent reality, that is experienced as ultra real, ultra intense and ultra personal and, perhaps most importantly, brings one close towards God's infinite reality. Such a transcendent moral order creates the psychological, ethical and social context for putting responsibility for the Other above one's infantile narcissistic needs, wishes and exaggerated self-interest.

These then are the coordinates of a Levinasian-inspired psychoanalysis, psychoanalysis conceived as "a difficult wisdom concerned with truths that correlate to virtues"[96]: the human condition, the self, or the subject, is "hostage" to the summoning other, responsible even for what he has not done; psychopathology is viewed as ethical disablement, impairment and blunting; treatment is about moving the analysand from a being that is "for-itself" to one that is "for-the-Other." That is, says Kunz,[97] it is the neediness and worthiness of others, calling us to responsibility prior to reason, decision, personal desire and the quest for happiness, and how these others form, influence and animate self-identity, that should be the main focus of psychoanalysis.

The analyst in this context is conceived, to use one of Levinas's preferred tropes, as in part, maternal presence: unconditionally loving, compassionate and emotionally containing, all within an atmosphere of trust, security and empathy; as in part, wise master teacher: mind-expanding, heart-opening and soul-deepening; and as messianic in inspiration. It is messianic in two senses of the term: the analyst is one who takes on the suffering of the other, "serving the universe" as

---

95 Michael Foucault, "The Subject and Power," in Hubert L. Dreyfus and Paul Rabinow, eds., *Michael Foucault: Beyond Structuralism and Hermeneutics*, 216; Foucault, "On the Genealogy of Ethics: An Overview of Work in Progress," 237.

96 Levinas, *Difficult Freedom*, 275.

97 Kunz, *The Paradox of Power and Weakness*, 11.

Levinas says,[98] and is also a messenger of hope. O'Connor beautifully captures the spirit of this first messianic sense as it relates to psychotherapy:

> The ethical dimension of suffering is that of opening the difference between suffering in the other, where for me it is unpardonable and solicits me, and suffering in me, whose uselessness becomes meaningful as the suffering for the suffering of someone else. This, I think, is why one can be a psychotherapist only through the inter-human emergence of one's own suffering.[99]

The point is that such a messianic sensibility does not simply mean responding to the analysand's suffering in terms of comfort, solace, or consolation, but rather as to "an open wound, a longing that connects us to the despair of the other."[100]

The analyst is also messianic in sensibility to the extent that he signifies to the analysand that when he has hit "rock bottom," when he most feels the burden of existence, the crushing heaviness of being, there is hope. "There is hope only when hope is no longer permissible." Moreover, he says, "The true object of hope is the Messiah, or salvation."[101] In other words, though the analyst cannot offer false reassurance that there will be an end to the analysand's anguish in the future, because he cannot predict or control the future, he can, however, be fully present in the analysand's hour of need, when he is intensely suffering in the here-and-now, utterly alone. To do so authentically is to offer the analysand a chance for a kind of salvation, at least in the immediacy of the present. The analysand's moment-to-moment awareness of what he is experiencing within the context of a caring and dedicated other, what the Buddhists call mindfulness, can be the beginning of a degree of self-acceptance and even tranquility of mind and heart. The analysand can come to understand that when all is said and done, one ultimately has the freedom to choose one's inner attitude towards one's suffering. In other words, the analysand can refashion himself, liberate himself (more or less) from deterministic causation and embrace a

---

98 Levinas, *Difficult Freedom*, 95.

99 Noreen O. Connor, "Who Suffers?" In Bernasconi and Critchley, *Re-Reading Levinas*, 232-233.

100 Smith, *Towards the Outside*, 121.

101 Levinas, *Existence and Existents*, 91, 93. I am indebted to Smith (203-204) for these citations and point.

new system of causality, one that is more in accordance with his needs, wishes and preferences.[102] This awareness, hard to assimilate and implement as it may be, is a form of empowerment that can foster new pain-reducing and strengthening of self-understanding.

No doubt, a Levinasian-inspired psychoanalysis is an extremely demanding psychoanalysis in terms of moral expectations, self-mastery, and life conducting, though as I have argued throughout this book, it is in harmony with the "other Freud," the extreme ethicist rarely appreciated by the psychoanalytic community. This is the Freud who always wanted psychoanalysis to be about transforming analysts, and by extension, analysands, to be "better, nobler, stronger" people, devoted to "goodness" and "kindness," as he wrote to James Jackson Putnam. Freud's frustrated expectation and disappointment, his deep ethical yearning for a different kind of psychoanalysis, should become the inspiration and basis for our discipline moving in a different direction than it is currently taking, one that Levinas has pointed us towards with magisterial brilliance, stunning moral clarity, and graceful pathos.[103]

102 Pinchas H. Peli, *Soloveitchik On Repentance. The Thought and Oral Discourses of Rabbi Joseph B. Soloveitchik* (New York: Paulist Press, 1984), 31.

103 Though this book has not focused on the limitations of Levinas's project, there have been thoughtful, scholarly criticisms of his position from a variety of perspectives. See for example, Alain Badiou, *Ethics: An essay on the Understanding of Evil*, trans, Peter Kathleen Blamey (Chicago, IL: Chicago University Press, 1992).

BIBLIOGRAPHY

WORKS BY EMMANUEL LEVINAS

Alterity and Transcendence. Translated by Michael B. Smith. New York: Columbia University Press, 2000.

Basic Philosophical Writings. Edited by Robert Bernasconi, Simon Critchley and Adriaan Peperzak. Bloomington, IN: Indiana University Press, 1996.

Beyond the Verse: Talmudic Readings and Lectures. Translated by Gary D. Mole. Bloomington, IN: Indiana University Press, 1994.

Collected Philosophical Papers. Translated by Alphonso Lingis. Pittsburgh, PA: Duquesne University Press, 1998.

Difficult Freedom: Essays on Judaism. Translated by Sean Hand. Evanston, IL: Northwestern University Press, 1989.

En Découvrant l'existence avec Husserl et Heidegger. Paris: Librairie Philosophique J. Vrin, 1949.

Entre Nous: Essays on Thinking-of-the-Other. Translated by Michael B. Smith and Barbara Harshav. New York: Columbia University Press, 1998.

Ethics and Infinity: Conversations with Philippe Nemo. Translated by Richard A. Cohen. Pittsburgh, PA: Duquesne University Press, 1985.

Existence & Existents. Translated by Alphonso Lingis. Pittsburgh, PA: Duquesne University Press, 2001.

Face To Face With Emmanuel Levinas. Edited by Richard A. Cohen. Albany, NY: State University of New York Press, 1998.

God, Death, and Time. Translated by Bettina Bergo. Edited by Jacques Rolland. Stanford, CA: Stanford University Press, 2000.

In The Time Of the Nations. Translated by Michael B. Smith. Bloomington, IN: Indiana University Press, 1994.

Is It Righteous to Be? Interviews with Emmanuel Levinas. Edited by Jill Robbins. Stanford, CA: Stanford University Press, 2001.

The Levinas Reader. Translated by Sean Hand. Oxford: Basil Blackwell Publishing, Inc., 1987.

Nine Talmudic Readings. Translated by Annette Aronowicz. Bloomington, IN: Indiana University Press, 1990.

Of God Who Comes to Mind. Translated by Bettina Bergo. Stanford, CA: Stanford University Press, 1998.

On Escape/De l'évasion. Translated by Bettina Bergo. Stanford, CA: Stanford University Press, 2003.

Otherwise Than Being: Or Beyond Essence. Translated by Alphonso Lingis. Pittsburgh, PA: Duquesne University Press, 1998.

Outside the Subject. Translated by Michael B. Smith. Stanford, CA: Stanford University Press, 1993.

Proper Names. Translated by Michael B. Smith. Stanford, CA: Stanford University Press, 1996.

Time and the Other. Translated by Richard A. Cohen. Pittsburgh, PA: Duquesne University Press, 1987.

Totality and Infinity: an Essay on Exteriority. Translated by Alphonso Lingis. Pittsburgh, PA: Duquesne University Press, 1969.

"The Trace of the Other." Translated by Alphonso Lingis. In *Deconstruction in Context: Literature and Philosophy,* edited by Mark C. Taylor. Chicago, IL: University of Chicago Press, 1986, 345-359.

SELECTED BIBLIOGRAPHY

Alford, C. Fred. *Levinas, the Frankfurt School and Psychoanalysis.* Ithaca, NY: Cornell University Press, 2002.

Alford, C. Fred. "Melanie Klein and the Nature of Good and Evil." In *Psychoanalytic Versions of the Human Condition: Philosophies of Life and Their Impact on Practice,* edited by Paul Marcus and Alan Rosenberg. New York: New York University Press, 1998, 118-139.

American Psychiatric Glossary. Edited by Jane E. Edgerton. 7th edition. Washington, D.C. American Psychiatric Press, 1994.

Améry, Jean. *At the Mind's Limits: Contemplations by a Survivor on Auschwitz and Its Realities.* Translated by Sidney Rosenfeld and Stella P. Rosenfeld. Bloomington, IN: Indiana University Press, 1980.

Aristotle. *Nicomachean Ethics* and *Eudemonian Ethics.* In *The Complete Works of Aristotle,* edited by J. Barnes. 2 volumes. Princeton, NJ: Princeton University Press, 1984.

Aron, Arthur, Elaine N. Aron and Christina Norman. "Self-expansion Model of Motivation and Cognition in Close Relationships and Beyond. " In *Blackwell Handbook of Social Psychology: Interpersonal Processes,* edited by Garth Fletcher and Margaret S. Clark. Blackwell Publishing, Inc., 2001, 478-502.

Atterton, Peter, Matthew Calarco and Maurice Friedman, eds. *Levinas and Buber: Dialogue & Difference*. Pittsburgh, PA: Duquesne University Press, 2004.

Atterton, Peter and Matthew Calarco. *On Levinas*. Belmont, CA: Wadsworth, 2005.

Attwood, George E. and Robert D. Stolorow. *Structures of Subjectivity: Explorations of Psychoanalytic Phenomenology*. Hillsdale, NJ: Analytic Press, 1984.

Badiou, Alain. *Ethics: An Essay on the Understanding of Evil*. Translated by Peter Hallward. London: Verso Books, 2001.

Bass, Alan. "Sigmund Freud: The Question of a Weltanschauung." In *Psychoanalytic Versions of the Human Condition: Philosophies of Life and Their Impact on Practice*, edited by Paul Marcus and Alan Rosenberg. New York: New York University Press, 1998, 412-446.

Bauman, Zygmunt. *Postmodern Ethics*. Oxford: Blackwell Publishing, Inc., 1993.

Beauvoir, Simone de. *The Second Sex*. Edited and translated by H. M. Parshley. Harmondsworth: Penguin Books, 1984.

Becker, Ernest. *The Denial of Death*. New York: The Free Press, 1973.

Benjamin, Jessica. *Like Subjects, Love Objects: Essays on Recognition and Sexual Difference*. New Haven: CT.: Yale University Press, 1995.

Beauvoir, Simone de. *The Second Sex*. Edited and translated by H. M. Parshley. Hardmondsworth: Penguin, 1984

Berger, Peter. *The Sacred Canopy*. Garden City, NJ: Doubleday, 1967.

Berger, Peter and Brigitte Berger. *Sociology: A Biographical Approach*. New York: Basic Books, 1972.

Bergmann, Martin S. *The Anatomy of Loving: The Story of Man's Quest to Know What Love Is*. New York: Fawcett Columbine, 1987.

Berkovitz, Eliezer. *With God in Hell*. Jerusalem: Sanhedrin Press, 1979.

Bernasconi, Robert and Simon Critchley, eds. *The Cambridge Companion to Levinas*. Cambridge: Cambridge University Press, 2002.

Bernasconi, Robert. "Levinas, Emmanuel." In *Routledge Encyclopedia of Philosophy*, edited by Edward Craig. 10 volumes. London: Routledge Books, 1998, 579-582.

———. "What is the question of which 'substitution' is the answer?" *The Cambridge Companion to Levinas*. Cambridge: Cambridge University Press, 2002, 234-251.

Bernasconi, Robert and David Wood, eds. *The Provocation of Levinas: Re-thinking The Other*. London: Routledge, 1988.

Bernasconi, Robert and Simon Critchley, eds. *Re-Reading Levinas*. Bloomington, IN: Indiana University Press, 1991.

Bernstein, Richard, "Evil and the Temptation of Theodicy" in Bernasconi, Robert and Simon Critchley, eds. *The Cambridge Companion to Levinas*. Cambridge: Cambridge University Press, 2002, 252-267.

Bettelheim, Bruno. *The Informed Heart*. Glencoe, IL: The Free Press, 1960.

_____. *Surviving and Other Essays*. New York: Knopf, 1979.

_____. "Schizophrenia as a Reaction to Extreme Situations," in *Surviving and Other Essays*, New York: Knopf, 1979, 105-111.

_____ "The Ultimate Limit," in *Surviving and Other Essays*, New York: Knopf, 1979, 3-18.

Blackwell Handbook of Social Psychology: Interpersonal Processes. Edited by Garth Fletcher and Margaret S. Clark. Oxford: Blackwell Publishing, Inc., 2002.

Bloechl, Jeffrey, ed. *In the Face of the Other and the Trace of God: Essays on the Philosophy of Emmanuel Levinas*. New York: Fordham University Press, 2000.

Boesky, Dale. "The Psychoanalytic Process and Its Components." *Psychoanalytic Quarterly*, 49 (1990): 527-531.

Bowie, Malcom. *Lacan*. London: Fontana Press, 1991.

Breton, Stanislas. In Richard Kearney, *Debates in Continental Philosophy: Conversations with Contemporary Thinkers*. New York: Fordham University Press, 2004.

Buber, Martin. *Between Man and Man*. Translated by Maurice S. Friedman. New York: Macmillan Company, 1965.

_____. *I and Thou*. Translated by Walter Kauffmann. New York: Charles Scribner's Sons, 1970.

_____. *The Knowledge of Man: Selected Essays*. Edited by Maurice S. Friedman. New York: Harper and Row, 1965.

The Cambridge Dictionary of Philosophy. Edited by Robert Audis. 2d edition. New York: Cambridge University Press, 2005.

Carr, David. "Husserl and Phenomenology." In *The Columbia History of Western Philosophy*, edited by Richard H. Popkin. New York: Columbia University Press, 1999, 675-681.

Caygill, Howard. *Levinas and the Political*. London: Routledge Books, 2002.

Chalier, Catherine. "Ethics and the Feminine." In Bernasconi, Robert and Simon Critchley, eds. *Re-Reading Levinas*. Bloomington, IN: Indiana University Press, 1991, 119-129,

_____. *What Ought I to Do? Morality in Kant and Levinas*. Translated by Jane Marie Todd. Ithaca, NY: Cornell University Press, 2002.

Cohen, Arthur A. and Paul Mendes-Flohr, eds. "Feminism." In *Contemporary Jewish Thought*. New York: Charles Scribner's Sons, 1987, 255-260.

Cohen, Richard A. "Maternal Psyche." In *Psychology-for-the-Other: Levinas, Ethics, and the Practice of Psychology*, edited by Edwin E. Gantt and Richard N. Williams. Pittsburgh, PA: Duquesne University Press, 2002, 32-64.

The Columbia History of Western Philosophy. Edited by Richard H. Popkin. New York: Columbia University Press, 1999.

The Concise Oxford Dictionary of Current English. Edited by R. E. Allen. 8th edition. Oxford: Clarendon Press, 1990.

Critchley, Simon. "Introduction." In *The Cambridge Companion to Levinas*, edited by Robert Bernasconi and Simon Critchley. Cambridge: Cambridge University Press, 2002, 1-32.

Critchley, Simon. "The Original Traumatism: Levinas and Psychoanalysis." In *Questioning Ethics: Contemporary Debates in Philosophy*, edited by Mark Dooley and Richard Kearney. New York: Routledge Books, 1999, 230-242.

Davies, Paul, "Sincerity and the end of theodicy: three remarks on Levinas and Kant." In *The Cambridge Companion to Levinas*, edited by Robert Bernasconi and Simon Critchley. Cambridge: Cambridge University Press, 2002, 161-177.

Davis, Colin. *Levinas: An Introduction*. Cambridge: Polity Press, 1996.

Davis, Mark H. *Empathy: A Social Psychological Approach*. Madison, WI: Brown and Benchmark, 1994.

Derrida, Jacques. *Adieu to Emmanuel Levinas*. Translated by Pascale-Anne Brault and Michael Naas. Stanford, CA: Stanford University Press, 1999.

_____. *The Gift of Death*. Translated by David Will. Chicago, IL: University of Chicago Press, 1995.

_____. *Of Grammatology*. Translated by Gayatri Chakravorty Spivak. Baltimore, MD: The John Hopkins University Press, 1976.

_____. *Writing and Difference*. Translated by Alan Bass. Chicago, IL: The University of Chicago Press, 1978.

Dovidio, John F. and Louis A. Penner. "Helping and Altruism." In *Blackwell Handbook of Social Psychology: Interpersonal Processes*, edited by Garth Fletcher and Margaret S. Clark. Oxford: Blackwell Publishing, Inc., 2002, 162-195.

Duck, Steve (ed.). *Handbook of Personal Relationships; Theory, Research and Interventions*. Chichester, England: John Wiley and Sons, Ltd., 1988.

Eagle, Morris N. "Attachment and Psychoanalysis. *British Medical Journal*, 70 (1997): 217-229.

Edelson, Marshall. *Psychoanalysis: a Theory in Crisis*. Chicago, IL: University of Chicago Press, 1988.

Eigen, Michael. "On the Significance of the Face," *Psychoanalytic Review*. 67 (1980): 427-442.

_____. *The Electrified Tightrope*. Northvale, NJ: Jason Aronson, 1993.

_____. *Emotional Storm*. Middletown, CT: Wesleyan University Press, 2005.

Eitinger, Leo. *Concentration Camp Survivors in Norway and Israel*. London: Allen and Unwin, 1964.

Eliach, Yaffa. "Jewish Tradition in the Life of the Concentration Camp Inmate," in *The Nazi Concentration Camps: Proceedings of the Fourth Yad Vashem International Historical Conference*. Jerusalem: Yad Vashem, 1980, 195-206.

Elliott, Anthony. *Psychoanalytic Theory: An Introduction*. Oxford: Blackwell Publishing, Inc., 1994.

Epstein, Mark. *Thoughts Without a Thinker: Psychotherapy from a Buddhist Perspective*. New York: Basic Books, 1995.

Erikson, Erik H. *Childhood and Society*. New York: W.W. Norton, 1950.

_____. *Insight and Responsibility*. New York: Norton, 1964.

Evans, Dylan. *An Introductory Dictionary of Lacanian Psychoanalysis*. London: Routledge Books, 1996.

Fagenblat, Michael and Nathan Wolski. "Revelation Here and Beyond: Buber and Levinas on the Bible." In *Levinas and Buber: Dialogue and Difference*, edited by Peter Atterton, Matthew Calarco and Maurice S. Friedman. Pittsburgh, PA: Duquesne University Press, 2004, 157-178.

Fairbairn, W. R. D. "Repression and the Return of Bad Objects.'" In *Object Relations Theory of the Personality*, edited by Martin S. Bergmann. New York: Basic Books, 1952, 327-341.

Faulconer, James E. "Levinas: The Unconscious and the Reason of Obligation." In *Psychology-for-the-Other: Levinas, Ethics, and the Practice Of Psychology*, edited by Edwin E. Gantt and Richard N. Williams. Pittsburgh, PA: Duquesne University Press, 2002, 102-117.

Federn, Ernst. *Witnessing Psychoanalysis*. London: Karnac Books, 1980.

Fine, Reuben. *History of Psychoanalysis*. New York: Columbia University Press, 1979.

Fisher, David J. *Cultural Theory and Psychoanalytic Tradition*. New Brunswick, NJ: Transition Publishers, 1991.

Fonagy, Peter. *Attachment Theory and Psychoanalysis*. New York: Other Press, 2001.

Foucault, Michel. *The Archaeology of Knowledge and the Discourse on Language*. Translated by A.M. Sheridan Smith. New York: Pantheon, 1972.

_____. "The Ethics of the Concern for the Self as a Practice of Freedom." In *Foucault Live: Collected Interviews, 1961-1984*, edited by Sylvère Lotringer. New York: Semiotexte, 1989, 432-449.

_____. "The Subject and Power." In Hubert L. Dreyfus and Paul Rabinow, *Michel Foucault: Beyond Structuralism and Hermeneutics*. 2d edition. Chicago, IL: University of Chicago Press, 1987, 208-228.

Fowers, Blaine J. *Virtue and Psychology: Pursuing Excellence in Ordinary Practices*. Washington, D. C.: American Psychological Association, 2005.

Freud, Sigmund. *The Freud/Jung Letters: The Correspondence between Sigmund Freud and C. G. Jung*. Translated by Ralph Manheim and R. F. C. Hull. Edited by William McGuire. Princeton, NJ: Princeton University Press, 1974.

_____. Letters to James Jackson Putnam, 5/14/11, 11/13/13, 6/17/15. *James Jackson Putnam and Psychoanalysis, Letters between Putnam and Sigmund Freud, Ernest Jones, William James, Sandor Ferenczi, and Morton Prince, 1877-1917*, Translated by Judith Bernays Heller. Edited by Nathan G. Hale. Cambridge, MA: Harvard University Press, 1971.

_____. Letter to Oscar Pfister, 10/9/18. In Ernest Jones, *The Life and Work of Sigmund Freud*. 3 volumes. New York: Basic Books, 1955, 457 (vol. 2).

_____. Letter to Princess Maria Bonaparte in 1934, quoted in Ralph Steadman, *Sigmund Freud*. New York: Paddington Press, 1979.

_____. Letter to Sandor Ferenczi, 1/10/10. In Ernest Jones, *Life and Work of Sigmund Freud*. 3 volumes. New York: Basic Books, 1955, 446 (vol. 2).

_____. *The Standard Edition of the Complete Psychological Works of Sigmund Freud.* Edited and translated by James Strachey. 24 volumes. London: The Hogarth Press and The Institute of Psychoanalysis, 1974. (*S.E.*)

Friedlander, Albert H. *Leo Baeck: Teacher of Theresienstadt.* New York: Holt, Rinehart, & Winston, 1968.

Friedman, Maurice S. *Martin Buber: The Life of Dialogue.* 4th edition. London: Routledge Books, 2002.

_____. Martin Buber and the Human Sciences. Albany, NY: State University of New New York Press, 1996.

Fromm, Erich. *The Anatomy of Human Destructiveness.* Greenwich CT.: Fawcett Crest Books, 1973.

_____. *The Art of Loving: An Enquiry into the Nature of Love.* New York: Harper Colophon Books, 1956.

Fryer, David Ross. *The Intervention of the Other: Ethical Subjectivity in Levinas and Lacan.* New York: Other Press, 2004.

Gantt, Edwin E, and Richard N. Williams, eds. *Psychology-for-the-Other: Levinas, Ethics, and the Practice Of Psychology.* Pittsburgh, PA: Duquesne University Press, 2002.

Gantt, Edwin E. and Richard N. Williams. "Pursuing Psychology as Science of the Ethical." In *Psychology-for-the-Other: Levinas, Ethics, and the Practice of Psychology,* edited by Edwin E. Gantt and Richard N. Williams. Pittsburgh, PA: Duquesne University Press, 2002, 1-31.

Gargiulo, Gerald J. "D.W. Winicott's Psychoanalytic Playground." In *Psychoanalytic Versions of the Human Condition: Philosophies of Life and Their Impact on Practice,* edited by Paul Marcus and Alan Rosenberg. New York: New York University Press, 1998, 140-160.

Geertz, Clifford. *The Interpretation of Cultures.* New York: Basic Books, 1973.

Goffman, Irving. *Asylums.* New York: Anchor Books, 1961.

Goldstein, Joseph, Anna Freud and Albert Solnit. *Beyond the Best Interests of the Child.* New York: Free Press, 1973.

Gordon, Neve. "Ethics and the Place of the Other." In *Levinas and Buber: Dialogue & Difference,* edited by Peter Atterton, Matthew Calarco and Maurice S. Friedman. Pittsburgh, PA: Duquesne University Press, 2004, 98-115.

Gouldner, Alvin W. "The Norm of Reciprocity: A Preliminary Statement." *American Sociological Review,* 25 (1960): 161-178.

Greenberg, Jay R. and Stephen A. Mitchell. *Object Relations in Psychoanalytic Theory*. Cambridge: Harvard University Press, 1983.

Grotstein, James S. "W. R. D. Fairbairn and His Growing Significance for Current Psychoanalysis and Psychotherapy." In *Psychoanalytic Versions of the Human Condition, Philosophies of Life and Their Impact on Practice*, edited by Paul Marcus and Alan Rosenberg. New York: New York University Press, 1998, 161-182.

Guerriere, Daniel. "Continental Theistic Philosophers." In *The Columbia History of Western Philosophy*. Edited by Richard H. Popkin. New York: Columbia University Press, 1999, 712-720.

Hadot, Pierre. *Philosophy as a Way of Life*. Oxford: Blackwell Publishing, Inc., 1997.

Hale, Nathan G., ed. *James Jackson Putnam and Psychoanalysis*. Translated by J.B. Heller. Cambridge: Cambridge University Press, 1971.

Halpern, Cynthia. *Suffering, Politics, Power. A Genealogy in Modern Political Theory* Albany: State University of New York Press, 2002,

_____. *The Rise and Crisis of Psychoanalysis in America: Freud and the Americans, 1917-1985*. Volume 1. New York: Oxford University Press, 1955.

Hand, Sean, ed. *Facing The Other: The Ethics of Emmanuel Levinas*. Richmond, Surrey: Curzon, 1996.

Handelman, Susan A. *Fragments of Redemption: Jewish Thought and Literary Theory in Benjamin, Scholem, and Levinas*. Bloomington, IN: Indiana University Press, 1991.

Hanly, Charles. "Ideology and Psychoanalysis." In *Psychoanalysis at the Political Border: Essays in Honor of Rafael Moses*, edited by Leo Rangell and Rena Moses-Hrushovski. Madison, WI: International Universities Press, 1996, 142-164.

Harasym, Sarah, ed. *Levinas and Lacan: The Missed Encounter*. Albany, NY: State University Press of New York, 1998.

Hartman, Heinz. *Psychoanalysis and Moral Values*. New Haven: CT: International Universities Press, 1960.

Hobbes, Thomas. *Leviathan*. Edited by Richard Tuck. Cambridge: Cambridge University Press, 1991.

Hutchens, Benjamin C. *Levinas: A Guide for the Perplexed*. London: Continuum International Publishing Group, 2004.

Huberband, Shimon, Jeffrey S. Gurock and Robert S. Hirt. *Kiddush Hashem: Jewish Religious and Cultural Life in Poland During the Holocaust.* Hoboken, NJ: KTAV Publishing House, 1987.

Ickes, William and Jeffry A. Simpson. "Empathic Accuracy in Close Relationships." In *Empathic Accuracy,* edited by William Ickes. New York: Guilford Press, 1997, 218-250.

Ickes, William and Jeffry A. Simpson. "Motivational Aspects of Empathic Accuracy." In *Blackwell Handbook of Social Psychology: Interpersonal Processes.* Edited by Garth Fletcher and Margaret S. Clark. Oxford: Blackwell Publishing, Inc., 2002, 229-249.

Jacobs, Jonathan. *Choosing Character: Responsibility For Virtue and Vice.* Ithaca, NY: Cornell University Press, 2001.

Jones, Ernest. *The Life and Work of Sigmund Freud.* New York: Basic Books, 1955, vol. 2.

James W. Jones, *Contemporary Psychoanalysis. Religion, Transference and Transcendence.* New Haven: Yale University Press, 1991.

Claire Katz, "Educating the Solitary Man: Levinas, Rousseau, and the Return to Jewish Wisdom." Jeffrey Bloechl, ed., *Levinas Studies. An Annual Review.* Volume 2, Pittsburgh: Duquesne University Press, 2007, 133-152.

Klein, Melanie. *Contributions to Psychoanalysis, 1921-45.* London: The Hogarth Press, 1948.

Kohut, Heinz. *Restoration of the Self.* New York: International Universities Press, 1977.

Kogon, Eugen. *The Theory and Practice of Hell.* New York: Berkley Publishing Corporation, 1980.

Kohut, Heinz. *The Analysis of the Self: A Systematic Approach to the Psychoanalytic Treatment of Narcissistic Personality Disorders.* New York: International University Press, 1971.

_____. *How Does Analysis Cure?* Edited by Arnold Goldberg. Chicago, IL: University of Chicago Press, 1984.

Kristiansen, Aslaug. "The Interhuman Dimension of Teaching: Some Ethical Aspects." *Martin Buber and the Human Sciences,* edited by Maurice S. Friedman. Albany, NY: State University Press of New York Press, 1996, 215-222.

Kugelman, Robert. "Pain, Exposure, and Responsibility." In *Psychology-for-the-Other: Levinas, Ethics, and the Practice of Psychology,* edited by Edwin E. Gantt and Richard N. Williams. Pittsburgh, PA: Duquesne University Press, 2002, 84-101.

Kunz, George. *The Paradox of Power And Weakness: Levinas and an Alternative Paradigm for Psychology*. Albany, NY: State University of New York Press, 1998.

Kunz, George. "Simplicity, Humility, Patience." In *Psychology-for-the-Other: Levinas, Ethics, and the Practice of Psychology*, edited by Edwin E. Gantt and Richard N. Williams. Pittsburgh, PA: Duquesne University Press, 2002, 118-142.

Kurzweil, Edith. *The Freudians: A Comparative Perspective*. New Haven, CT: Yale University Press, 1989.

Lacan, Jacques. *The Four Fundamental Concepts of Psychoanalysis (The Seminar of Jacques Lacan, Book 11)*. Translated by Alan Sheridan. London: The Hogarth Press and Institute of Psychoanalysis, 1977.

_____. *The Seminar, Book I. Freud's Papers on Technique, 1953-54*, trans. with notes by John Forrester, New York: Norton; Cambridge: Cambridge University Press, 1988.

_____. *The Seminar, Book II. The Ego in Freud's Theory and in the Technique of Psychoanalysis, 1954-55*, trans. Sylvana Tomselli, notes by John Forrester, New York: Norton; Cambridge University Press, 1988.

Laing, R. D. *The Divided Self*. Baltimore, MD: Penguin Books, 1959.

Landes, Daniel. "Spiritual Responses in the Camps." In *Genocide: Critical Issues of the Holocaust*, edited by Alex Grobman and Daniel Landes. Chappaqua, NY: Russell Books, 1983, 261-278.

Langer, Lawrence L. *Holocaust Testimonies: The Ruins of Memory*. New Haven, CT: Yale University Press, 1987.

Lear, Jonathan. "Philosophy." In *Textbook of Psychoanalysis*, edited by Ethel S. Person, Arnold M. Cooper and Glen O. Gabbard. Washington, D.C.: American Psychiatric Publishing, 2005, 513-524.

Lechte, John. *Fifty Key Contemporary Thinkers: From Structuralism to Postmodernity*. New York: Routledge Books, 1994.

Legato, Marianne J. "The Weaker Sex." *New York Times*, 17 June 2006, A, 13.

Levi, Primo. *The Drowned and the Saved*. New York: Summit Books, 1988.

Llewelyn, John. *Emmanuel Levinas: The Genealogy of Ethics*. New York: Routledge Books, 1995.

Mitchell, Stephen. *Relationality: From Attachment to Intersubjectivity*. New York: Analytic Press, 2000.

Macquarrie, John. *Twentieth-Century Religious Thought*. Harrisburg, PA: Trinity Press, 2001.

Madison, G. B. "Hermeneutics: Gadamer and Ricoeur." In *The Columbia History of Western Philosophy*, edited by Richard H. Popkin. New York: Columbia University Press, 1999.

Marcus, Paul. *Ancient Religious Wisdom, Spirituality and Psychoanalysis*. Westport, CT: Praeger Books, 2003.

_____. *Autonomy in the Extreme Situation: Bruno Bettelheim, the Nazi Concentration Camps and the Mass Society*. Westport, CT: Praeger, 1999.

_____. "I'm Just Wild About Harry: A Psychoanalyst Reflects on His Relationship With His Dog," in *Psychoanalytic Review* 94, 4 (2007): 515-528.

_____. "Psychoanalysis and Social Psychology." *Journal of The American Academy of Psychoanalysis*, 14, 1 (1986): 115-123.

_____. "The Religious Believer, the Psychoanalytic Intellectual, and the Challenge of Sustaining the Self in the Concentration Camps." *Journal for the Psychoanalysis of Culture and Society*, 3, 1 (Spring, 1998): 61-75.

Marcus, Paul and Alan Rosenberg, eds. *Psychoanalytic Versions of the Human Condition: Philosophies of Life and Their Impact on Practice*. New York: New York University Press, 1998.

May, Rollo, ed. *Existence*. New York: Basic Books, 1958.

Meissner, W. W. *The Ethical Dimension of Psychoanalysis: A Dialogue*. Albany, NY: State University of New York Press, 2003.

Meir, Ephraim. "Buber's and Levinas's Attitudes Towards Judaism." In *Levinas and Buber: Dialogue and Difference*: Pittsburgh, PA: Duquesne University Press, 2004, 133-156.

Meltzer, Donald. *The Kleinian Development: Books I, II and III in One Volume*. Perthshire, Scotland: Clunie Press, 1978, as paraphrased in C. Fred Alford, "Melanie Klein and the Nature of Good and Evil." In *Psychoanalytic Versions of the Human Condition: Philosophies of Life and Their Impact on Practice*, edited by Paul Marcus and Alan Rosenberg. New York: New York University Press, 1998, 118-139.

Meskin, Jacob. "The Role of Lurianic Kabbalah in the Early Philosophy of Emmanuel Levinas." Jeffrey Bloechl, editor, *Levinas Studies. An Annual Review. Volume 2*, Pittsburgh: Duquesne University Press, 2007, 49-78.

Monte, Christopher F. *Beneath the Mask: An Introduction to Theories of Personality*. 2d edition. New York: Holt, Rinehart and Winston, 1980.

Moore, Burness E. and Bernard D. Fine, editors. *Psychoanalytic Terms and Concepts*. New Haven, CT: The American Psychoanalytic Association and Yale University Press, 1990.

Moyn, Samuel. *Origins of the Other: Emmanuel Levinas Between Revelation and Ethics*. Ithaca, NY: Cornell University Press, 2006.

Nicholi, Armand M., Jr. *The Question of God: C.S. Lewis and Sigmund Freud Debate God, Love, Sex, and The Meaning of Life*. New York: The Free Press, 2002.

Nietzsche, Friderich. *On the Genealogy of Morals*. Translated by Walter Kaufmann. New York: Random House, 1957.

O'Connor, Noreen O. "Who Suffers?" In *Re-Reading Levinas*, edited by Robert Bernasoni and Simon Critchley. Bloomington, IN: Indiana University Press, 1991, 229-233.

Oliner, Marian M. "Jacques Lacan: The Language of Alienation." In *Psychoanalytic Versions of the Human Condition: Philosophies of Life and Their Impact on Practice* edited by Paul Marcus and Alan Rosenberg. New York: New York University Press, 1998, 362-391.

Oliner, Samuel P. and Pearl M. Oliner. *The Altruistic Personality: Rescuers of Jews in Nazi Europe*. New York: The Free Press, 1988.

Ornstein, Anna. "Survival and Recovery." *Psychoanalytic Inquiry*, 5, 1 (1985): 115.

Oshry, Ephraim. *Responsa from the Holocaust*. Translated by Y. Leiman. New York: Judaica Press, 1983.

Passover Haggadah: The Feast of Freedom. Edited by Rachel Anne Rabinowicz. 2d edition. New York: Rabbinical Assembly. 1982.

Pattison, E. Mansell. "The Holocaust as Sin: Requirements in Psychoanalytic Theory for Human Evil and Mature Morality." In *Psychoanalytic Reflections on the Holocaust: Selected Essays*, edited by Steven A. Luel and Paul Marcus. Hoboken, NJ: University of Denver and KTAV Publishers, 1988, 71-94.

Pawelczynska, Anna. *Values and Violence in Auschwitz: A Sociological Analysis*. Translated by Catherine S. Leach. Berkeley, CA: University of California Press, 1979.

Peli, Pinchas H. *Soloveitchik. On Repentance*. New York: Paulist Press, 1984.

The Pentateuch and Haftorahs. Edited and translated by J. H. Hertz. London: Soncino Press, 5720/1960.

Peperzak, Adriaan. "Emmanuel Levinas." In *The Cambridge Dictionary of Philosophy*, edited by Robert Audis. New York: Cambridge University Press, 2005.

_____. To The Other: An Introduction to the Philosophy of Emmanuel Levinas. West Lafayette, IN: Purdue University Press, 1993.

_____. Beyond: The Philosophy of Levinas. Evanston: Northwestern University, 1997

Person, Ethel S., Arnold M. Cooper and Glen O. Gabbard, eds. Textbook of Psychoanalysis. Washington, D. C.: American Psychiatric Association, 2005.

Person, Ethel Spector. "Forgiveness and its Limits: A Psychological and Psychoanalytic Perspective." Psychoanalytic Review. 94(3), June 2007, 389-408.

Pingel, Falk. "The Destruction of Human Identity in Concentration Camps: The Contribution of the Social Sciences to the Analysis of Behavior under Extreme Conditions." Holocaust and Genocide Studies, 6, 2 (1991): 167-184.

Polen, Nehemia. The Holy Fire, The Teachings of Rabbi Kalonymus Kalman Shapira, the Rebbe of the Warsaw Ghetto, Northvale, NJ: Jason Aronson, 1994.

Pollak, Richard. The Creation of Dr. B: A Biography of Bruno Bettelheim. New York: Simon and Schuster, 1996.

Putnam, Hilary. "Levinas and Judaism," in The Cambridge Companion to Levinas, edited by Robert Bernasconi and Simon Critchley. Cambridge: Cambridge University Press, 2002, 33-62.

Psychoanalytic Terms and Concepts. Edited by Burness E. Moore and Bernard D. Fine. New Haven, CT: The American Psychoanalytic Association and Yale University Press, 1990.

Raines, Theron. Rising to The Light: A Portrait of Bruno Bettelheim. New York: Knopf, 2002.

Reis, H.T. and P. Shaver, "Intimacy as interpersonal process," in S Duck, (ed), Handbook of personal Relationships: theory, Research and Interventions. Chichester, England: Wiley, 1988, 367-389.

Richards, P. Scott and Allen E. Bergin. A Spiritual Strategy for Counseling and Psychotherapy. Washington, D. C.: American Psychological Association, 1997.

Ricoeur, Paul. Oneself as Another. Translated by Kathleen Blamey. Chicago, IL: University of Chicago Press, 1992.

Robinson, Daniel N. The Great Ideas of Philosophy, Part II. Springfield, Virginia: The Teaching Company, 1997.

Robinson, Daniel N. "The Idea in Freedom." In *The Great Ideas of Philosophy*. Part IV." Springfield, VA: The Teaching Company, 1997.

_____. "Aristotle on the Perfect Life." In *The Great Ideas of Philosophy*. Part II." Springfield, VA: The Teaching Company, 1997

Rorty, Richard. *Contingency, Irony, and Solidarity*. New York: Cambridge University Press, 1989.

Rose, Nikolas Rose. *Inventing Our Selves*. Cambridge: Cambridge University press, 1996.

Roth, Paul A. "The Cure of Stores, Self-Deception, Danger Situations, and the Clinical Role of Narratives in Roy Schaefer's Psychoanalytic Theory." In *Psychoanalytic Versions of the Human Condition: Philosophies of Life and Their Impact on Practice*, edited by Paul Marcus and Alan Rosenberg. New York: New York University Press, 1998, 306-331.

Routledge Encyclopedia of Philosophy. General Editor, Edward Craig. 10 volumes. London: Routledge Books, 1998.

Rubin, Jeffrey B. *The Good Life: Psychoanalytic Reflections on Love, Ethics, Creativity, and Spirituality*. Albany, NY: State University of New York Press, 2004.

Rubin, Jeffrey B. *Psychotherapy and Buddhism: Toward an Integration*. New York: Plenum Press, 1996.

Rycroft, Charles. *A Critical Dictionary of Psychoanalysis*. Middlesex, England: Penguin Books, 1968.

Sandford, Stella. "Levinas, Feminism and the Feminine." In *The Cambridge Companion to Levinas*, edited by Robert Bernasconi and Simon Critchley. Cambridge: Cambridge University Press, 2002, 139-160.

Sartre, Jean-Paul. *Nausea*. Translated by Lloyd Alexander. New York: New Directions: 1949.

_____. *Being and Nothingness*. Translated by Hazel E. Barnes. New York: Washington Square Press, 1953.

Scarfone, Dominique. "Psychoanalysis in the French Community." In *The American Psychiatric Publishing Textbook of Psychoanalysis*. edited by Ethel Spector Person, Arnold M. Cooper and Glen O. Gabbard. Washington, D. C., American Psychiatric Publishing, Inc., 2005, 423-435.

Schafer, Roy. "The Psychoanalytic Visions of Reality." In *A New Language for Psychoanalysis*. New Haven, CT: Yale University Press, 1976.

_____. *The Analytic Attitude*. New York: Basic Books, 1983.

Scott, Charles E. "Continental Philosophy at the Turn of the Twenty-First Century." In *The Columbia History of Western Philosophy*, edited by Richard H. Popkin. New York: Columbia University Press, 1999, 745-754.

Shapiro, Susan. "Emmanuel Levinas." In *Holocaust Literature*, edited by S. Lillian Kremer. 2 volumes. New York: Routledge Books, 2003, 759-762.

Silberstein, Lawrence J. *Martin Buber's Social and Religious Thought*. New York: New York University Press, 1989.

Smith, Michael B. *Toward the Outside: Concepts and Themes in Emmanuel Levinas*. Pittsburgh, PA: Duquesne University Press, 2005.

Steadman, Ralph. *Sigmund Freud*. New York: Paddington Press, 1979.

Stern, Daniel. "Intersubjectivity." In *The Textbook of Psychoanalysis*, edited by Ethel S. Person, Arnold M. Cooper and Glen O. Gabbard, eds. Washington, D. C.: American Psychiatric Association, 2005, 77-92.

Sutton, Nina. *Bettelheim: A Life and a Legacy*. New York: Basic Books, 1996.

Taylor, Mark C., ed. *Deconstruction in Context: Literature and Philosophy*. Chicago, IL: University of Chicago Press, 1986.

Todd, Sharon. *Levinas, Psychoanalysis, and Ethical Possibilities in Education*. Albany, NY: State University of New York Press, 2005.

Todorov, Tzvetan. *Facing the Extreme: Moral Life in the Concentration Camps*. New York: Henry Holt and Company, 1966.

Wallwork, Ernest. "Ethics in Psychoanalysis." In *Textbook of Psychoanalysis*, edited by Ethel S. Person, Arnold M. Cooper and Glen O. Gabbard. Washington, D. C.: American Psychiatric Publishing, Inc., 2005, 281-300.

_____. *Psychoanalysis and Ethics*. New Haven, CT: Yale University Press, 1991.

Walsh, Lisa. "Between Maternity and Paternity: Figuring Ethical Subjectivity," *Differences* 12 (Spring): 79-111.

Weinstein, Fred. *History and Theory After the Fall: An Essay on Interpretation*. Chicago, IL: University of Chicago Press, 1990.

Werber, Jack and William B. Helmreich. *Saving the Children: Diary of a Buchenwald Survivor and Rescuer*. New Brunswick, N.J.: Transaction Publishers, 1996.

Wiesel, Elie. "Talking, and Writing and Keeping Silent." In *The German Church Struggle and the Holocaust*, edited by Franklin H. Littell and Hubert G. Locke. Bloomington, IN: Wayne State University Press, 1974, 269-277.

Wirzba, Norman. "Emmanuel Levinas." In *World Philosophers and Their Works*, edited by John K. Roth. 3 volumes. Pasadena, CA: Salem Press, 2000, 1090-1096.

Wolf, Arnold Jacob. "Heschel's 'Torah from Heaven.'" *Judaism*, 53, 3-4, (Summer/Fall 2004): 303-304.

Worthington, Everett L., Jr., *Forgiving and Reconciling: Bridges to Wholeness and Hope*. Downers Grove, IL: InterVarsity Press, 2003.

Wyschogrod, Edith. *Emmanuel Levinas: The Problem of Ethical Metaphysics*. 2nd edition. New York: Fordham University Press, 2000.

INDEX